Telecommunications Reform in India

Edited by Rafiq Dossani

Quorum Books
Westport, Connecticut • London

Library of Congress Cataloging-in-Publication Data

Telecommunications reform in India / edited by Rafiq Dossani.
    p. cm.
   Includes bibliographical references and index.
   ISBN 1–56720–502–X (alk. paper)
   1. Telecommunication—India. 2. Telecommunication policy—India. I. Dossani, Rafiq,
1954–
HE8374.T45 2002
384′.0954—dc21   2001049183

British Library Cataloguing in Publication Data is available.

Library of Congress Catalog Card Number: 2001049183
ISBN: 1–56720–502–X

First published in 2002

Quorum Books, 88 Post Road West, Westport, CT 06881
An imprint of Greenwood Publishing Group, Inc.
www.quorumbooks.com

Printed in the United States of America

The paper used in this book complies with the
Permanent Paper Standard issued by the National
Information Standards Organization (Z39.48–1984).

10 9 8 7 6 5 4 3 2 1

Copyright Acknowledgments

The author and publisher gratefully acknowledge permission for use of the following:

"Privatization and Market Liberalization in Asia" by J.P. Singh reprinted from *Telecommunications Policy*, Volume 24, 2001, pp. 885–906, Copyright 2001 with permission from Elsevier Science.

This book is dedicated to India's poor, long in want of good governance, and to its bureaucrats—who want good ideas.

Contents

Tables

Figures

Foreword

In the present age of an information-based society, telecommunication – which provides the infrastructure for the flow of information – is a sine qua non of socio-economic development. India has come a long way in telecommunications development, mostly in recent years.

The history of telecommunications development in India is fascinating though somewhat chequered. Although the use of telecommunications commenced almost simultaneously with the invention of the telephone, growth was slow, uneven and intermittent, and it remained a state monopoly. A process of reforms was begun in the 1980s and its pace increased in the 1990s. The most important phase of reforms began with the New Telecom Policy of 1999, which ushered in a series of advanced, third-generation reforms that started yielding results during the past two years. The underlying theme of reforms was to usher in full competition through unrestricted entry in almost all service sectors. As a result, teledensity has doubled since 1999, with a particularly high growth rate in mobile services. These days, 1000 new telephone lines are added every hour and the rate is rising. This is still not enough. We intend to further accelerate roll-out, with an improvement in quality and with widespread distribution of services.

It is important that the fruits of telecommunications development reach those in all economic levels and in all regions of the country. This is not only a political maxim but a socio-economic necessity. Expectations are, naturally, rising. In a country with enormous human resources and IT potential, the advantages of globalization and of an information-based society can only be derived from quick, all-round and high-quality roll-outs. This raises issues of the efficient management of resources and technologies, requiring regular mid-course corrections to achieve optimal results.

I am indeed happy to go through this publication. There may be several issues and observations where there could be more than one view. However, it does outline the work of practitioners with policymakers and scholars, to present a cogent understanding of the process of telecommunications reform in India, and the opportunities and challenges that these present. The experiences of many other countries are examined to understand best practices . I compliment everybody concerned with this venture for the task accomplished.

I am sure that this publication will be of great interest and use not only in India but in other countries with similar problems, and will provide the template for those that want to develop their telecommunications infrastructure.

Pramod Mahajan
Minister   of   Parliamentary   Affairs,   Information   Technology   and Communications

Preface

In September 2000, I visited a village, Chandrampet, 10 miles from Sircilla town in the Karimnagar district of Andhra Pradesh and 90 miles from Hyderabad. I was surprised to find that, of the approximately 200 homes in the village, none had a telephone. There was not even a public telephone within 5 miles. But every home had cable TV – a service provided by a village entrepreneur who had a franchise from a large satellite TV firm and who had connected each home by coaxial cable to a central dish antenna.

To the western observer, this relative proliferation of cable TV over telephones would seem very unusual. Americans, for example, typically pay at least $40 per month to access cable (or satellite) TV whereas a phone line (for basic services) costs only about a third of this. Of course, most homes in the US have both cable TV and a telephone, but given a choice, the telephone is the more essential commodity and is cheaper, so would always be chosen.

But in this Indian village, cable TV costs Rs.50 (a little over $1 at end-2001 exchange rates) per month for 4 channels. Even in nearby Hyderabad, a subscription to 50 channels also costs only about Rs.50 per month. The business is profitable and flourishing, with over 70 million national subscribers, growing at 20% per year. It is also unregulated.

Meanwhile, a telephone connection in Hyderabad, also–for basic services– costs the user Rs.50 per month. The difference with cable TV is that the telephone company (which is state-owned) loses a lot of money at this price and its true cost is closer to $15 per month (or Rs.2400), i.e., the American cost. So the telephone company rations the telephone lines to loss making areas and is particularly slow in making telephones available in rural areas like Chandrampet where set-up (last-mile) costs are estimated to be 50% higher than in urban areas. Where it does service rural areas, it is almost invariably through a public telephone, usually without direct long-distance dialling.

The same village entrepreneur who provided the cable connections could be on to a big thing here: for a small additional cost for routers and related equipment, he could connect up the village's residents to each other and also connect up nearby villages over the cable network, providing, at least, Internet-protocol based telephony. Since India already has a well-developed fiber optic backbone network (in this case, accessible within 10 miles of Chandrampet), the village could also be easily and cheaply connected nationally and globally and provide voice, data and Internet services.

The entrepreneur would not, however, be allowed to do so. Using the cable TV network to provide even village telephony requires a special circle or state-wide license (there are only two such licensees in the whole state of Andhra Pradesh–with a population of 80 million–and no more licenses are likely to be given in the near-term). Interconnection with the national fiber-optic network requires a long-distance service provider's license, given only to national providers. The entrepreneur could try to obtain concessions or a franchise from the big state-wide or national licensees to cobble together the service at some additional cost, but he would likely fail because these licensees have not been interested in disturbing the phased roll-out of their public switched telephone network (PSTN) with which the proposed system would ultimately compete because of its intrinsically lower costs.

To the cable TV entrepreneur contemplating adding phone lines, the much talked about "last-mile problem" is a myth because his subscribers are already wired-up at the last mile, while policy barriers are the real problem. But, as the above example shows, making a few changes in policy can have a rapid impact on connectivity and, as argued in the book, without affecting the profitability of the big licensees.

Can such changes happen? The inertia of India's bureaucracy is legendary and Indians are the first to say "It cannot happen here!" Much of this view is based on past experiences and not all of it applies to the future. It is true that, by 1991, the Indian economy had suffered the weight of over four decades of poor, though not always poorly-intentioned, independent political governance. The state either stifled private initiative through limiting what could be done or by taxing the majority of the profits away, even by unhesitatingly levying special taxes on unexpectedly successful industries. Despite a huge, growing and democratically active population with a well-educated fringe, initiatives for substantial change had, therefore, usually come from outside the country and, lacking domestic support, quickly stagnated. The Green Revolution in agriculture began in the sixties with the work of Norman Borlaug, but, after helping India become self-sufficient in food, has not yet succeeded in giving the average Indian adequate nutrition. Even the remarkable Indian information technology (IT) industry began in the early eighties to service overseas demand, and an American firm, Texas Instruments, was the first to be given a broadband connection. But a stifling tariff regime has prevented the benefits from reaching domestic users and the industry, as of 2002, primarily existed to service overseas demand–an oddity given the size of the population.

The 1991 currency crisis began a remarkable process of change whose primary beneficiary has been the Indian civil service. Under pressure from the IMF and other multilateral lenders (again, the foreign factor resurfaces), the first bold steps were taken, particularly the delicensing of industry.

A decade later, something new is noticed in political governance: the ability of the politician and bureaucrat to say "I do not know the why and how of all things, but I am willing to cooperate with the outside world, such as practitioners and scholars, to learn." I do not know the origins of the change. It may that a decade of reform finally produced a suitable bureaucratic cadre; or it might be the decline in centrist politics due to coalitions and the consequent competition among the individual states.

The significance, though, is momentous. For the first time, citizenry do not have to make their business decisions of buying, selling, saving and investing with the anticipation that their success will lead to a negative reaction from the government. Business leaders from the IT field, such as Azim Premji and Narayan Murthy, are hailed as respected citizens and their advice eagerly sought by policymakers. The diaspora, once vilified for taking the benefits of their state-subsidized Indian education overseas, has an improved status, with persons such as the Silicon Valley-based IT-entrepreneur, Kanwal Rekhi, able to be heard in policymaking.

As a researcher in policy reform to enable entrepreneurship in India, telecommunications reform is a subject close to my heart. There is perhaps no other sector, with the possible exception of the power sector, where the leverage to success is so high. As the example of Chandrampet shows, there are no obvious models, no single set of best practices, that a policymaker can bring to bear. Rapid technological change, sectoral heterogeneity (Chandrampet's needs and solutions seem worlds apart from Bangalore's IT industry), the influence of legacy systems in the developed world and different starting points for reform imply the need for carefully thought out policies. So, while India still has a very long way to go in "getting it right", it also needs intellectual support – and that is the purpose of this book.

Several persons cooperated in the production of this book. For his quality of thought and passion for the cause, in addition to financial support for a conference on the subject of telecommunications reform in India held at Stanford University in November 2000, I would particularly like to thank the above-mentioned Kanwal Rekhi. I am also thankful to my fellow contributors and others who contributed their ideas and funds, including Anil Godhwani, B.V. Jagadeesh, Suhas Patil, Sun Microsystems and the US India Business Council. Harry Rowen, Director Emeritus of the Asia/Pacific Research Center, has been my intellectual mentor for the past three years and I owe him a constant debt for this. For production support, I would like to thank Bill Berry, Nina Duprey, and Rafael Ulate. The latter, in his role of administrative assistant, was a pleasure to work with. To my wife, Khairunessa, I owe the debt of time cheerfully given.

Abbreviations

AC	access center
ADSL	asymmetric digital subscriber line
AN	access network
ARB	Area Relay Base Station
AT&T	American Telephone and Telegraph
ATM	asynchronous transfer mode
AU	access unit
BDSU	basic rate digital subscriber unit
BJP	Bharatiya Janata Party
BN	backbone network
BRTA	Bangladesh Rural Telecommunications Authority
BSNL	Bharat Sanchar Nigam Ltd.
BTS	basic telephone service
C-DOT	Center for Development of Telematics
CAC	carrier access codes
CAGR	compounded average growth rate
CALLS	coalition for affordable local and long-distance services
CBS	connected base station
CCLR	carrier common line rates
CCS7	common channel signalling system

CCS	hundreds of call seconds
CDMA	code division multiple access
CLASS	custom local area signaling services
CLEC	competitive local exchange carrier
CMSP	cellular mobile service provider
COFETEL	Federal Telecommunications Commission
CPE	customer premises equipment
CRTC	Canadian Radio-television and Telecommunications Commission
CSP	cable service provider
D&I	drop and insert
DBS	direct broadcast by satellite
DECT	digital enhanced cordless telecommunications
DEL	direct exchange line
DIAS	direct Internet access system
DIU	DECT interface unit
DOT	Department of Telecommunications, India
DOTC	Department of Transport and Communication
DPNC	Dirección de Politicas y Normas de Communicación
DTH	direct to home
DSL	digital subscriber line
DSP	digital signal processing
DSU	digital subscriber unit
DTS	Department of Telecommunications Services
DWDM	dense wavelength division multiplex
EUCL	end user common line
FCC	Federal Communications Commission
FDI	foreign direct investment
FITEL	Fondo de Inversion de Telecomunicaciones
FSP	fixed service provider
GATT	general agreement on tariffs and trade

GCI	General Communications Incorporated
GDP	gross domestic product
GMPCS	global mobile personal communication services
GNP	gross national product
GSM	Global System for Mobile Communications
HCPM	hybrid cost proxy model
HDSU	high—bit rate digital subscriber unit
HFCL	Himachal Futuristic Communications Ltd.
IAN	Internet access unit
IDRC	International Development Research Center (Canada)
IIT	Indian Institute of Technology
ILEC	incumbent local exchange carrier
IP	Internet protocols
ISD	international subscriber dialing
ISDN	integrated services digital network
ISP	Internet service provider
IT	information technology
ITU	International Telecommunication Union
KMTC	Korea Mobile Telecom Corporation
KT	Korea Telecom
KTA	Korea Telecom Authority
LATA	local access and transport area
LDC	less developed country
LEC	local exchange carrier
LECOM	local exchange cost optimization model
LIBOR	London inter-bank offer rate
LSP	local service provider
MARR	multi-access radio relay
MIC	Ministry of Information and Communications
MII	Ministry of Information Industry
MNC	multi-national corporation

MPT	Ministry of Posts and Telecommunications
MSC	Multimedia Super Corridor
MTNL	Mahanagar Telephone Nigam Ltd.
MWS	multi-wallset
NAFTA	North American Free Trade Agreement
NECA	National Exchange Carriers Association
NEP-1991	New Economic Policy, 1991
NFAP-2000	National Frequency Allocation Plan, 2000
NGO	nongovernmental organizations
NIB	national internet backbone
NIC	newly industrializing country
NIE	new institutional economics
NIP	New Industrial Policy
NITP	National Information Technology Plan
NMS	network management system
NTC	National Telecommunications Commission
NTP-1994	National Telecom Policy 1994
NTP-1999	New Telecom Policy 1999
OECD	Organization for Economic Corporation and Development
OFTEL	Office of Telecommunications
OFTA	Office of the Telecommunications Authority
PBX	private branch exchange
PCO	public call office
PCS	personal communications systems
PDH	plesiochronous data hierarchy
PICC	primary interexchange carrier charge
PLDT	Philippines Long-Distance Telephone Company
PMRTS	public mobile radio trunk services
POTS	plain old telephone service
PSTN	public switched telephone network
PTIC	public tele-info center

PTO	public telephone operators
PTT	post telephone and telegraph
PUC	public utility commission
QOS	quality of service
R&D	research and development
RAS	remote access switch
RAX	Rural Automatic Exchange
RBOC	Regional Bell Operating Companies
RJ-11	U. S. standard telephone connector
RPSP	radio paging service provider
RS 232	a standard serial interface
SATCOM	satellite communications
SDH	synchronous data hierarchy
SINGTEL	Singapore Telecom
SLC	subscriber line charge
SNMP	simple network management protocol
SONET	synchronous optical network
SP	service provider
STD	subscriber trunk dialing
STM-16	16-channel statistical multiplex
SU	subscriber unit
TDSAT	Telecom Dispute Settlement and Appellate Tribunal
TEC	Telecommunication Engineering Center
TELMEX	Tel fonos de M xico
TELRAIC	total element long-run incremental cost
TENET	Telecommunications and Computer Network Group
TMN	telecommunications management network
TRAI	Telecom Regulatory Authority of India
UNDP	United Nations Development Program
UNESCO	United Nations Educational, Scientific, and Cultural Organization

USAID	U.S. Agency for International Development
USO	universal service obligation
USTR	U.S. Trade Representative
UT	Urban-Targeted
VDSL	very high data rate digital subscriber line
VOIP	voice over Internet protocols
VPT	village public telephone
VRU	versatile remote unit
VSAT	very small aperture terminal
VSNL	Videsh Sanchar Nigam Ltd.
WARTELS	Warung Telekomunikasi
WLL	wireless-in-local-loop
WPCC	wireless planning coordination committee
WS-IP	wallset with Internet port
WTO	World Trade Organization

Introduction

The objective of this book is to analyze Indian public policy on telecommunications. India's telecommunications sector is still mostly state-run, despite a decade-long process of reforms that ended the state monopoly, allowed private entry, and introduced independent regulation. The result has been inefficiency and under investment—India and China had similar numbers of telephone lines in 1990 (6 million), but, a decade later, India had 28 million lines, while China had 120 million.

Why has reform not delivered? The answers, as discussed in this book, lie in the choices made by policymakers on reforming the existing institutions that provided telecommunications products and services and what was done to enable new institutions (especially from the private sector) to be created—in particular, the degree of competition allowed and the rules that govern both old and new institutions.[1]

As we shall show, India's policymakers cannot easily be faulted for making bad choices since it may be argued that in ending the state monopoly, allowing private investment, and introducing independent regulation, they—after a complex process—ended up duplicating the experiences of other successful countries, such as in most of Europe. Given that telecommunications reform is relatively new—the U.S. Telecommunications Act dates to 1996—this was perhaps a natural choice for rational policymakers in a hurry, yet they risked making choices that had not been adequately field-tested. During the latter half of the 1990s, there was a new factor that had been unexpected at the start of reform in 1991: a rapid change in technology with potentially significant impact on the possibility of competition and achieving universal service goals.[2] These developments have made the experience of other countries an even riskier guide than earlier.

The main policy conclusions of the book are, first, that cookie-cutter solutions derived from rich-country experience do not always work in poorer countries (however pro-market the latter may be) and that good analysis relevant for the country at hand can lead to much better outcomes. For example, universal service goals suffered from an effort to use developed-country solutions in India, in particular, the subsidizing of rural users through telecommunications-related taxes on urban users. In India, where less than 3% of the population can afford a circuit-switched telephone line, it is irrational to use such a strategy. On the other hand, strategies such as cross-subsidies within rural areas through interconnection-charge design, using Internet protocol-based telephone services and line-sharing among subsidized users, can be shown to be better strategies.

Second, some of the choices made by policymakers were rational given the circumstances of the time but turned out to be inefficient due to changes that were unanticipated, such as in technology. Such was the case with the initial decision to create large service areas for basic service providers.

A final category of choices is shown to be inefficient, given both the initial conditions and anticipated events. Such was the case of the decision to license service providers prior to the creation of a regulator. These choices were probably most influenced by the need for immediate revenue due to budgetary shortfalls rather than the interests of consumers.

We believe that this book's lessons on reforming policy are relevant not just for India but for many similar countries reforming their telecommunications sectors, such as Indonesia, Mexico, and the Philippines. In addition, since some of the drivers of reform—such as the Internet economy and competition for basic services—are still very recent global phenomena, the book discusses many unexplored issues, adding to the literature on introducing competition, promoting universal service, implementing differential regulation between the former monopoly and newcomers, reaching agreement on power-sharing between lawmakers and regulators, encouraging appropriate technology choice and convergence, and the sequencing of reform.

This introductory chapter describes how the drivers of reform were introduced in India through changes in the institutional structure and the rules of the game. It is based on the contributions of Ghosh, Verma, and Dossani and Manikutty. We then discuss Singh's analysis of India's political economy and its effect on the pace of private investment, the effects of choices on policy goals and an analysis of the remaining required policy changes; and competition, based on the chapters by Casanueva, Jhunjhunwala, Hudson, and Rosston and Wimmer. Finally we discuss the introduction of universal service, based on the chapters by Braunstein; Gasmi, Laffont, and Sharkey; Khosla; and Kumar, Pernyeszi, Rao, and Yadagiri.

INTRODUCING REFORM

Telecommunications services and products up to 1991 were provided by a state-owned monopoly that was a division of the Department of Telecommunications, itself an arm of the Ministry of Communications.[3] The goal of telecommunications reform was to increase private investment; the strategies were to change the laws that had created a state-owned monopoly and create instead a new environment, consisting of new laws and rules, and create a regulator that would enforce them fairly.

Changing the Rules of the Game

In this section, we describe the complex process by which the laws and rules were changed to induce the private sector to invest in providing telecommunications services.

Initial Focus on Private Sector Equipment Manufacture. The reform of India's telecommunications sector began in 1991, when the government opened up exchange-level switch manufacturing to the private sector and welcomed foreign investment. Earlier, only customer-premises equipment (i.e., handsets and office switchboards) had been allowed for private manufacture (in 1986). Policymakers' approach to telecommunications prior to 1991 was to view it as a luxury good:

The primary need of the people is food, water and shelter. Telephone development can wait. In place of doing any good, development of the telecommunication infrastructure has tended to intensify the migration of population from rural to urban areas. There is a need to curb growth of telecom infrastructure particularly in the urban areas. (*Approach Paper to the Sixth Plan*, quoted in Balashankar, 1998, p. 30)[4]

The success of China in the 1990s in inducing foreign telecommunications equipment makers to set up shop through local-content requirements was probably an important motivator of initial Indian policies on local content. This was, apart from saving on costs, expected to bring in new capital, develop local manufacturing capabilities and save on foreign exchange. The National Telecom Policy of 1994 (NTP-1994) stated:

The additional resources required to achieve (teledensity) targets (are) beyond the capacity of Government funding. Private initiative would be used to complement the (Government's) efforts to raise additional resources through international generation. (Section 6) Telecommunication is a vital infrastructure. It is also technology intensive. It is, therefore, necessary that India not lag behind in getting the full advantage of the emerging new technologies. (Section 12)

The provision of telephone services was, however, retained as a state monopoly. This was, at the time, believed to be an adequate strategy for telecommunications development. An Indian policymaker looking around the world could be excused for thinking thus; China had similarly opened up only its manufacturing sector to private firms. Most of the advanced countries of Asia, including Japan and South Korea—Hong Kong being an exception—were similarly organized, as was all of Western Europe. Where such a strategy succeeded, foreign equipment suppliers competed fiercely with each other to set up manufacturing facilities and fulfill the demands for equipment from the state-owned monopoly. In addition, they provided finance, thus allowing the service provider to effectively leverage its limited resources.

China succeeded in attracting foreign investment, while India did not; the difference was that India did not offer a large-enough market. Although the two countries started out with similar numbers of phone lines in 1990, China was already a richer state, and its growth rate in demand for telephony was higher. This was also partly due to competition for service provision among various state organs. There were as many as 30 arms of different ministries and state governments providing telecommunications services. This probably resulted in a higher demand for equipment than a monopoly would want (see Wallsten, 2000, for general evidence on the effect of monopolies on line rollouts). These service providers had the additional advantage of being able to use the advanced stock markets of Hong Kong as a means to partly finance its state-owned service providers' demand for equipment. Second, unlike China, the Indian service provider—itself a part of the Ministry of Communications—also owned the only manufacturing firms and faced a conflict of interest when it placed orders for new equipment.

As Indian policymakers later discovered, equipment manufacturing was to become a very competitive field internationally, and it became possible to procure equipment as cheaply as having it made locally. Hence, in retrospect, it appears that the failure to attract foreign investment in manufacturing did not directly affect the growth of teledensity, although it kept the focus of policymakers on strategies to improve foreign investment in equipment manufacture rather than on improving line rollouts.

Introducing the Concept of Private Service Provision. The evolution of reform through the 1990s in response to this shortfall, as policymakers searched for ways to induce new private investment, led to a rejection of manufacturing-led investment in favor of a new focus on enabling private investment in services. This was not an easy evolution because of opposition from unions and the state-owned incumbent. But, slowly, the concept of allowing private provision in basic services came to be a politically acceptable route for accessing private investment.

Initially, when private service provision was first contemplated in July 1992, the policymaker's goal was not to allow competition in basic services but instead to supplement basic services by allowing private providers to offer premium services at high prices (such as mobile services). The revenue earned by the state through license fees and other charges on private providers was to be used to fulfill the state-owned incumbent's targets of providing both universal service and high-quality value-added services, the latter to also meet the needs of India's increasingly important information technology industry. That is why mobile service, which did not compete with basic services (at least, that was the perception at the time, in 1992, while the reality has been different), was the first private service to be allowed.[5] Licenses were issued to those who bid the highest up-front fees.

India's unexpected success in information technology also assisted the acceptance of private service provision by putting pressure on the government to enable solutions that would raise the quality of services faster than was possible for the government on its own. By March 2000, the software industry in India had output of $5.7 billion, growing at 50% per year (Nasscom, 2000). Improving the availability of bandwidth was a goal of the New Telecom Policy of 1999 (NTP-1999), which stated that the new policy would:

Strive to provide a balance between the provision of universal service to all uncovered areas, including the rural areas, and the provision of high-level services capable of meeting the needs of the country's economy (Section 2.0). In addition to some of the objectives of NTP 1994 not being fulfilled, there have been far-reaching developments in the recent past in the telecom, information technology (IT), consumer electronics, and media industries world-wide. The new telecom policy framework is also required to facilitate India's vision of becoming an IT superpower and develop a world-class telecom infrastructure in the country. (Section 1.3)

The solution implemented by the Department of Telecommunications (DOT) was to open up data services to the private sector while retaining basic service provision in the public sector (in order to continue with the policy of cross-subsidy). Hence, data traffic was the earliest wireline service allowed to private providers (in 1998), even though technological developments at the time made it possible for voice traffic to be sent as data traffic.

The concept of private service provision suffered a setback when none of the mobile service licensees were able to pay the fees that they had bid, apparently due to overbidding. Similarly, private basic service licensees, who had been awarded their licenses in 1994, also failed to pay the promised fees. It took another six years and an important policy change in 1999 before the private sector started supplying services at significant levels.

Doing Away with Local-Content Requirements. Meanwhile, the focus on private equipment manufacture continued to lose importance, partly because it did not happen and partly because policymakers shifted their reliance to rules that would enable the private sector to provide services.

NTP-1999 made private service provision possible through three new principles. First, the government accepted the spread of telecommunications as a necessity rather than a luxury and no longer looked for high up-front fees in return for franchises. Second, new entrants from the private sector were to be put on par with the incumbent state-owned provider, and, third, a hitherto contentious and ineffective regulatory body was strengthened and made independent. As part of the second initiative, NTP-1999 did away with local-content requirements for all providers, whether private of state-owned.[6]

It was a difficult process even for local content to be done away with as official policy, even if the effectiveness of implementation—particularly within the incumbent—has yet to be judged as of this writing. As noted earlier, an important reason that private equipment manufacturers stayed away despite favorable terms of entry offered in 1991 (similar to those offered by China, such as the promise of orders in return for increases in local-content manufacture) was limited demand. The state-owned provider, which was the only buyer of exchange-level equipment, could not afford the full price of high-quality private equipment as it was under a political obligation to provide subsidized service to large classes of the population and to protect employment, both within its basic service provider and within its equipment-manufacturing subsidiaries.

In this context, a decision, made as early as 1991, to allow private service provision in mobile services without constraints on the local content of equipment was to later have a major positive impact on rollout and on subsequent local-content rules for wireline equipment manufacturers as well. The decision was, at the time, a relatively easy one for policymakers given their political constraints (and their wish to demonstrate a case of successful and speedy outcome of reform). Mobile service was perceived to be a supplementary service for wealthier segments of the population and would, therefore, not hurt demand for the basic services provided by the state-owned incumbent. Conveniently, the state-owned equipment manufacturing industry had no investment in cellular equipment since it was focused entirely on wireline-related equipment. Finally, politicians representing rural interests viewed the sale of mobile licenses as a source of revenue to fund rural services. The decision was reiterated in NTP-1999, which stated:

The CMSP (cellular mobile service provider) shall be free to provide, in its service area of operation, all types of mobile services including voice and non-voice messages, data services and PCOs (public call offices) *utilizing any type of network equipment* including circuit and/or packet switches, that meet the relevant International Telecommunication Union (ITU)/Telecommunication Engineering Center (TEC) standards. (NTP-1999, Section 3.1; emphasis added)

The reason that this decision on de-linking service provision with local-content requirements turned out to be important is that it could otherwise have led to some fundamental contradictions between policies. While local-content policies make sense when all users of exchange-level equipment (i.e., the service providers) are controlled by the state (as in China), it does not work when service providers are private.[7] Private service providers, expected to compete with each other and the state-owned incumbent, will not invest in line rollout unless they have the freedom to choose equipment (and, along with it, the technology that is used to make it). In some cases, this might be technology that they are already familiar with rather than the policymakers' view of what is appropriate. For example, mobile service providers in India include European, Asian, and American firms, each with experience in different legacy systems. Hence, the policymakers' decision to allow any technology provided it met the basic Global System for Mobile Communications (GSM) standard was, in hindsight, a sensible one. Of course, abandoning local-content rules also meant, therefore, abandoning control over the technology to be implemented. This, too, was a favorable outcome of reform.

In wireline services, however, the political issues on technology and equipment choice were more difficult since the affected segments—the incumbent state-owned provider and the state-owned equipment manufacturers—were politically powerful. New forces with their own interests in opposing competition also quickly developed. As a result, there were constant slowdowns due to policymakers' insistence on local content and on appropriate technologies. For example, supplying voice services over the Internet (technically, voice over Internet protocols, or VoIP) ought to be a natural solution for improving the affordability of a telephone call. China, for example, has had great success with this as it has brought down the cost of making calls by as much as 70% (Chapter 3). Thus, a VoIP caller in China typically buys a prepaid card that takes him or her, via any phone line (including a public phone), to the Internet and finally to the recipient's phone line. Yet, DOT—apparently under pressure from the state-owned incumbent that fears a loss in revenue—has not permitted VoIP. Similarly, in March 2001, a policymaker-recommended technology for rural provision, fixed wireless access technologies (also known as wireless-in-local-loop or WLL), was strongly opposed by a new political force, the mobile service providers, arguing that it would affect their business. Private wireline licensees, who wanted the flexibility of using any available technology, including WLL, threatened to delay rollout in return.

The situation has improved since the year 2000, when the regulator (as opposed to the policymaker, DOT, which was the agency recommending technologies, including WLL) declared itself to be "technology-neutral" (Chapter 2). This should, over time, resolve the contradiction in a sensible way, despite DOT's continued activism on the subject, via acceptance of the regulator's view. This is an interesting case of the regulator's setting policy in an area that the DOT has not explicitly delegated to it and reflects its greater capability (vis-à-vis DOT) to be able to understand the implications of trying to dictate technological choice.

Being technology-neutral also means that the government has abandoned plans for local-content manufacture (since locally manufactured products of necessity cannot encompass the full range of technologies available globally).

The reforms in local-content manufacture and technology choice also illustrate a case of reforms that were incomplete initially (in this case, for political reasons) and then were completed (after costly delays).

By the year 2000, when some landmark reforms occurred, including the corporatization of the state-owned provider (hitherto a division of DOT), the beginning of private provision in land-line services, the flourishing of private (including foreign-owned) cellular service provision, and the opening up of domestic long-distance services to private providers, the concept of private service provision combined with a level playing field with the incumbent (not necessarily an easy concept to implement, as discussed later) had come to be firmly established as a policy goal.

Introducing Revenue Sharing. Revenue sharing as a form of taxation of service providers, in replacement of up-front license fees, was introduced in

NTP-1999. NTP-1999's first objective, improving affordability of services, was sought to be achieved by foregoing up-front license fees earlier agreed to be paid by licensees (but which remained unpaid). Instead, the new policy offered licensees the opportunity to migrate to a new regime of sharing revenue (in return, licensees had to agree that there could be an unlimited number of new licensees). The new rule made sense given the failure of the first one, but it also reflected a new economic reality, that the immediate need for government revenue had lessened relative to the need for teledensity over the decade.

In 1991, when reform began, there was a much greater need for up-front revenue. At the time, India's motive for reform was to find a solution to its balance-of-payments problems and to pay for the costs of higher unemployment that arose from the economic slowdown. Then, the need of the hour was to earn high up-front revenue to ease the pains of reform.

Accordingly, it is not surprising that licenses for service provision were initially sold (in 1992 and 1994 for mobile and wireline services, respectively) for a high up-front fee (Chapter 3). In return, licensees were guaranteed that a duopolistic structure would be implemented, although mobile and wireline services were considered separate services.

This strategy did not work because winners overbid, leading to defaults in paying license dues, when service providers realized that they had overestimated revenue and began to renege on their contracts. As NTP-1999 acknowledged:

the government recognizes that the result of the privatization has so far not been entirely satisfactory. While there has been a rapid rollout of cellular mobile networks in the metros and states with currently over 1 million subscribers, most of the projects today are facing problems. The main reason, according to the cellular and basic operators, has been the fact that the actual revenues realized by these projects have been far short of the projections, and the operators are unable to arrange financing for their projects and therefore complete their projects. Basic telecom services by private operators have only just commenced in a limited way in two of the six circles where licenses were awarded. As a result, some of the targets as envisaged in the objectives of the NTP-1994 have remained unfulfilled. The private sector entry has been slower than what was envisaged in the NTP-1994 (NTP-1999, Section 1.2).

As court cases against defaulting licensees by DOT piled up, licensees—all of whom had earlier, strong connections with bureaucracy and politicians—had continued to pressure the government to resolve the issue in a different way rather than through the courts. The government responded as stated in NTP-1999 by offering licensees "migration" to a new policy in which the government would surrender its claim on license fees and take a revenue share. In return for this concession, licensees had to agree to the end of the duopoly. All the licensees in both mobile and wireline services subsequently agreed to the change, and the court cases were dropped by DOT.

The turnaround by the government was sensible and also possible given the changed macroeconomic environment. By 1999, the government's financial position was considerably different from that at the time of its crisis in 1991. By

March 1999, foreign reserves were in excess of $29 billion compared with less than $300 million in early 1991, and economic growth had stabilized at 6% versus 0.8% for the fiscal year ended March 1992; hence, the government could afford to take the view that up-front revenue was less important than a more balanced plan that led to speedier development in return.

Allowing Foreign Service Provision. In the early days of reform, foreign value-added was believed to be greatest in equipment quality, whereas service provision was viewed as a low-technology job best fulfilled in the interests of saving foreign exchange by the state-owned incumbent or local firms.[8] Thus, NTP-1994 focused on improving customer service through better customer service but restricted basic service provision to companies registered in India (NTP-1994, Section 10). By 1999, foreign ownership was seen as a necessary element of the service sector, offering two advantages: better technology and better access to capital. Foreign ownership in manufacture was permitted up to 100%, while, in basic and cellular services, it was restricted to 49% (unless special approval was obtained). For E-mail, voice mail, and other value-added services, the limit of foreign ownership was 51%. Even 49% was enough for control since the balance did not have to be held by the state or a single private firm but could be widely distributed.

It should also be recognized that a changed attitude toward foreign service provision was not just caused by local events. Telecommunications reform for market-driven economies such as India became globally significant only after the U.S. Telecommunications Act of 1996, which was designed to promote competition and reduce regulatory burdens. Since then, similar waves of reform swept several countries as they attempted to keep up with the United States' capabilities in communications. Concurrently, changes in technology led to new, economical solutions for poorer countries, particularly using wireless access and networks based on Internet protocols. The Indian government, by 1999, recognized that it could not keep up with the pace of change through its own organizations and private domestic firms and needed the foreign private sector if rapid and affordable technological change was to take place in India.

It was expected that India's IT sector would play a role in improving the quality of telecommunications services, especially bolstered by the investment activities of nonresident Indians, many of whom were global pioneers in the field. To some extent, this had happened by 2000, as evidenced by the growth of private Internet service providers and portals. However, some developments were resisted by policymakers. As noted earlier, NTP-1999 did not open up VoIP for private sector provision. Policymakers also responded to new ideas with great conservatism. For example, an innovative Silicon Valley start-up, Naveen, offered a low-cost product in 2000 particularly suited to emerging-country conditions of low teledensity. An Indian resident, using Naveen's technology, could record a voice mail by calling a local number. The voice mail was then transmitted over the Internet to the designated recipient (who could be anywhere in the world).

Policymakers did not allow Naveen to begin operations on the grounds that the service that it offered required it to have a license to deliver basic services. Such licenses were available only on a circle-wide basis and required large up-front capital investments.[9]

Summing Up. Why was it so difficult to get the rules right? Politics has played an important role in the evolution of telecommunications policy. In particular, firms with political linkages rather than proven telecommunications capabilities (of which there were several, particularly from the newly developing IT segment) have gathered the bulk of the licenses. Singh (Chapter 5) provides a justification for the slow pace of private investment in India based on its political economy and the property rights that have evolved. Singh provides a detailed analysis of six Asian countries, China, India, Malaysia, the Philippines, Singapore, and South Korea, to demonstrate his case. For example, in China, the agenda was driven by the shifts in political fortunes of the Ministry of Posts and Telegraphs. When its fortunes waned, competition sprang up (and has been sustained) through the involvement in telecom service provision by other powerful ministries such as industry, defense and railways. As a result, there has been strong competition within state-owned firms leading to high rollout rates, though with a neglect of the politically weak rural areas. Hence, the exclusion of foreigners from service provision did not matter. In addition, Hong Kong has been a favored stock market for state-owned telecom firms to raise capital (although management control is firmly in the hands of the state). Other countries have often had a simpler time thanks to the overwhelming political power of a single class, such as the *Chaebol* in South Korea and the Bumiputeras in Malaysia. Singh finds India's case to be the most complex of the six countries; with the Department of Telecommunications a battleground between several powerful groups: multinational and new economy firms asking for better service, supported by urban users from outside the formal coalition who exert pressure through the media, and the state-owned sector trying to protect its market share, supported by unions and politicians (who may be supported by domestic businesses continuing to benefit from inward-oriented policies and with a stake in keeping multi-national corporations out of the market). Politicians also represent the rural sector, where teledensity is only 0.4 but where over two-thirds of voters live, in their demands for subsidized services.

Singh concludes that (1) introducing market competition is slow, messy, and difficult to manage, but, where present, it is better for growth than privatization alone, and (2) network expansion and efficiency are most noticeable where adequate property rights and enforcement mechanisms are in place. He also conjectures that the East Asia model toward network expansion may not be easily generalizable.

Independent Regulation

Achieving independent regulation was an important part of reform efforts. It should have happened as one of the first steps of reform but, in fact, came later.

As Ghosh states in Chapter 1, unlike the European countries, where the setting up of an independent regulator preceded the opening up of the market, in India there was a reversal of sequence, and an independent statutory regulator was established only in 1997. The DOT was initially keen to undertake regulatory functions as well. This was probably the main reason for the absence of an independent regulatory body. One of the motives for finally doing so was that the licenses for private fixed-line and cellular services that had been issued earlier in 1992 and 1995 were not being used; this was widely attributed to the absence of clear, independent regulation (later, there was evidence of corrupt issuance as well). The Telecom Regulatory Authority of India (TRAI), charged with promoting nondiscriminatory competition, enabling private sector participation and promoting universal access, was set up in 1997.

The period 1997–2000 was a difficult time for TRAI. There were constant conflicts between the regulator and policymakers. Some of the conflicts had to do with differences in interpretation of the rights of the regulator vis-à-vis the policymaker, DOT. This was particularly so in the case of licensure, where TRAI questioned the terms of licensure of some of the licenses awarded by DOT and was taken by DOT to court (DOT won all the cases on the grounds that the government had explicitly given it jurisdiction over licensure). Other conflicts occurred even in areas that seemed to be within TRAI's jurisdiction but were opposed by DOT. For example, in March 1999, TRAI announced a tariff rebalancing that raised local call charges and reduced long-distance charges. Although TRAI legally had the right to rebalance rates, the government faced an uproar in Parliament on the issue and subsequently disallowed TRAI from making the changes (which, post-NTP-1999, have become relatively routine). When asked how the government could justify its action of overruling a legally independent regulator, such an action implying that the government did not think the regulator's existence to be necessary, a DOT source replied that:

the people's interests are supreme, and the spirit is more important than the institution. An increase in rentals and local call charges cannot be allowed because it will make telephones unaffordable, and a drastic cut in subscriber trunk dialing/ international subscriber dialing (ISD/STD) (long-distance) rates cannot be allowed as it will adversely affect the revenues of DOT, rendering it incapable of undertaking the development of services in rural and backward areas (*Times* of India, March 12, 1999).

NTP-1999 sought to resolve the issue by stating, "The Government is committed to a strong and independent regulator with comprehensive powers and clear authority to effectively perform its functions" (Section 7.0). The amendment to the TRAI act in 2000 clarified that the regulator's role was limited to tariffs. NTP-1999 stated, "TRAI has the powers to issue directions to Government (in its role as service provider) and further to adjudicate all disputes arising between Government (in its role as service provider) and any other service provider" (Section 7.0). In the previous example of tariff rebalancing, therefore, the regulator was well within its rights to amend tariffs, and such rebalancing had become a routine regulatory activity by the year 2000. The problems that its tariff orders created in 1999 appear to have been due to the government's being suspected of abdicating its responsibility of serving the underprivileged by shifting politically difficult issues onto the regulator, which might lack the capacity to be politically sensitive. Equally important, the new regulator (Verma, appointed in 2000) was able to develop a strong working relationship with policymakers, particularly Ghosh, showing perhaps the importance of having the right people in place in the early stages of institution building. The regulatory environment in 2000 thus differed greatly from its initial situation.

India's chief telecom regulator, Maya Verma, chairman of TRAI, has argued that achieving independent regulation takes time because regulatory discipline is a comparatively new phenomenon in most countries (Chapter 2). He also stresses the importance of good regulation in developing economies. He argues that good regulation in telecommunications is important because it is widely recognized that a competitive private sector can do better than a monopoly (either state or private). Developing countries have the additional burden of undercapitalized telecommunications, a problem that cannot be solved by continued state involvement. At the same time, the private sector, particularly from overseas, tends to be more cautious about investing in telecommunications in developing countries than in developed countries. The reason is that investments in telecommunications service provision are by their nature long-term investments, requiring considerable confidence in the stability of the rules and regulations. Hence, independent regulation becomes a critical requirement. As Verma shows, the recent spurt of growth in India of the private cellular sector (which includes several overseas providers) can clearly be traced to the setting up of a regulatory body in 1997, albeit with a lag while outsiders verified its independence.

Although the regulator, since 2000, has been given complete independence in some areas (e.g., tariff-setting), it is restricted in others (e.g., it cannot issue or cancel service providers' licenses, which is to be done by elected officials). NTP-1999 states, "The functions of licensor and policy maker would continue to be discharged by Government in its sovereign capacity" (Section 7.0). In the United States and other advanced countries, regulatory independence from lawmakers for license criteria and issuance is built into the initial design of the regulatory structure (although regulatory capture by market participants may later occur). The hybrid Indian structure where policymakers decide on the licensing structure and on who gets licenses requires a much closer and more frequent interaction between the regulator and policymakers if the system is to work, if indeed it can work. It also raises issues of regulatory capacity vis-à-vis that of policymakers, the division of powers between the regulator and lawmakers, and the possibility of regulatory recapture by the state.

Technology choices are another gray area between the regulator and DOT, with TRAI preferring to remain technology-neutral, while DOT continues to recommend technologies.

The conclusion in examining regulatory reform in India is that reforms have not been well structured and that the division of powers between the regulator and the policymakers is inefficient. A good structure would give adequate authority to the regulator and allow the regulator to build up its institutional capabilities. The role of policymakers—as distinct from the regulator—should be to provide only broad guidelines, such as the need to create a pro-competitive environment, to provide lifeline services adequately, and to maximize the role of market forces, leaving it to the regulator to define these directives in the Indian context and create and implement the necessary mechanisms. Instead, the policymakers have kept key roles for themselves in the reform process, such as determining who gets licenses in the private sector and recommending technologies. This not only reduces the accountability of both the policymaker and the regulator but is a challenge to policymakers' institutional capability as well, with an adverse, long-term impact on efficiency and investment in the telecommunications sector.

Some of the changes needed to resolve the problem areas have been incorporated in a communications convergence bill that was expected to be introduced in Parliament at the end of the calendar year 2001. The draft version is encouraging: the regulator will be empowered to issue licenses and to make decisions on technology. With these changes, the gaps in regulation of the carriage of telecommunications services will have been filled.[10]

It may appear from the preceding discussion that telecom reform in India is incomplete, but this is not how policymakers see it. The government's chief policymaker, Shyamal Ghosh, states that the various reforms committed under NTP-1999 were almost complete by March 2001, some months ahead of schedule. In consequence, the first years of the new millennium are expected to be a period of growth and consolidation (Chapter 1). Yet, reforms have not delivered on their objectives (though it may be argued that it is too early to pass judgment given that the most significant reforms took place in the period 1999–2000). This is the subject of the next section.

REFORM AND THE ACHIEVEMENT OF POLICY GOALS

The foremost objective of policymakers was increasing teledensity to satisfactory levels. NTP-1994 projected 7.5 million telephone lines by 1997, while 8.73 million lines were provided. While this looks satisfactory relative to targets, this was still a teledensity of only 0.9 lines per 100 persons. All 600,000 villages were to be provided with at least one public telephone by 1997, while only 310,000 villages were covered (NTP-1999, Section 1.2). By 2000, teledensity had risen to 3.5, while rural teledensity was 0.4.

As noted earlier, there has been a shortfall in private investment. There is almost no private investment in equipment manufacture, with limited private investment in fixed lines. Up to March 2000, private service providers had installed only 140,790 lines against a license commitment of 1.36 million (TRAI, 2000, Table 3.A). Of these, only 12 were village public telephones against a license commitment of 24,303 (calculated from total lines actually installed rather than committed). Thus, private licensees have simply reneged on their obligations. The state-owned service provider is still the only serious investor. It is also inefficient, as Table 1 shows.

Table 1
Efficiency of DOT

	Capital costs/ line $	Number of lines/ employee
DOT, India (3/98)	657.6	44
Philippines long-distance Telephone Company, the Philippines	2951*	113
Telmex, Mexico	885	201
SBC, USA	781	351

* Includes revaluation reserve.
Figures as of December 1999, except where indicated.
Source: Chapter 3, An Institutional View.

We discuss the needed policy changes in this section. The starting point for our analysis is to look ahead from the changes that were adopted following NTP-1999 through to the end of the year 2000. These changes, as discussed earlier, allowed private service providers to convert their fee-based licenses to one based on revenue sharing. The policy on the number of licensees was also changed to allow multiple licensees. Universal service was to be funded by a revenue tax of 5%.

Introducing Competition

The standard way to introduce competition, as favored by, say, the U.S. Telecommunications Act of 1996, is to allow open access to any provider and impose stringent obligations on incumbent network providers to interconnect with new entrants on just and reasonable terms. However, developing countries such as Mexico and India have decided to license new providers in phases. There is a fear that, otherwise, entry will be deterred by the prospect of unfettered competition. How real is this fear? On the face of it, it seems a groundless one. In a country with low teledensity and long waiting lists indicating unmet demand, there surely ought to be enough profitable business for all entrants, while licensed exclusivity will most likely lead to under investment, thus failing to solve the problem. Second, it has been shown that the largest share of a network's cost and the largest potential benefits of competition are in "last-mile" access (Chapter 4), and competition for the last mile will not be realized through exclusivity. Indian policymakers, after initially arguing for limited licensing, changed their approach (in 2001) in favor of greater competition, although providers still need to have access to large amounts of capital. This is because the licenses are given out for large circles, each with a population of about 50 million. Will this ensure competition; or are further structural changes needed?

The real fear for policymakers (and new private providers) is not competition from other newcomers but that the incumbent will refuse to play fairly with newcomers. This requires that special attention be paid to the regulation of the incumbent.

Casanueva (Chapter 9) has examined regulatory reform in Mexico as an instructive example for newly reforming countries like India that have a dominant incumbent. In the last two decades the Mexican telecommunications industry has experienced substantial transformation. These changes have been triggered, to a large extent, by the privatization of Teléfonos de México (Telmex), the country's original public telecommunications operator, and by the opening of the telecommunications markets to competition. The profound changes in the telecommunications markets have been sometimes ushered in by, and sometimes followed by, regulatory reform. However, some key aspects of the regulatory process have not resulted in the efficient use of the available infrastructure and its further expansion. Nor have they resulted in a higher penetration of telephone lines (mainly residential), which represents access by the end users to a more diversified array of telecommunications services, with better quality and lower prices. The causes appear to be the state's political economy, in which Telmex has historically been a powerful force. For example, the concept of dominant-carrier regulation (i.e., differential regulation of the dominant carrier due to its superior market power) was successfully resisted until 2000, over a decade after reform. The result has been under investment, although efficiency seems to have markedly increased within Telmex as a result of privatization. The experience of Telmex offers important lessons for India, which has a dominant carrier that seems to be exercising, through policymakers, influence over the pace of reform. For example, policymakers have chastised private fixed-line licensees for initially focusing on "cherry-picking" or luring away the incumbent's best customers, instead of serving those who have never had service earlier.

Issuing licenses to newcomers with large franchised populations is also likely to create problems. First, as noted, newcomers will need large amounts of capital if they are to qualify as licensees. Second, even well-funded newcomers will not be able to move as fast in covering less affluent areas as small newcomers.

The solution is to delicense service provision along with franchises for newcomers that want to resell bulk lines purchased from large providers. This is what the U.S. Telecommunications Act of 1996 enabled, but this solution has a longer history. While American Telephone and Telegraph's (AT&T) success in providing universal service in the twentieth century is often cited as the premier example of the success of regulated monopoly, the more appropriate model for Indian reform may not be that of the United States up to 1984 (prior to the breakup of AT&T) but the United States before 1913. The end of the Bell patents in 1894 had a profound impact on U.S. telecommunications, leading to the growth of over 3,000 independent companies by 1913, often with no interconnection facilities with the dominant carrier, AT&T. Yet, the positive impact of this development was deep: independent firms competed actively with AT&T, offering better local service in return for being unable to offer long-distance service. For example, they led AT&T in introducing new technologies, including implementing the Strowger exchange, a fundamental switching technology of the time. Their biggest impact was through an externality: their competition led to the installation of an extensive local network that would add significant value to AT&T's long-distance network (that AT&T as a monopolist would not have been able to achieve on its own), which AT&T could capitalize on through its later acquisitions of independent firms.

Had a regulated monopoly been an appropriate model for development, surely some of the European countries, such as Germany and Britain, which created monopolies as soon as the Bell patents expired in Europe (i.e., in 1894) would have done as well as the United States. The evidence is otherwise. Beginning with the same teledensity as in the United States in 1894, Europe saw limited growth (its teledensity grew from 0.5 to 0.75 by 1913, while the United States went from 0.5 to 13 (Lipartito, 1997).

Another fundamental reason for preferring a competitive over a monopolistic service provider is that technological developments have continued to reduce the economies of scale at the last mile. For example, technology developed by Jhunjhunwala (Chapter 4), among others, is based on wireless (and in use in over 20 countries), which provides voice telephony and adequate Internet access at speeds up to 70 kbps (which is about 50% of the speed of standard, developed-country solutions as of the year 2000 but considerably below the 45 mbps offered by latest-generation wireless technology) and costs $250 per line, a saving of 75% over standard solutions. These savings are generated by bundling several services at the last mile, such as voice and data traffic, as well as limited upside data speed capabilities (but still well above the acceptable minimum for broadband). But, as Jhunjhunwala argues, such technology will not be adopted widely in India unless there are changes in the competitive structure. The most important change that he argues for is competitive access at the local loop. Under current rules, private licensees are given statewide licenses (with average population of 50 million). Given the installed cost of $1,000/line, only 2% of the Indian population can afford telephones. The strategy of the private licensees, who face such widely heterogeneous populations, has been to "cherry-pick" off the state provider by offering wealthier segments developed-country service quality (at developed-country prices). Only after the cherry-picking is complete will they move on to cover poorer clients using technologies of the type developed by Jhunjhunwala. This could take several years given the low teledensity of just 8 lines per 100 urban residents (i.e., there is enough business for them to do in richer urban areas before covering poorer rural areas). The solution to the problem of slow deployment is to delicense last-mile provision so that strategies that price service according to quality can be implemented by new providers.[11] Such a strategy would have the additional advantage of reducing subscriber costs since the small independents typically have much lower costs than large licensees, particularly given the absence in economies of scale at the level of the local loop. Jhunjhunwala (Chapter 4) discusses several other benefits of the decentralized structure proposed by him, including a boost to local manufacturing and research and development (R&D) efforts.

Hudson (Chapter 7) provides a primer of positive and cautionary lessons for India's reformers. She begins with an analysis of how information is critical to development, particularly rural development, as has been well documented for India. Taking examples from several countries, she shows that teledensity is not by itself sufficient for development, other infrastructure needing to be in place. But market forces by themselves may be inadequate to drive other infrastructure, as the case of South Africa shows. The solution is joint inter-ministerial planning, something that market-driven economies may find difficult. Independent regulation is also an important requirement but is often hard to achieve. In practice, the regulator tends to be staffed with personnel from the erstwhile state monopoly and may favor it. Second, while a conceptually neat division exists between regulators and policymakers, in practice, as has happened in Canada and the United States, regulators often set policy due to the absence of timely policymaker involvement. In India, by contrast, the regulator's powers have been limited, and there is the risk that it will not be able to make timely decisions. Other cautions are offered in terms of following old paradigms that are no longer relevant, such as the distinguishing of services between fixed-line (also called "basic" service) and mobile services (in fact, as Hudson shows, mobile service has become the basic service in several countries) and long exclusivity periods. Unfortunately, India has chosen to adopt both these paradigms. Similarly, a reliance on the dominant carrier may not be the most efficient way to provide universal service (although India has chosen this method), as shown by Chile, in which bidding mechanisms have worked and which has shown the world that rural demand is often much stronger than revealed in the presence of a state-owned monopoly. There is also considerable heterogeneity within rural areas, and some areas may be viable. For example, in Bangladesh, the rural providers are allowed to prioritize customers by financial capability and to charge a substantial upfront connection fee. The result is that the Bangladesh Rural Telecommunications Authority is profitable despite having to provide at least one public call office in each village that requests one.

Rosston and Wimmer (Chapter 8) look at the impact of social-pricing policies on competitive entry in United States markets following the Telecommunications Act of 1996. They find that regulators' interest in preserving local subsidies in certain areas reduces, as expected, new entry into telecommunications in those areas. The Telecom Act also introduced portable universal service funding, which should affect competitors' decision to enter rural settings. They also find that federal subsidies to cover high costs of entry, which are yet to be targeted, still seem to be having an impact on competitors' decisions to enter. The authors conclude that implicit subsidies are untenable in competitive markets; eliminating them should be a primary regulatory task.

In summary, policymakers' fears about unfettered competition might be overstated, and the balance of both theoretical and empirical evidence favors more, rather than less, competition in service provision.

Providing Universal Service

In India, universal service is funded through a tax (currently 5%) on the revenue of all service providers. Given that only 2% of the country's population can afford to pay the full cost of basic telephone service (Chapter 4), the tax collected is obviously insufficient to provide connections for those who cannot afford it. Different solutions are needed. Some of these can be based on new, cheaper technologies, while some can be based on clever structuring of tariffs and different institutional structures. We discuss next the chapters that deal with these issues.

Braunstein (Chapter 10) focuses on the use of interconnection charges as a device for promoting universal service. As new entrants enter a telecommunications market, the problem of interconnection has two dimensions, technical and economic. Braunstein focuses on the latter. Users wish to communicate with others regardless of which firm(s) provides them services and connects them to the network. The terms of interconnection between and among network operators directly influence both the costs to the users and the financial prospects of the operators, both incumbents and new entrants. It is in the national interest to encourage the widespread diffusion of the network and to promote access by users who might not be considered economically viable by operators. There are various ways of encouraging this "universal service," but it is likely that the specific mechanisms needed after liberalization will be different from those that have been used in a monopoly regime.

Historically, the standard model was to have a single provider of local telephone service, using central offices (switches) and wires to provide service to those regions in the service area that were profitable, at least on average, to serve. Local requirements and/or national policy may also have encouraged or required the provision of service to remote regions or to neighborhoods with lower purchasing power, thus extending the reach of telephone services. These local telephone operators then connected to trunk (long-distance) carriers and international carriers, who may or may not have had common ownership with the local carrier(s).

Domestic policies have, of course, varied from country to country, but it was common to see some or all of the following:

- Local tariffs were averaged across customers despite the fact that the cost of serving one region might be different from the costs of serving another. In addition, the non-traffic-sensitive portion of the tariff (the monthly subscriber fee or "line rental") was often kept artificially low.

- The tariffs for trunk calls were sufficiently higher than costs so as to enable the costs of local service to be kept low. This could be accomplished either by having an integrated entity with an implicit cross-subsidy or by having the trunk carriers pay call origination and/or termination fees to local carriers that were significantly above the costs of the local carriers.

- International rates were many times the cost of service. These high rates, when combined with a traffic imbalance on certain routes, led to a hard-currency inflow to monopoly carriers in several countries.

This pattern of tariffs had several effects. While it might have helped address national policy goals such as universal service, it also provided incentives for new entrants to provide services at below current price levels, thereby making the situation unstable.

The liberalization in many countries of specific parts of the market, often starting with trunk and international services, and the growth of mobile services and new access technologies have made the situation ever more complex. In each case the payments between carriers (whether called access fees, settlements, termination charges, or interconnection fees) and the bases for those payments have become explicit and subject to scrutiny. At the same time, the entry of new carriers and new services, especially mobile telephony, has forced many regulatory and policy bodies to reopen the issue of how to finance universal service. This has also, in some cases, included the reexamination of what universal service means (or should mean) in the current circumstances.

For example, the old sharing models of interconnection fees included cost-based or revenue-sharing mechanisms. Under a liberalized environment, new options such as bill-and-keep (the originator of the call collects and keeps all the payments received) or negotiated payments have been used. The problem that these new mechanisms have for universal service is that they lead to a reduction in producers' surplus and, therefore, in the funds available to provide universal service. Hence, in order to provide a surplus to fund universal service, it may be necessary for the regulator to step in and impose a schedule of interconnection fees.

Interestingly, the experiences of Israel, Sweden, and the United States documented by Braunstein, show that interconnection fees are heavily influenced by the relative powers of the incumbent. In the United States, the tradition of independent regulation has made the incumbent somewhat less powerful than in Israel and Sweden. Another important conclusion is that while it is important to get the prices "right," it is probably even more important to have the rules clear and fairly enforced.

Gasmi, Laffont, and Sharkey (Chapter 11) have focused on the use of an innovative contractual structure to achieve universal service, that of using cross-subsidies among economic classes, as compared with India's current approach of creating a universal service fund funded by all taxpayers. Local telecommunications service has traditionally been provided by a monopoly under a regulated price structure. In most countries and jurisdictions, an explicit goal of regulation has been the provision of service to customers in high-cost areas at "affordable" prices, achieved by cross-subsidies within the regulated monopoly. Recent moves toward deregulation and competition, along with changing technologies, have threatened the viability of this traditional method of universal service funding. Approaches that retain responsibility on the incumbent to provide universal service have the following disadvantage: the absence of competition within areas eligible for universal service gives the incumbent an informational advantage over the regulator, allowing it to appear less efficient and, therefore, eligible for greater subsidies. An option is to replace responsibility on the incumbent (funded by taxes) with putting the responsibility for universal service on all providers, financed by cross-subsidies from urban to rural areas. The authors show that while using cross-subsidies from wealthy urban areas to poorer rural areas creates distortions (the severity of which depends on the elasticity of demand in urban areas), this may be less distorting than using relatively costly public funds (due to inefficiencies in the tax system). They provide conditions under which urban-to-rural cross-subsidies may still prove to be a powerful tool for financing universal service under competition. An important conclusion of the chapter is that those conditions are often met by developing countries where rural density is high.

According to Khosla (Chapter 6), the goal of giving all Indians access to telecommunications within the next 20 years is unrealistic. He notes that many countries that have been in India's current position have tried at one time or other to provide telecommunications services to everyone and have failed. China is the most recent example,[12] but over the twentieth century, the developed countries of Europe and Japan also went through this route unsuccessfully. Each ended up putting its limited resources in the big cities.

Noting that the existing political economy will result in a primary role for the state-owned incumbent, which has the additional advantage of easy access to licenses and already owns most relevant rights-of-way, it makes sense to find solutions that make efficient use of the state's resources. Khosla proposes that the state take responsibility for providing the fiber-optic lines that connect switching systems to key areas of the country (dark fiber). Dark fiber requires little maintenance and can be contracted out for implementation by the private sector; the other portions of the system, such as switches and last-mile provision that will "light up" the dark fiber, should be the responsibility of the private sector.

Different though it must be, the appropriate approach for India will rely heavily on markets. Suppose, starting ab initio, one draws 5,000 circles on a map of India, each with an indicated radius of 40 kilometers, to cover the whole country. Each circle would, on average, cover 120 villages with an average population of 150,000 people. Note that both a rail infrastructure and a trunk fiber backbone are already in place in each such circle in India. Khosla proposes that the state build 5,000 communications centers or "work centers" and link these to the rail and fiber infrastructure. These centers would then be available for private sector service provision.

Under Khosla's approach, universal service would be defined as the provision of access at the 5,000 centers. Rural services would not be subsidized at all. Instead, populations in rural areas that have the most need for telecommunications services would access the nearest work center.

Khosla's argument is that this approach would maximize social welfare. Since 85–90% of the cost of telecommunications is in the last mile, these costs would be saved, in addition to the costs of subsidizing ongoing access. In return, the heavily subsidized, but already established, rail/road system would enable a self-selecting mechanism to operate, inducing those with the greatest need to travel to an access center to use its facilities for entrepreneurship and social services.

Kumar, Pernyeszi, Rao, and Yadagiri (Chapter 12) have studied the impact of changing the strategy of providing village public phones as widely as possible to a new strategy of linking clusters of villages together first. Telephone users in Parvathagiri Mandal, a cluster of 13 villages in the Indian state of Andhra Pradesh, were surveyed on their use of telephones, revenue, and benefits. A comparison with the privately run cable television (TV) systems in the same area was also done. The findings support the view that rural demand is often viable, although there is considerable heterogeneity among rural users. Network value does depend on distance but in a nonlinear way, being highest for intervillage traffic within the nearest cluster and then for communications with the district headquarters or nearest town. The policy implication is that the network should be geared toward completing connections within the local cluster followed by connecting to the nearest town. While competition would normally lead to this outcome, the state-owned provider has followed a policy of connecting villages by a thin line to the district headquarters (with too little capacity to handle intracluster traffic via the district headquarters). This suggests that private provision of service to individual villages and clusters of villages should be allowed, rather than the present policy of licensing providers only over very large areas with an average population of 50 million. A second implication of non-linear value is that providers should be allowed to provide service to small clusters with flexibility to set prices based on demand, in contrast to current policy, which sets rates based on distance. The chapter's survey supports the arguments of others discussed earlier, such as Jhunjhunwala, favoring delicensing of service provision at the village level in order to provide varying qualities and levels of telephone service at different prices.

Technology Choices and Convergence

As already noted, an important objective of national policy is that up-to-date technology be used in the telecommunications sector. The strategy is to encourage technology inflow through private (including foreign) investment. Since private investment has been low, the state-owned incumbent has set its own technology standards based on standards in use in the United States and Europe.

While the United States, most other advanced countries, and even developing countries such as Mexico have continued with their reliance on circuit-switched technology, countries such as China and Brazil have used technology based on Internet protocols (IP), such as voice over IP. This reflects perhaps the reality that the standard United States model of providing a high basic service level may be unaffordable in poorer countries, leading to the need for solutions where different qualities of service are provided at different costs. As such, IP technology, for example, may be appropriate for poorer countries. Given the conservatism of the incumbent in India, this is unlikely to be used until the private sector becomes a significant service provider. Policymakers meanwhile have banned the use of VoIP, pending a resolution of convergence issues.

In several developing countries, such as Colombia and Malaysia, wireless technologies are used to supply basic service. This defies conventional logic since wireless networks that use scarce spectrum have higher costs. However, it does have the advantage of quick installation. It may be argued, also, that if spectrum scarcity competes with the alternative of overloaded wirelines, and if—especially in the early days of usage—usage rates are low, spectrum may not be relevant to pricing. This could explain its widespread adoption in many countries, to the point where it has become a form of basic service. If wireless technologies are to play an important role in providing basic telecommunications services in India, several policy and regulatory changes will be needed. For example, the policy of charging wireless providers a higher tax than wireline providers may need to be changed.

CONCLUSION

Although telecommunications reform in India has come a long way, this volume shows that there is yet a long way to go. A fundamental starting point for the analyses in this book is that, at least in telecommunications, India has chosen a structure that is closer to the pure competition model of the United States–Chile system and different from the "restricted competition" approaches favored by Mexico, China, and several Southeast Asian countries. This is a bold step since its logical outcomes include abandoning the phased-competition approach that was earlier favored and, along with it, the protection that it afforded the incumbent. However, political will at the stage of implementation is still needed and will be needed for some years to come. The reason is that anticompetitive forces in the form of unions and the management of the state-owned incumbent remain. They are being supplemented by newly formed anticompetitive forces, such as the cellular service providers, who, as noted, have actively opposed WLL-based expansion of private provision of basic services. This, of course, is only a part of the tasks yet undone. The other key issues that remain to be tackled are the regulatory role in licensing, introducing competition at the last mile, allowing flexibility in pricing of services, financing universal access, and dominant carrier regulation. We have discussed various approaches to tackling each of these issues. Some of the solutions would not have been possible in eras of different technology, such as the use of VoIP solutions, some required evidence of the mistakes of other countries, such as Mexico's experience with the structuring of Telmex, while still others can be understood only in India's unique political and economic contexts, such as the ongoing role of the Department of Telecommunications in licensing new providers. Implementing the proposals recommended will correspondingly require political will in some cases, such as delegating licensing functions to the regulator; a buildup of regulatory capacity in other cases, such as on the use of interconnection charges to finance universal service; and the taking of risks in still other cases, such as yielding to the market on technology choices and allowing competitive access at the local loop. This chapter, despite pointing out the immense policy problems that India's telecommunications sector faces and the severe complexities of the political system and the condition of property rights, nevertheless offers hope by describing achievable solutions to these problems.

NOTES

1. We are directly interested not in analyzing the political bases for the choices made, although these were very important, but in explaining why the choices made had the economic outcomes that resulted. In a democratic country, all choices have to be politically acceptable (i.e., they are a mix of the influence of relevant vested interests such as unions, political parties, and old economy firms on reform). Such interests often work with different objectives. For example, unions may try to block reform in state-owned firms that employ them, due to worries about unemployment. Politicians may direct reform to protect incumbent, state-owned firms from which they or their constituents receive favors. Different ministries may work at cross purposes. In the early stages of reform, there are usually high costs to be paid for reform, leading to a rise in the political powers of the finance ministry. This has certainly been the case in India. The government may decide to sacrifice a longer-term benefit with a higher net present value for one with immediate revenue benefits (e.g., retain monopolistic structures in telecommunications and realize higher immediate revenues even when such decisions lead to lower line rollouts in the long term) (see Wallsten, 2000). Old-economy firms may try to control the pace of reform to match their ability to respond. Finally, their combined influence has an effect; in India, we shall show that it has led to policymakers' choosing inefficient institutional structures and bad rules and regulations.

2. The U.S. Telecommunications Act and the rapid changes in technology that succeeded it were probably closely linked, as some writers have pointed out (e.g., Hundt, 2000).

3. The names of the departments and their functions went through minor changes up to 1991, which we do not discuss. For details, see Balashanker, (1998).

4. By contrast, the National Telecom Policy 1994 stated, "It is necessary to give the highest priority to the development of telecom services in the country" (Section 1).

5. This was different from the Chinese approach, which had been to sell a minority stake in its state-owned mobile service company on Hong Kong and other overseas stock markets

6. Instead, NTP-1999 stated that "the government will provide necessary support and encouragement to promote indigenous telecom equipment manufacturing, including

incentives to the service providers utilizing indigenous equipment" (NTP-1999, Section 8.2).

7.   This may be why China has been facing conflicts over equipment choice ever since it allowed expanded competition between service providers, for example, the conflict over allowing China Unicom, a competitor to the incumbent, China Mobile, to use the code division multiple access (CDMA) standard.

8.   Security concerns may have been an issue, although this is only hinted at in NTP-1994, Section 12, which states that, apart from telecommunications being a "vital infrastructure," an "equally important aspect is the strategic aspect of telecom, which affects the national and public interests."

9.   Information provided by Naveen Chairman, Suhas Patil, in a conversation with Rafiq Dossani, November 2000.

10. The draft convergence bill also gives the regulator powers over content. This is likely to make the bill more difficult to pass.

11. If VoIP is also simultaneously delicensed, it will likely lead to a great reduction in costs, of the order of 70%, as experienced by China.

12. According to He (1997), 46% of China's telephone lines are in seven coastal provinces, and the ratio of rural phones to the total is only 18%. According to Rohlen (2000, p. 15), Guangdong Province, with only 5.5% of China's population, has almost a third of the country's lines.

BIBLIOGRAPHY

Balashankar, R. *Golden Era of Indian Telecommunications.* Department of Telecommunications, Government of India, 1998.

He, B. "Democracy, Transnational Problems and the Boundary Question: Challenge for China—An Interview with David Held." *Social Alternative* 16, no. 4 (1997): 33–37.

Hundt, R. *You Say You Want a Revolution.* New Haven, CT: Yale University Press, 2000.

Lipartito, K. "Cutthroat Competition, Corporate Strategy, and the Growth of Network Industries." *Research on Technological Innovation, Management and Policy,* ed. R. Burgelman, and R. Rosenbloom. Amsterdam, Holland, JAI Press, 1997.

Nasscom, Statistics – Indian IT Industry, www.nasscom.org, 2000.

Rohlen, T. "Hong Kong and the Pearl River Delta: One Country Two Systems in the Emerging Metropolitan Context." Working Paper, Asia/Pacific Research Center, Stanford University, July 2000.

Telecom Regulatory Authority of India, "Consultation Paper on Issues Relating to Universal Service Obligations." July 2000.

Wallsten, S. J. "Telecommunications Privatization in Developing Countries: The Real Effects of Exclusivity Periods" Stanford Institute for Economic Policy Research Working paper, SIEPR Policy paper No. 99-21, May 2000, available at http:// siepr.stanford.edu/papers/pdf/99-21.html.

Chapter 1

The Policy Agenda

Shyamal Ghosh

Policy reforms, particularly during the year 2000, are expected to rapidly transform the Indian telecommunications sector. The objective of these reforms is to reach a teledensity of 7 by 2005 and 15 by 2010, compared with the March 2001 teledensity of 3.3, while managing a transition to higher technologies that will allow for higher voice and data traffic volumes and improving the spread of services to all parts of the country. The strategies include (1) a continuing important role for the public sector in all aspects of telecommunications, particularly in service provision to rural areas but also as the major investor in existing and new value-added services and (2) free and open competition for all participants in all sectors. This chapter describes how these strategies will be implemented.

THE THREE PHASES OF REFORM

Historically, the invention of the telephone in 1876 and the commencement of the use of telecommunications in India were almost simultaneous. By the beginning of the twentieth century, telecommunications had come to be universally accepted as a natural monopoly—whether in the public or private sector. In India, as in many other countries in Europe and Asia, telecommunication services were operated by a government department. The expansion of the network was excruciatingly slow, being managed and used primarily by the government. This continued till the early 1990s, by which time the concept of natural monopoly was increasingly challenged in many countries by technological change. This led to reforms for ushering in competition through the dismantling of both private and government monopolies. The outcome was greater consumer welfare, particularly in terms of lower tariffs and improvements in the quality of service.

In many ways the year 2000 was the most significant period in the Indian telecommunications sector, when a series of consecutive reform measures were taken with speed and in a short time, totally redefining the rules of the game.

Phase 1: The 1980s

The process of telecom reforms in India began in the 1980s, when "Mission Better Communication" was launched by the government. During this period, private manufacturing of customer premise equipment was allowed (in 1984), the Center for Development of Telematics (C-DOT) was established (in 1984) for the development of indigenous technologies, and proliferation of public call offices for local and long-distance service (the now-ubiquitous "STD/ISD/PCO" network) was undertaken on a large scale across the country through private individual franchisees. Two large corporate entities were spun off from the Department of Telecommunications (DOT). These heralds of corporatization were the Mahanagar Telephone Nigam Ltd. (MTNL) to provide basic services in Delhi and Mumbai and Videsh Sanchar Nigam Ltd. (VSNL) to provide overseas services. A high-powered Telecom Commission was set up in 1989 with all the powers of the state for directing the ongoing growth of telecommunications.

Phase 2: 1990–1998

The second phase coincided with the liberalization of the economy in the early 1990s and announcement of the New Economic Policy (NEP-1991). The emphasis was on allowing private sector access followed by delicensing where appropriate. Telecom equipment manufacturing was delicensed in 1991. Licensed access to the private sector was permitted in value-added services in 1992 and for radio paging, cellular mobile, and basic telephony services gradually thereafter. In general, licenses were issued against license fees for qualified participants through a bidding process. The intent was to create at least two viable service providers in each circle of operation (each circle is roughly congruent with individual states, in addition to the four metros). Internet services were opened to the private sector in 1998 on a nearly delicensed basis and without any entry fee. During this phase, a National Telecom Policy was announced in 1994, its emphasis being on universal service and qualitative improvement in services. However, unlike the European countries, where the setting up of an independent regulator preceded the opening up of the market, in India there was a reversal of sequence, and an independent statutory regulator was established only in 1997.

Phase 3: 1999–2001

The most important landmark in telecom reforms came with the New Telecom Policy 1999 (NTP-1999), which may be termed the third generation of reforms. NTP-1999 is not just a policy document. It reflects a new philosophy, a new vision, a new direction, and a new commitment. The government has undertaken its implementation with utmost earnestness, in letter and spirit. Its theme is to usher in full competition through unrestricted private entry in almost all service sectors unless restricted by spectrum availability, with the full protection of a strong regulator. Its purposes are to manage the imminent convergence of various transmission media that technological change has wrought and to strengthen the still somewhat weak presence of the private sector. NTP-1999 allowed existing private service providers to migrate from the earlier fixed license-fee regime to revenue-sharing of licensee revenue, while duopoly rights were discontinued in order to allow for unlimited competition. The private sector may provide domestic long-distance and (from April 2002) international long-distance voice services, with no limit on the number of participants. Wireless-in-local-loop (WLL)-based limited mobility has been allowed for basic service providers. Data services have been fully opened to the private sector. Cellular service providers are permitted to carry their own long-distance traffic within their service area. The duopoly in cellular service is to be augmented by allowing the public sector entities in basic service provision to provide cellular services, and a fourth cellular license is to be issued. The licensing and service provision functions of government have been fully separated, and the latter have been corporatized. There is no restriction on the number of global mobile personal communication services (GMPCS) licenses, but the gateways for the GMPCS are to be located in India. A National Frequency Allocation Plan (NFAP-2000) came into force on January 1, 2000. The Indian Telegraph Act 1885 has been reviewed, and a new bill based on convergence has been drafted. A panel has been set up to facilitate the opening of Internet telephony. The preparation for issuance of 3G spectrum has started.

With all these measures, which have come one after another in quick succession, the various reforms committed under NTP-1999 were almost complete by March 2001, some months ahead of schedule. In consequence, the first years of the new millennium are expected to be a period of growth and consolidation.

REFORMS AND THE ROLE OF THE REGULATOR

The completion of policy reforms shifts much of the responsibility for their efficient implementation—through creating an environment of free and open competition with a level playing field—onto a strong regulator. After NTP-1994 had opened the doors for participation of the private sector, the restructuring process was continued with the establishment of the Telecom Regulatory Authority of India (TRAI) in 1997. An amendment of the Telecom Regulatory Authority of India Act in the year 2000 paved the way for reconstitution of the Telecom Regulatory Authority of India and creation of the Telecom Dispute Settlement and Appellate Tribunal (TDSAT). The TRAI has been empowered to provide recommendations on various aspects relating to the functioning of telecom service providers and to discharge certain regulatory functions. The TDSAT has been empowered to adjudicate on disputes between the licensor and licensee; between two or more service providers; and between a service provider and a group of consumers. It is also the appellate authority in respect of any direction, decisions, and orders of TRAI. It has a mandate for time-bound resolution of disputes within 60 days, and further appeals lie only with the Supreme Court.

REFORMS AND THE ROLE OF THE PUBLIC SECTOR

The corporatized entity Bharat Sanchar Nigam Ltd. (BSNL), which was spun off from DOT in October 2000 and is the country's largest basic and domestic long-distance service provider, is expected to play an important and dominant role in achieving the objectives of NTP-1999. It will provide not only lifeline services but also value-added and cellular services. As it has shown in the past, the capabilities exist in BSNL to do justice to this role. Corporatization is intended to allow BSNL to reconstruct its business strategies based on best commercial principles. Along with MTNL, it will continue to be the biggest contributor toward increasing teledensity. To top it all, the new corporation, along with MTNL and VSNL, will utilize their synergies to open up new vistas for operations in other countries.

With the formation of BSNL, the biggest question is how the affordability of its services will be maintained while providing rural services in an environment that is market-driven and competitive. In such a scenario, universal service will be a challenging task to accomplish. As the teledensity in India is low, the challenge is correspondingly bigger. A universal service obligation (USO) fund will be created by levying a percentage of revenue from various service providers. However, with government control, the dominant operator will provide the major part of universal service. The government is committed to provide services in unviable areas by increasing volumes in viable areas. But the best option is to increase the rural market base with a long-term economic perspective. The rural-sector telecommunications market is expected to see a faster rate of growth in the coming years from its present teledensity of just about 0.65 per 100 population.

As noted, under NTP-1999, all telecom services have been opened up for private sector participation except international voice telephony. This segment was earlier scheduled to be reviewed by the year 2004, but it was later decided that the monopoly of VSNL over international telephony would end by March 2002.

Technology development in the public sector is spearheaded by an autonomous body, C-DOT. C-DOT has developed a wide range of Digital Switching Systems for rural and urban applications. The range extends from a 200-line Rural Automatic Exchange (RAX) to a 40,000-line switching system for urban applications. Complete with integrated service digital network (ISDN), network synchronization, and inter-exchange networking based on state-of-the-art interfaces and switching (ITU common channel signalling [CCS7] and version 5.x interfaces), the switching systems based on C-DOT technology have a large presence in Indian telecom network. They account for over 40% of the total lines of the network. In terms of exchanges, the share is above 90%, as C-DOT technology enjoys a leadership position in the rural network comprising small exchanges. The switches are being used in about 20 developing countries other than India. Its rural switches are most suitable for Indian weather conditions. Besides the efforts of C-DOT, India's acknowledged prowess in information technology (IT) adds to the potential for telecommunications R&D in India.

POLICY ON BANDWIDTH

Adequate bandwidth is critical, and the government has taken a number of steps to ensure its availability on demand in national and international segments. Besides setting up a Bandwidth Advisory Committee, DOT has permitted Internet Service Providers (ISP)s to take bandwidth directly from foreign satellites for setting up international gateways. ISPs have also been permitted to set up submarine cable landing stations for international gateways. VSNL has the responsibility to ensure that there is no shortage of international bandwidth through suitable agreements with its international counterparts. For example, earlier, bandwidth was procured following registration of user demand, whereas now it is procured in anticipation of demand. As part of national long-distance policy, unrestricted entry has been permitted to infrastructure providers who provide infrastructure: towers, buildings, dark fiber, and so on (Category I), as well as those (Category II) who provide end-to-end bandwidth. Right-of-way procedures have been streamlined. At present, all the 579 district headquarters of the country are connected to reliable media, out of which more than 80% are on fiber. To provide a backbone for national information infrastructure, National Internet Backbone (NIB) and Sanchar Sagar projects were conceived. Under NIB, 331 revenue districts out of 585 districts of the country have been provided with Internet nodes. Sanchar Sagar Phase I has been completed, providing 10 rings of 2.5 gbps capacity with standard 16-channel statistical multiplex (STM-16) systems covering a route length of 17,000 kilometers, and connecting 33 large cities (including 13 major state capitals). Sanchar Sagar Phase II Project, under implementation as of March 2001, covers about 36,000 route kilometers. connecting an additional 150 cities by creating 33 rings. Also 40GB dense wavelength division multiplex (DWDM) rings will cover the four metros and 30 major cities of the country by 2002.

THE STATUS OF TELECOMMUNICATIONS IN INDIA

As is evident from Table 1.1, the growth of the telecommunications network in India has been synchronous with reforms. The teledensity, which was 0.03 in 1951, grew slowly to 0.31 in 1981, but more quickly thereafter, reaching 2.20 in 1999. As of March 2001, it was over 3, and if mobile telephony is taken into account, teledensity was 3.3. The growth rate in this sector has been consistently more than 20% from 1994–1995 onward, as indicated in Figure 1.1. All the exchanges in the country are now electronic. The total investment by the government alone in the telecom services during the year 1999–2000 was US$3.39 billion, and the estimate for 2000–2001 is US$4.35 billion. Foreign direct investment in this sector has been over US$1 billion. Public sector investments during the last five years is indicated in Table 1.2. The current status of the network is indicated in Table 1.3. It is the second largest network among developing countries and the ninth largest in the world.

Table 1.1
India Population, Direct Exchange Lines and Teledensity

Year	Population (in million)	Direct Exchange Lines (DELs) (in million)	Teledensity (in percent)
1951	361.1	0.16	0.04
1961	439.2	0.33	0.08
1971	548.2	0.98	0.18
1981	683.3	2.15	0.31
1991	846.3	5.07	0.60
1992	863.2	5.81	0.67
1993	880.4	6.80	0.77
1994	898.0	8.04	0.90
1995	915.9	9.80	1.07
1996	934.2	11.98	1.28
1997	949.4	14.54	1.53
1998	964.7	17.80	1.85
1999	980.4	21.59	2.20
2000	996.2	26.51	2.66
Feb'01	1000.0	34.26*	3.43

* February 2001 figures include cellular phones.

Sources: Economic Survey, 1998–1999; Indian Telecommunication Statistics, 1999; Ninth Plan (1997–2002) Document, Planning Commission.

There is potential for much faster growth. As envisaged in the New Telecom Policy 1999, the teledensity in India is expected to rise to 7 by 2005 and 15 by the year 2010. This will result from an active partnership between the public and the private sector and an increasing role for the latter, and is expected to involve an investment of US$35 billion by 2005 and US$75 billion between 2005 and 2010.

Figure 1.1
Growth of the Telecommunications Network in India

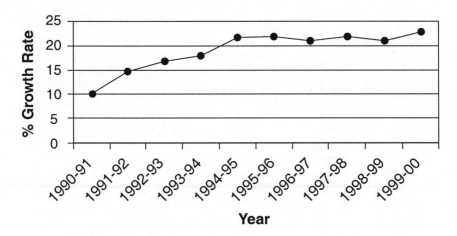

Table 1.2
Investments in Telecommunication Services by the Public Sector, 1995–1999

Year (fiscal-year ends March 31)	Public Sector Investment	
	(in Rs. billion)	(in US$ billion)
1995—1996	84.65	2.48
1996—1997	89.67	2.50
1997—1998	99.66	2.52
1998—1999	111.89	2.64
1999—2000	14,672	3.39
2001—2001 (Est)	202.53	4.35

Table 1.3
Network Status in India

Number of telephone connections	30.99 million
Number of Telephone Exchanges	30,462
Switching capacity (fixed lines)	37.7 million
Village public telephone	397,537
Public Call Offices	817, 470
Cellular	3.27 million
Pager	0.6 million
Internet Customers	2.5 million
Internet Service Providers	111
Optical fiber route Length	207,777 kilometers
UHF & Microwave Route Length	182,634 kilometers
Television sets	75 million
PCs	4.5 million
Cable TV connections	37 million

THE STATUS OF PRIVATE SECTOR PARTICIPATION (MARCH 2001)

Prior to the third phase of reforms, basic services by private operators had started in six circles. This sector was opened for unlimited competition in January 2001, and more than 145 new applications were received by March 2001. The telephones in 15 state capitals of the country are available on demand, and teledensity has almost doubled since 1998. WLL has been allowed for faster rollout of services. In cellular mobile, licenses have been awarded to two operators in each circle, and services are being run in 18 telecom circles and four metro cities. A third operator—state-owned MTNL in Delhi and Mumbai and BSNL in the rest of the country—began services in 2000. A fourth operator is to be appointed in each circle based on bids received in 2001. As of March 2001, the subscriber base was 3.27 million, increasing by 150,000 each month. Thus, cellular mobile services are flourishing in the country and are likely to grow beyond the big cities due to participation of the incumbent service provider and competition. About 450 ISP licenses had been granted by March 2001, and more than 111 of them were providing services to about 2.5 million subscribers. More than 240 clearances have been given to ISPs for setting up their own international data gateways. Access to Internet is available practically throughout the country on local call access basis. With better availability of bandwidth, IT-enabled services like e-commerce, call-centers, tele-education, tele-medicine, tele-banking, and so on are growing rapidly.

THE EMERGING SCENARIO AND FUTURE CONVERGENCE

By 2010, teledensity will increase more than five-fold, and traffic volume will increase several times more. Data services are still nascent and should grow rapidly. The tremendous potential of IT in India and its aspirations to become a world superpower in IT will have a direct bearing on future telecommunications growth in the country. These two sectors—IT and telecommunications—will grow hand in hand in the era of convergence. The broadcasting sector will later slip into the continuously changing mold of digital clay. Private sector participation and investment are the key to realize this scenario. BSNL, with its dominant market share, will provide the best network reach. It is expected to be able to face competition by adapting to the competitive environment. The technological developments are likely to make services more and more affordable. Therefore, India is likely to emerge as a strong force in telecommunications and continue to be strong in IT.

As mentioned earlier, steps are being taken for rapidly moving toward enacting a comprehensive statute—a communications convergence bill to address the convergence of technologies and markets. The new act will replace the Indian Telegraph Act 1885 and several other related acts. It will cover both carriage and content of transmitted information. This will be a major step forward in the development of a national infrastructure for an information-based society and establishment of a licensing and regulatory framework in the context of convergence. The broad framework of this enactment was under finalization as of March 2001. Convergence will also provide challenges for the regulator to ensure competition and for regulating tariffs. Inroads made by the expansion of cable networks while providing for convergence and broadband access can create situations of technology lock-in and preempt future competition. The access alternatives for businesses are far greater than for individual households. The debate for use of cable versus DSL may continue for a long time, but in many countries the trend seems to be for rapid rollout of cable for broadband access. This will throw up the issue of whether content providers should be in the business of access provision. Vertical integration could lead to monopolistic conditions such as ownership of direct to home (DTH) platform by a content provider. Similarly, fixation of tariff in a packet switched data/voice network will pose a new dimension. In the Indian context, the relationship of Internet telephony and providing universal access would be areas of immense concern for policymakers. While regulation should necessarily facilitate utilization of new technology, the simultaneous need to make the technology universally accessible, particularly in rural, backward, and remote areas, will need focused attention.

CONCLUSION

The telecommunications sector in India has reached a stage where the environment for competition and private sector participation has been maximized. The reform cycle is on the verge of completion. The time has come when the Indian telecommunications sector is ready to leap forward and realize its enormous growth potential. This is a huge opportunity for industry and investors. It is expected that the new environment will catalyze growth and provide the best telecommunications services in the world.

Chapter 2

TRAI's Objectives and Policy Focus in a Changing Environment

M.S. Verma

It is a widely held view that we are presently experiencing a technological revolution that will change the way humankind lives and does business. Telecommunications and related activities are one of the main drivers of these changes. As its regulator for India, the Telecom Regulatory Authority of India (TRAI) not only is a witness but has the privilege of being associated with, and of giving some speed and direction to, these powerful forces of change.

It is not a simple task. Regulatory discipline and related institutions are relatively new phenomena in most countries. The United States and Canada excepted, even developed countries such as the United Kingdom and most of Europe have had only about two decades of experience with infrastructure regulation. In developing countries, the experience is of even shorter duration and restricted to only a few countries. Even these offer limited lessons for India for several reasons: their political structures differ from India's, raising government revenue is a lower priority than in India, and the universal services obligations acceptable to India are such that it would be very difficult to fulfill these only with contributions from the country's wealthier segments.

However, regulatory discipline and the need to build up related institutions are being increasingly recognized as important for telecommunications growth in both the developed and developing countries. The change has been driven by a recognition that telecommunication services, which have so far been delivered mostly by monopolies, either government or private, are better delivered in a competitive environment. The days of monopolies in telecommunication services are over. In such a situation there is a growing appreciation among countries that regulation and regulators have a very important role to play. They not only facilitate the transition from monopoly to multipoly but ensure that, through transition and onward, the principles of fair competition are observed. The outcome of this appreciation is reflected in the report published by the International Telecommunication Union (ITU), which states that by late 1999 there were 84 separate regulators in ITU member states, and more than 150 countries introduced new or modified telecommunications legislation during the 1990s.

This chapter sets out the background to the development of TRAI and its agenda.

TELECOM REGULATORY AUTHORITY OF INDIA

Formation

In India, TRAI was established in 1997 by an act of Parliament as a part of ongoing changes in telecommunications policy. By then, licenses for private provision of basic and cellular services had already been issued. A common view in 1997 was that TRAI should have been established earlier, that is, prior to opening up the sector. This was for several reasons. First, winners of the licenses already issued for cellular services through what had appeared to be a successful round of bids found that their winning bids were based on overestimated revenue assumptions. These same bidders realized that their bids would have been more realistic if a regulatory agency had existed at that time, since the regulator would have been a source of scarce information on the potential of the Indian telecommunications market. Second, unlike in China, where there is no separate regulator but where service provision has been the prerogative of state-owned agencies only, there is a greater need in countries like India for a regulator to prepare the groundwork for liberalization through initiatives that address interconnection, a level playing field for various service providers, provision of universal service, tariff rebalancing, quality of service, and other conditions under which various services would be open to entry by the private sector. Third, a need had also been felt for a forum at which disputes among service providers could be settled. TRAI was seen as fulfilling all these needs.

The Initial Years

The earliest steps taken by TRAI were to initiate tariff rebalancing for basic services and to issue a regulation on interconnection that specified certain important principles governing commercial aspects of interconnection. Groundwork was initiated also in a number of other areas such as evolving quality of service parameters, funding of universal service obligations, development of a number policy, maintenance of register on interconnection agreements and basic terms of license for different telecom services.

TRAI emphasized a transparent, participatory, predictable, and equitable policy framework. These four principles were important in the Indian environment for the following reasons:

1. In a nascent market where the incumbent has immense possibility to be anticompetitive, equity among service providers, transparency as to costs, and predictability as to process were needed to ensure new entry. To build up stakeholders' support for the regulatory process, which, after all, sought to replace the existing protective umbrella of the state with a market-driven process, it was important to maintain the principles of equity, transparency, and participation.

2. Given that telecommunications is a field where market economics as well as technologies are changing with breathtaking rapidity, the most important method of infusing an acceptable degree of certainty is to state clearly the underlying principles that will determine policy. This imparts predictability to the policy framework, so that even if the market situation is evolving rapidly, policy uncertainty is reduced. TRAI did this by specifying certain principles that emphasized the need for a level playing field with focus on preventing anticompetitive activities, basing interconnection charges and tariffs on costs, encouraging competition where possible, and emulating competitive conditions wherever competition is not yet fully established or cannot, for reasons such as incumbent monopoly, be immediately established.

What is important also is that these principles were established not by fiat but through a transparent and participatory process that involved widely distributed consultation papers followed by open house discussions with all stakeholders. In this regard, the TRAI process established high standards of transparency in public policy, which will be emulated over time in other regulatory bodies as well.

One issue that arose in TRAI's early years was about the limits of its legal power. This included whether TRAI had the power to settle disputes between the licensor and the licensees and whether TRAI could alter or specify interconnection conditions overriding those mentioned in the license. The former issue went to the heart of the matter as to which authority ultimately determined the choice and terms of a licensee. International experience varied greatly enough to not be an adequate guide. For example, in Mexico, the telecommunications regulator Cofetel has no tariff-setting authority but merely recommends tariff structures to the government. The government is not bound to seek or to abide by these recommendations. At the other extreme, in the United States, the Federal Communications Commission is the licensor and has high policy-making powers.

Not surprisingly for a democracy, the intervention of the judiciary was sought in order to determine the limits of TRAI's powers. The courts ruled against TRAI on both counts on the grounds that the government needed to determine the powers of TRAI, and since the licensor (the Department of Telecommunications, DOT) was an arm of the government, it was the government's, (DOT's), prerogative to set limits on its own powers. Since DOT had sought the courts' intervention, it followed that DOT should prevail in such a situation.

However, the government remedied the situation substantially by passing an amendment to the TRAI Act in 2000, that clarified TRAI's overriding powers in respect of interconnection and also provided for setting up a separate Telecom Disputes Settlement Appellate Tribunal with powers to settle disputes between the licensor and the licensees.

The other significant change was a commitment by the government that it would be obliged to seek the recommendation of TRAI on the issues that TRAI had powers over and would act on these recommendations in a predictable way. The new TRAI became functional in March 2000 and has since addressed a number of issues, including opening up national long-distance service to private operators and issuing licenses to additional cellular mobile and fixed-service providers under the new Telecom Policy announced by the government in 1999. More recently, in the last quarter of 2000, following a due process of consultation papers and open house discussions, TRAI provided to the government its recommendations on public mobile radio trunking services (PMRTS) and very small aperture terminal (VSAT) services and issues related to licensing thereof under the New Telecom Policy of 1999.

The Agenda for TRAI in the New Millennium

TRAI as of 2000 was well advanced in the process of formulating its recommendations on issues relating to universal service obligations and on separate, service-wise, unbundled network-elements-based accounting.

In July 2000, TRAI published regulations on quality of service (QOS) parameters. Compliance with these parameters by all service providers will be monitored either directly by TRAI or through an external agency to be appointed by TRAI. This will include customer satisfaction surveys on a countrywide basis, the results to be published periodically. In 2000, for example, a QOS analysis was done of Internet service providers to identify the issues that affect Internet services in India and recommend corrective actions.

Looking ahead, the policy laid down by DOT favors competition for all services, with a phased-in process depending on market conditions. Such a phase-in will rely heavily on TRAI to achieve a timing that is fair to both incumbents and consumers. Although all-out competition may be an ultimate goal, there are concerns that need to be addressed about its effects on a nascent industry. TRAI's task will be to address this issue and to help create an industry structure that most quickly resembles a competitive one, without a cumbersome and costly regulatory process. Rapid changes in technology will ultimately dictate a quicker, rather than a slower, move to competition since the economies of scale in service provision are disappearing. There is no doubt that the country's new policy relating to domestic long-distance telecommunications and basic services will result in a multi operator environment. This would call for clear guidelines on technical compatibility, inter-operability, and effective interconnection between different service providers.

Some of the important areas of TRAI's concerns and activities in the near future are, therefore, going to be the following:

- Interconnection arrangements between access providers such as basic/ cellular and national long-distance operators, including carriage charges on the interconnection link between the point of presence of the basic service provider and that of a national long-distance operator.

- Routing, charging, and numbering in a multioperator environment and its conformance to national fundamental plans.

- Allotment of carrier access codes (CAC) to various national long-distance operators.

- Charting a migration path from CAC to carrier preselection for ensuring equal ease of access to the customer.

- Technical arrangements for proper settlement of carriage charges in a multioperator environment and implementation of an intercarrier charge billing system.

- Radio paging services in India have so far not proved as successful as at some other places in Asia. This service is of considerable relevance to India given its low costs and considering India's vast geographical spread, low existing teledensity, and limited affordability of the majority of the users. Despite its limited range, radio paging can, therefore, provide quick and usable connectivity to certain classes of users.

- Consumer education about the role and importance of regulators in general and that of TRAI in particular. The monopolistic character of telecommunication services in the country has severely constrained consumer awareness about the range and quality of services, as have other obligations of the service provider. TRAI appreciates the role that nongovernmental organizations (NGOs) and consumer organizations can play in the evolution and maintenance of standards of service and is, therefore, keen to support and develop consumer organizations that will act as watchdogs of the quality of services and of the service providers' responses to consumers' needs and expectations.

Year 2000 policy initiatives have allowed free entry to service providers in almost all areas of telecommunications, including fixed services, national long-distance services, VSAT services, and PMRTS. Some services, particularly basic, long-distance, and cellular mobile, need large investments, as a result of which the number of service providers automatically becomes limited. In a developing country like India it becomes a difficult balancing act for the regulator to simultaneously create conditions for inflow of high-value, long-term investments in the sector and the growth of a highly competitive market focused primarily on consumers. While one tends to limit the number of market participants, the other requires just the opposite, that is, a larger number of operators. TRAI is trying to handle this dilemma by providing franchisees at the point of customer interface so that even if the main licensees and the backbone operators remain limited in number, they can appoint large numbers of franchisees who will compete for customer attention and provide the customer with choice of service. We believe that such an approach will help faster market penetration and achievement of higher teledensity within a much shorter time. The existence of a large number of franchisees catering to customer needs in different areas is expected to be highly advantageous, as it will be possible for the service providers to cover the market comprehensively as well as rapidly through multiple franchisees who may also use multiple technologies (TRAI is technology-neutral).

Another area that is engaging TRAI's attention is the opportunity for leapfrogging technologies. To leapfrog or not is a difficult choice to make. Information technology, and with it, telecommunication technology are moving at an extremely fast pace, overtaking implementation of many plans and projects, and giving rise to serious dilemmas in which one has to choose between infructuous costs, if one were to abandon a project midway, and loss of opportunities, if adoption of the latest technology was to be delayed. The problem assumes much greater proportions in situations where financial resources are limited. The march of technology and its benefits to the masses must not be denied, but, at the same time, the value of investment already made cannot be overlooked all that easily. In TRAI, therefore, there is an attempt to handle the situation in a manner that affords flexibility for seamless migration from one technology to another and finally their convergence.

Changes in technologies and their convergence apart, it is also becoming difficult to anticipate the shape and character of the market as new methodologies are being developed for pricing and generation of revenue from services. These weaken the existing links between the revenue earned by a service provider and the amount paid by the customer for the services used. In most cases not only a single service but a set of services given as a package make costing of any specific service to the customer rather difficult. This both complicates pricing and makes it difficult to estimate universal service obligations of the service provider. Regulation has to deal with these complexities.

CONCLUSION

TRAI's objective, therefore, is to create an environment of ever-increasing competition in the market so that the market itself becomes the main regulator. Regulatory policies in the future will have to be less and less intrusive. TRAI firmly believes that regulation should do nothing more than provide a framework for operation to the market and leave it free to operate. The framework must provide enough flexibility to the service providers while respecting certain key regulatory principles, most important among which will be improving all-around transparency, ensuring a level playing field for all players, fair and nondiscriminatory availability of interconnections, consumer care, and universal service obligations.

TRAI has set for itself a heavy agenda, but—given fast and far-reaching changes—there is little choice. India has approached the situation with confidence and clarity. The policymakers, the service providers, the consumers and the regulators, together, feel the excitement of the dynamic possibilities that lie ahead and are determined to realize them.

Chapter 3

An Institutional View

Rafiq Dossani and S. Manikutty

There is little doubt that the telecommunication sector in India witnessed major reforms during the 1990s. But has India done enough, given the opportunities, to reform this vital sector? Or have the reforms fallen short of what was needed or could have been done?

It has been argued by policymakers that, after a shaky start, telecommunications reform by the year 2000 looked complete.[1] While the outcomes of reform are awaited, and many things will have to go right, such as good-quality regulation, it is believed that the process of creating the right kinds of institutions and structures is in place.

However, this chapter takes a different view. Despite significant progress, equally significant institutional reform is still needed. The sequence of this chapter is first to set the reforms in an institutional context and then to explore how institutional factors affected the progress of reforms in India. This allows us to deal with the issues of institutional capability and structure.

ROLE OF INSTITUTIONS IN MANAGEMENT OF CHANGE

The term "institutions" refers to agencies that participate in a system, and "institutional structure" refers to the rules and procedures that determine the relationships between different participants in a system and mediate the outcomes. Institutions could be economic institutions[2] that govern economic relationships and sociological institutions that govern social relationships. Economic institutions consist of market institutions that govern relationships between buyers and sellers, financial institutions that govern the transactions of finance, labor market institutions that govern the relationships between labor and management, supply institutions, and institutions to curb opportunism, free riding, and shirking and to ensure that gains are shared equitably among the participants. Sociological institutions have formal institutions such as legal institutions that define what is permitted and not permitted under law and informal institutions such as negotiating forums, public hearings, and means of exchanging information and knowledge such as seminars, discussion meetings, and roundtables.

The institutional structure might evolve on its own over time, or it might be, at least in part, determined by decisions of policymakers and regulators. In the case of telecommunication, there is almost invariably some role for policy-making and regulation. This might be because telecommunications is viewed as a natural monopoly that is too important for social welfare to be left alone, or it might also be in the national interest for the government to provide some subsidized services. In general, policy—however politically determined—usually seeks to fulfill some or all of the following objectives: competition, efficiency, viability of the sector, coverage of underprivileged segments of the population, quality of service, and adequacy of investment. The regulator's mandate is to implement policy; the regulator is assumed to be answerable to the policymaker. Firms play out the intentions of policymakers and regulators through their economic activities. Usually, there will be participants outside the institutional structure who can influence the workings of the industry, as for example, shareholders, unions that may directly influence firms and indirectly influence policymakers, and so on.

Our view is that the progress of any initiative is not merely a function of the policy-making skills of the individuals who are involved in such policy making. They are also influenced by the institutional structure.[3] Institutional forces affect organizations' processes and decision making; *and* hence, decisions, however well thought out they may be even as a group, will not be effective unless unaccompanied by reforms undertaken on the institutional structure. It is necessary, therefore, to view the reforms in the context of the institutions that enable or hinder these reforms, so that attention is paid to building the necessary institutions (also to properly sequence reforms).

The reason that an analysis of institutional structure is particularly important for emerging economies such as India is that it can affect competition. Reform in these countries usually creates new private participants that compete with an incumbent in the public sector. These new firms have the potential to (even if that is not the policymaker's intention) to replace old ones from the public sector as the dominant providers rather than merely supplement them.[4] This has been observed in the airline and power industries, for example. Even in telecommunications services, where the incumbent may be thought to have the advantage of a valuable capital asset (the line network), new entry (often coupled with new technology, such as wireless communications) has led to a rapid decline in the incumbent's market share. This may be viewed as a good outcome, but not necessarily the best possible one, since competition is also an important consideration in reform. Competition does not come merely by adding a single private provider to an existing monopoly. As Wellenius (1997) has shown, there is evidence that countries that offer their telecommunications operators exclusivity periods see slower rollout of services than countries that do not. For example, Chile, which did not grant an exclusivity period, saw a faster rollout than Argentina, Mexico, and Venezuela, which did grant exclusivity to newly privatized firms. Wallsten's (2000) study of 20 firms that had been given exclusive licenses either for local fixed telephone service or international long-distance service showed that exclusivity reduces network growth by between 20–40% compared with countries that did not grant exclusivity.

Hence, it is important that the institutional structure be chosen so that it enables new firms to be viable financially, operate within a level playing field vis-à-vis the incumbent, and compete with other providers in the private sector, while fulfilling the policymakers' objective of improving the efficiency, levels of investment, and service provision.[5]

This is not easy to achieve. For one thing, the envisaged institutional arrangements may not turn out as expected. For example, the breakup of American Telephone and Telegraph (AT&T) in 1984 was supposed to have freed it to enter new value-added businesses, while the straightforward, boring, regulated business of owning the "wires" was hived off to the Baby Bells. Instead of AT&T's flourishing, this led to AT&T's rapid decline due to competition, while the regulated portion under the Baby Bells flourished and indeed consolidated back to monopolistic structures more similar to the pre-breakup scenario.[6] The opposite seems to be happening in America's electric power industry, where the intention of reform in 1996 was to create a competitive institutional structure in generation and thus bring costs down. Instead, the generators seem to be benefiting the most from reform, while distribution companies are struggling to meet the higher costs of purchased power.

A second reason that outcomes may be different from the expected ones is that the regulatory structure can have as significant an impact as institutional arrangements on the resulting industry structure. For example, in 1994 in India, the policymakers issued licenses to private cellular providers. At that time, there was no independent regulator (the Department of Telecommunications [DOT] was the regulator as well as the policymaker) in place, and the result was an uncertain number of participants and costs (since DOT never specified its competition policy either explicitly or through specifying interconnection arrangements). This led to very low investments by private licensees, which rose only after an independent regulatory body took effect. By contrast, for example, the institutional structure that was envisaged for the telecommunications industry after AT&T was granted a monopoly in 1913 worked as expected because it was possible for the regulator to acquire knowledge of the cost structures of the industry and thus enforce tariff structures that led to adequate investment, services, and viability for the industry.

In some cases, even though the work of policymakers and regulators is usually divided up neatly between policy-making and policy implementation, there can be some substitutability. This may reflect differences in institutional capabilities, real or perceived. For instance, the policymaker may arrogate some powers of implementation to itself in the belief that the regulator would not do as good a job. As an example, in the Indian telecommunications sector, the "neat" division on licensing of new service providers is that the policymaker ought to set certain broad goals, for example, that new participants be selected on the basis of their competence, that providers be allowed to earn returns that are fair, and that competition be encouraged. The regulator, in consequence, should set certain competence-based criteria, such as net worth and experience, and determine the basis of return (e.g., rate of return on assets) and the initial number of entrants. Once the criteria for selection and reward have been publicly debated and approved by policymakers, the regulator ought to be able to move ahead with a process of inviting bids, evaluating them, making awards of licenses, setting tariffs, and so on. However, in India, the policymaker awards licenses.[7] This leads to lack of transparency and conflicts of interest since DOT does not have to reveal the basis of its choice or the criteria for choice to the public; it may choose a financially weak competitor in order to help the incumbent survive better. Also, its ongoing control over the licensure means that it can pressure newcomers on an ongoing basis to adapt their strategies to assist the incumbent (which it owns) to survive better.

It is much more difficult for the regulator to assume policy-making functions because the regulator reports to policymakers. This has happened, though. For example, venture capital policy-making in India was, till recently, done independently by various arms of the Ministry of Finance: the Reserve Bank, the Securities and Exchange Board, the Central Board of Direct Taxes and the Department of Economic Affairs. Only the last-named has a policy-making mandate, while the rest are regulators or bodies implementing laws and regulations. Yet, when policy was substantially changed in June 2000, it happened at the behest of the Securities and Exchange Board rather than the Department of Economic Affairs.[8]

Just as the roles of the policymaker and regulator are somewhat substitutable, so may the roles of the regulator be partly substituted with a change in institutional structure. This may also be what policymakers intend to happen over a period of time. For example, the recent trend toward deregulating certain components of the power industry in the United States, notably, generation, has been done by policymakers with the intention of creating a competitive generating industry. If successful, the hope is that intensive regulation of the power sector, as currently practiced in the United States, will be replaced by a much lighter hand.

THE NATIONAL CONTEXT: INDIA'S ECONOMIC REFORMS

From being a pre-dominantly state-controlled economy, India moved toward a more pro-market and open economy during the 1990s, spurred initially by an economic crisis and a potential payment default in 1991.[9]

The first step was a New Industrial Policy (NIP) issued in August 1991, which removed some controls, such as industrial licensing, that had been a prominent feature of India's post-independence industrial policy.[10] Later reforms progressively supported markets and competition through:

- Introduction of competition in sectors hitherto reserved for the state,

- Promotion of competition in other sectors,

- Reduced role for the state in areas such as determination of prices and directing investment,

- Lowering tariff and nontariff barriers to trade,

- Reduction of barriers to foreign investment, and

- Liberalization of the means of raising finance, especially from overseas markets.[11]

By 1994, the areas still reserved for the state were only defense, sectors of strategic concern, and petroleum.[12] Barriers on imports, tariff and nontariff, were progressively reduced. The unweighted average nominal tariff came down from 125% in 1991 to 55.5% by 1994; the peak rates came down from 355% to 65%.[13] Restrictions on direct foreign investment and on the terms for forming joint ventures with Indian firms were also progressively reduced, and foreign direct investment (FDI) doubled every year between 1991–1992 and 1995–1996.[14] These steps resulted in an increase in the level of competition for Indian firms, from imports, and from multinationals investing in new ventures, singly or jointly with other Indian companies. The compounded average growth rate (CAGR) in the industrial sector between 1991 and 1999 was 5.7%.[15] It was against this general policy of liberalization that the reforms in the telecommunications sector were enacted.

SECTOR CONTEXT: REFORMS IN INDIAN TELECOMMUNICATIONS

Up to 1991, the Department of Posts and Telegraphs and its successor, the DOT under the Ministry of Communications, had a monopoly, enabled by the Indian Telegraphs Act, 1885, which entitled the government of India to be the sole agency to operate, or license others to operate, telecommunications services. Annual reports of DOT (and its predecessors) justified the monopoly on the grounds of equity or meeting universal service obligations (USO). But DOT's record hardly scintillates: its own reports indicate that teledensity was an abysmal 0.8 in 1990; only 140,000 out of 576,000 villages had a phone connection; even when there was a connection, in many cases it was just one connection of low quality. Wait times for new connections extended to seven to eight years, and quality of service was low. Access charges and long-distance tariffs were among the highest in the world. The only positive developments during this period were the success of the Center for the Development of Telematics in developing cheap rural branch exchanges in the mid-1980s and the installation, also during the 1980s, of a wide network of public call offices (PCOs) all over the country, including rural areas with long-distance direct dialing facility. By 1999, there were 515,000 PCOs in the network. These were operated as privately owned franchises licensed by the DOT and, by unofficial estimates, generated 20% of DOT's revenue.

There were attempts at improving efficiency. Two corporate entities were created from DOT in the mid-1980s: Mahanagar Telephone Nigam Ltd. (MTNL) for providing services in the metropolitan cities of Mumbai and Delhi, and Videsh Sanchar Nigam Ltd. (VSNL), for international long-distance services. Both firms were later listed on the stock exchanges through a minority divestment.[16] Although corporatization was believed to be good for MTNL, there was no follow-through to the rest of the country, mainly due to union pressure.

The changed mind-set of the government was reflected, though with less intensity, in telecommunication, after the general reforms of 1991. The private sector was allowed into telecommunications equipment-manufacture (earlier a monopoly of the state-owned Indian Telephone Industries) in 1991 and into value-added services such as fax, E-mail, and radio paging in 1992–1993. Thus, until the first National Telecom Policy was announced in 1994 (NTP-1994), a limited liberalization took place, reflecting the thrust of general economic reforms that liberalized the manufacturing sector but not the services sector. Although the private sector was licensed to provide cellular services from 1992, this was not implemented by any private firm until NTP-1994 owing to disputes over license fees (the successful bidders having overbid) and interconnection charges. Meanwhile, the tariff structure continued to penalize long-distance voice and data transmission, and the power of the unions led to resistance on technological progress. The members of unions enjoyed the special protection of being government employees: under Article 14(2) of the Indian Constitution, they were virtually immune from prosecution.

DOT's role as dominant equipment manufacturer, sole service provider, and sole rule-maker thus created an institutional structure within which it was the only participant. The other arms of the executive did not intervene because it generated profits that helped subsidize other government departments. Politicians ensured that DOT set tariff structures to provide cross-subsidies for local service. While there were external bodies for grievance redressals such as consumer courts, these were ineffective due to the general problems of the Indian legal system.

NATIONAL TELECOMMUNICATIONS POLICY, 1994

The 1994 policy marked the second phase of reforms in the telecommunications sector. NTP-1994 stated five objectives, but only two were specific: (1) to make telephones available on demand, cover all villages, and provide one PCO for every 500 persons in urban areas by the year 1997 and (2) to make all value-added services "available internationally" by 1996.[17]

The other objectives were stated in general terms; such as "telecommunication within the reach of all," "quality of services should be of world standard," and ensuring that "India emerges as a major manufacturing base."[18]

The two clearly stated objectives were simply unattainable. There was no way that telephones could be provided on demand in two years when the waiting time for a connection in 1994 was six to seven years; similarly, covering all the villages in three years from a starting point of about 25% was virtually unattainable. In this sense, the policy did not contain any meaningful and attainable objectives at all.

The policy did not envisage any substantial change in the institutional structure. For the first time, the policy talked about private sector participation in basic services (as already noted, from July 1992, the private sector had already been licensed to operate certain value-added services such as E-mail, voice mail, data and text services, paging, and cellular services). But the approach of NTP-1994 was that the private sector would *supplement* DOT (rather than *compete*) in providing telecommunications services, on such terms as DOT laid down. There was no institutional structure to define these relationships or to have a body for settlement of disputes. Although the policy did not explicitly say so, the government made it clear that the private sector would be allowed only in local services (which were loss-making due to the cross-subsidy) and not in the lucrative long-distance sector. This almost ensured that no private sector player would be able to enter the field and pose any meaningful competitive threat to DOT. There was no regulatory mechanism put in place to ensure fair competition or prevent unfair exploitation of DOT's dominant position.

DOT thus continued to be a monopoly in basic telecommunications. DOT itself, as an institution, did not have the capability either to build or even to operate such a vastly increased network by 1997 as was envisaged by NTP-1994. The private sector was envisaged as aiding resource generation, but under the framework offered by NTP-1994, it was difficult to see how the private sector would find it worthwhile to make any substantial investments. Foreign service providers were not allowed.

A major failure of NTP-1994 was its not addressing the issue of a regulatory authority. Although the document talks of consumer complaints and dispute resolution receiving special attention, there was no mention of an institutional arrangement for achieving this objective. DOT itself would continue to be the regulator and dispute settler.

PROGRESS IN INDIAN TELECOMMUNICATIONS SECTOR, 1994–1999

Soon after the announcement of NTP-1994 in January 1995, the government invited tenders from private sector operators to participate in basic services. An important objective seems to have been to maximize revenues for the state since the highest bidders would be chosen (although the criteria for selection were not publicly specified). The continued absence of a regulator meant that DOT was charged with selecting (and, later, regulating) its own competitors. An additional problem was that DOT, unlike an independent regulator, was subject to political influences in its choice.

Did DOT do its job well? Consider the following: after the bidding was over, DOT declared a ceiling of 3 circles per bidder, ostensibly to prevent undue dominance by any single player across the country. It is not clear why DOT did not think of a cap before issuing tender conditions. Similarly, in an incredible announcement after the tendering was over and bids had been received, DOT stated that it had fixed reserve prices for each circle and that those bids that did not meet these reserve prices would be rejected. On this basis, the bids for 10 circles were rejected. Not surprisingly, both the caps and reserve prices were challenged in the courts.

While in 10 circles the bids were below reserve prices, in some of the others they were extremely high. One company, Himachal Futuristic Communications Ltd. (HFCL), bid very high: in the 4 circles that it had bid, the total of its bids was Rs.285.5 billion ($8.1 billion at exchange rates prevailing in December 1995). HFCL was a small and unknown company with no financial capabilities of this magnitude, and it was doubtful whether it would be able to discharge its obligations. Yet DOT could not reject these bids without exposing itself to charges of corruption and objections by audit and parliamentary committees. Some other companies had also bid very high amounts and secured licenses. But after the contracts were awarded, the companies backed out of 18 state circles and 8 metros of the country, so that in only 6 circles were licenses given. Only 2 had started functioning as the end of 1998, and 4 by the year 2000.[19]

Further, the terms of licensure did not include qualifying terms for bidders (such as net worth requirements) nor penalty clauses for noncompliance. Even such clauses that existed were weak and were challenged later in the courts on one count or other. Had there been a strong regulatory authority, perhaps the contracts would have been drafted better, and compliance enforced.

The question of assignability of the licenses awarded showed again how weak DOT's tendering processes were. In the tenders, no lock-in periods or restrictions on transfer of licenses were mentioned; bidders perhaps assumed (and even planned) that they could resell the licenses after these were awarded. After the award of tenders, DOT imposed a total ban on such transfers, but the financial institutions refused to finance projects unless assignability was permitted. Only after 33 months of delay was an agreement reached to permit transfer of licenses.

Lastly, while the tender documents mentioned no fees payable to DOT other than the license fees, after the licenses were awarded, the licensees were charged a onetime levy of Rs.136,000 per connection. This would amount to Rs.1.36 billion for a circle with 10,000 connections, clearly an amount that could seriously upset the calculations of any bidders. After much negotiation, DOT agreed to reduce the fees to Rs.54,000 plus an installation fee, effectively giving a figure of about Rs.100,000 per connection.

In summary, DOT's erratic and arbitrary behavior during the licensing process certainly seems to have been influenced by its role as a service provider, while also exposing its lack of institutional capability to handle a license-award process. Although legal intervention did finally sort out the mess created, neither was the organization nor any of its functionaries held accountable for their mistakes.

In the cellular sector, the story has been similar. The license fees for the private operators were fixed at high rates, as may be seen from Table 3.1.

In addition to the license fees, operators had to pay charges for carrying calls on the DOT network. Since even within the same circle, cellular operators were not allowed to carry their own traffic, DOT had to be paid for any call outside one town or city (this rule has since been changed, and cellular operators can carry calls in their own network within a circle).

Table 3.1
License Fees Payable by Cellular Service Operators

Service Area	Year 1	2	3	4 - 6	Year 7 onwards for each year
Mumbai	30	60	120	180	240
Delhi	20	40	80	120	160
Calcutta	15	30	60	90	120
Chennai	10	20	40	60	80

Source: Tender documents of DOT.

The result was unduly high costs for cellular operators. This led to a very slow buildup of subscriber base and use of airtime. The cellular companies all incurred heavy losses for the next three to four years. Only after the license regime was changed into a revenue share regime in 1999 and after cellular operators were allowed to carry traffic within their own circle did the system start growing (over 2 million subscribers by end-2000, growing at over 50% per year).[20]

Internet services were opened to the private sector, thus offering competition to VSNL. But VSNL, in an attempt to stifle competition, was allowed to continue its monopoly over the international gateways. Internet service providers (ISPs) had to route all their international traffic through VSNL. Only in 1999 were these restrictions released, permitting ISPs to have their own gateways.

The outcome of the preceding policies was an institutional structure in which DOT continued as the dominant incumbent as well as rule-maker and arbitrator. The resulting outcomes were predictable: both long-distance and cellular calls continued to be among the most expensive in the world. Even USO, the oft-cited justification for DOT, was a failure: between 1985–1986 and 1998–1999, while the overall number of direct exchange lines (DELs) in the country increased from 3.48 million to 21.53 million, the number of village public telephones even as on January 2000 was still only 0.35 million or 1.6 percent; the number of DELs in rural areas was 3.6 million or 16.7%.[21] Nearly 40% of the rural areas did not have a telephone connection by 1999. The rural network expansion could perhaps have proceeded faster had other technologies—especially wireless-in-local-loop (WLL)—been used, but DOT was slow to adopt these cost-effective technologies. DOT's cost per line was Rs.26,800 per DEL,[22] and the cost per rural line was perhaps 50% higher.[23] But the WLL promoters claimed to be able to provide connections at about Rs.18,000 per line.[24] It seems that DOT had no incentive to use these cheaper technologies due to its monopolistic position.

Thus, the events between 1994 and 1999 show that it is not sufficient to formulate policies; there is also a need for different competent institutions, each with its own role, competence and powers to discharge its functions. The merging of institutions of regulation, licensing, and adjudication all in one body, which was also an operator, was bound to lead to perverse decisions, slow development of the network, and neglect consumer interest, especially when this body lacked competence.

DEVELOPMENT OF TRAI AS AN INSTITUTION

An independent institution to discharge the function of regulation, called the Telecom Regulatory Authority of India (TRAI), was set up in January 1997 through an act of Parliament. The chairperson of TRAI was to be a judge of the Supreme Court or High Court (serving or retired). The members were to be persons with "special knowledge of, and personal experience in telecommunication, industry, finance, accountancy, law, management and consumer affairs"[25] and could be ex-government servants. The government had the power to appoint the members (although the procedure for doing so was not laid down, and there was a lack of transparency about the entire process), but once appointed, they could not be removed prior to their term of five years.

The TRAI Act, 1997, was an exercise in ambiguity and contradictions. According to the act, TRAI could recommend certain actions and play an adjudicating role regarding certain others. Though it was given certain functions such as "ensuring technical compatibility and effective interconnection between providers" and "regulating arrangements among service providers of sharing their revenue derived from providing telecommunications services,"[26] precisely how it was to discharge these functions was not clear. Similarly, it could call for any information from any service provider "relating to its affairs as the Authority may require,"[27] but what exactly it could do if the service provider refused to furnish such information was not made clear. This was a glaring omission, since one of the service providers was DOT, an arm of the government itself. TRAI could not revoke any license of an operator if the operator failed to conform to some standards of service; it could only make a recommendation to the government. If the defaulting service provider was the DOT itself, such a recommendation made little sense.

Licensing was also not within the purview of TRAI, although, as one of its functions, it was to recommend the terms and conditions of licenses of a service provider. It, therefore, tried to issue directives to DOT regarding the terms and conditions of licenses for private service providers, but this was challenged by DOT in the Delhi High Court. Arguing that licensing was a sovereign prerogative of the government, DOT won the case. Thus, TRAI could not play any role in defining the terms under which DOT could issue licenses to its own competitors.[28]

The act laid down that TRAI could notify in the *Official Gazette* the domestic and international tariffs,[29] but when it did so, involving substantial reductions in the long-distance charges but increases in the rentals and local call charges, including those from villages, there was a furor in the Parliament, many members of Parliament arguing that tariff-setting was an issue of public policy and hence within the domain of the government. Eventually, the government rolled back the increases and retained the reductions. This was permissible, since the TRAI rates were only ceilings and not the exact rates to be applied. The act also contained a provision[30] that the government could issue to the authority "such directions as it may think necessary in the interest of sovereignty and integrity of India, the security of the State, friendly relations with foreign States, public order, decency or morality." In fact, it went further in clause 25(2), wherein it was laid down that "without prejudice to the foregoing provisions, the Authority would, in exercise of its powers or the performance of its functions, be bound by such directions on questions of policy as the government may give in writing from time to time." Thus, it was not the regulator who could issue directions to the operator, but the other way round!

NEW TELECOM POLICY 1999 (NTP-1999)

On March 26,1999, a new policy, namely, the New Telecom Policy 1999 (NTP-1999) was announced. This took effect from May 1, 1999. NTP-1999 was more reformist and realistic than NTP-1994.

NTP-1999's main objectives were to:[31]

- Provide a telephone on demand by 2002.

- Achieve a teledensity of 7 by the year 2005 and 15 by the year 2010.

- Increase rural teledensity from 0.4% to 4% by the year 2010 with greater reliability.

- Cover all villages by 2002.

- Provide Internet access to all district headquarters by the year 2000.

- Provide high-speed data and multimedia capability using the latest technologies to all towns with a population greater than 200,000 by the year 2002.

- Encourage rural telecommunications through affordable tariffs and imposing rural coverage obligations on all fixed-service providers.

The main strategies of NTP-1999 were the following.

National Long-Distance Services

National long-distance telecommunication was to be opened to full competition from January, 1 2000,[32] with no limit on the number of providers, no up-front license fees, and only a revenue share (since achieved on the scheduled date—see Chapter 1 in this volume). All local-access providers would be required to interconnect to all long-distance providers. Resale was to be permitted for domestic long distance, while for international telephony, resale would be permitted after 2004, when VSNLs monopoly ended (since advanced to April 2002).

International Long-Distance Services

International long distance would be opened up for competition only from the year 2004[33] (since advanced to April 2002).

Cellular Services

Cellular mobile service providers (CMSPs) were allowed to carry their own long-distance traffic within their own service areas without any need for additional licenses, to interconnect with any other intracircle CMSPs or any other type of service providers, to provide all types of mobile services including voice and nonvoice messages, data services, public call offices, and to use any type of network equipment that would meet the standards of the International Telecommunication Union (ITU)/Telecommunication Engineering Center (TEC).[34] But interconnectivity between CMSPs of different circles (even if the same company operated in two circles) was not permitted; this traffic had to go through DOT's lines. However, they would be permitted to connect directly with VSNL after January 1, 2000, when national long-distance would be opened.[35]

NTP-1999 proposed that cellular providers be allowed to move from a license-fee regime to a revenue-sharing regime.[36] All providers subsequently undertook to do so. The percentage of the revenue to be shared would be based on the recommendations of TRAI. The revenue sharing was implemented from August 1999, tentatively with a revenue share of 15% going to DOT, of which 10% would be a contribution to the general budget of the government, and 5% would go to a USO fund. The final share agreed to by TRAI and the Telecommunications Commission is 17%.[37]

NTP stated that DOT/MTNL could also enter the cellular service area or circle as a third operator in addition to two private operators (only two private operators had been licensed per circle).[38] Since then, a fourth cellular provider has been permitted.

Fixed Services

The number of fixed service providers (FSPs) was to be increased (at the time, there was one private operator in each of 6 circles), based on TRAI's recommendations (since then, TRAI's recommendation of an unlimited number was accepted on January 25, 2001—see Chapter 1 in this volume). All new FSPs were put on par with the state-owned incumbent by allowing them to interconnect with other FSPs/CMSPs and with domestic and international long-distance providers. They could provide all types of services, including voice and data. They could use alternative technologies, such as WLL, in which case they would have to pay a onetime fee for the usage of spectrum for WLL, in addition to the normal entry fee. They would also have to share revenues, as in the case of CMSPs.[39]

In addition to FSPs, cable service providers (CSPs) would be allowed to establish last-mile linkages, freely interconnect with all other service providers, and provide Internet services. They could also apply for FSP licenses.[40]

Radio Paging

NTP-1999 permitted direct interconnectivity between licensed radio paging service providers (RPSPs) and other types of service providers in the area of operation. After August 15, 1999, connectivity among RPSPs in different service areas would be considered.[41]

NTP-1999 permitted and liberalized other areas for private sector participation, such as public mobile radio trunk services (PMRTS), global mobile personal communication services (GMPCS), and very small aperture terminals (VSATs), and applications such as tele-banking, tele-medicine, tele-trading, and e-commerce.

The Role of TRAI

TRAI's role was to promote the government's policy of nondiscriminatory access and the promotion of competition.[42] NTP-1999 stated that TRAI would be given full powers to issue directions to all service providers, including government service providers (DOT/MTNL/VSNL), and to adjudicate disputes among service providers (including DOT and other providers) and between any service providers (SPs) and the government. But decisions on the number of licenses (i.e., competitors to DOT) to be issued, the timing for issue of licenses (i.e., how far competition could be controlled), and who would get the licenses would be made by the government alone, although TRAI's recommendation would invariably be sought on number and timing. But TRAI could give its recommendations only if *sought by DOT and not on its own. In all cases where TRAI's role was to give recommendations, it would not be mandatory on the part of the government to seek its recommendations.*[43]

NTP-1999 and the Institutional Structure. NTP-1999 went much further than NTP-1994. While in 1994 DOT was seen as the major service provider, and the private service providers were seen as supplementing the efforts of DOT, in 1999 the new institutional structure envisaged DOT as one among the service providers. The question remained as to whether the envisaged structure would, in fact, occur and, if it did, whether it would be adequate. In addition, of course, it would be up to the regulator to ensure a level playing field.

NTP-1999 committed the government to the corporatization of DOT by the year 2001. It also stated the government's intentions to restructure DOT, separating its policy-making and licensing functions from its operating entity that provided telecommunications services.[44]   NTP-1999 thus recognized the difficulties posed by the multiplicity of roles vested in DOT.

DEVELOPMENTS AFTER NTP-1999

A number of key developments have taken place after NTP-1999.

Amendment of the TRAI Act and Reconstitution of TRAI.[45]

From the institutional point of view, this was the most important development. In January 2000, the government of India issued an amendment ordinance, that led to major changes in the institutional structure of TRAI. The following were the major changes.

TRAI was split into two agencies, a "new" TRAI, divested of all its adjudicatory and dispute-settling powers and to a newly created agency named Telecommunications Disputes Settlement and Appellate Tribunal. The chairperson of the new TRAI was no longer required to be a serving or retired judge but could be a civil servant or one with experience in relevant fields.[46]

The term of the TRAI team was reduced to three years.[47] The old TRAI was dissolved.[48] A fresh set of persons became the members of the new TRAI.

The following recommendatory functions were given to the new TRAI:[49]

- Need and timing for the introduction of a new service provider; terms and conditions of the license to a new SP;

- Revocation of license to an SP;

- Measures to facilitate competition and promote efficiency in telecommunications services, suggesting technological improvements and the types of equipment to be used; and

- Efficient management of spectrum.

TRAI was given full authority over the following functions:[50]

- Tariff fixation;

- Ensure compliance of the terms and conditions of the license;

- Fix the terms and conditions of interconnectivity between two service providers, including DOT and others;

- Regulate the arrangements among the SPs regarding revenue sharing when required;

- Ensure effective compliance of the USOs;

- Lay down and ensure the quality of service and conduct a periodical survey on service quality provided by SPs; and

- Lay down and ensure the time period for providing local and long-distance circuits of telecommunications between SPs.

TRAI's recommendatory functions were not binding on the government. However, regarding licensing, government had to seek TRAI's opinion, and TRAI had to give its recommendations within 60 days of reference by the government. If the government did not find it possible to accept TRAI's recommendations, it had to return the same to TRAI for reconsideration. TRAI would reconsider within 15 days and give its new recommendations. The government could make a final decision on its own, which might be different form TRAI's recommendations, old or revised. TRAI could seek such documents from SPs, including DOT, as were needed to enable them to give their recommendations, and the SPs had to give these documents within 7 days.

Thus, the new act went a long way in overcoming some of the earlier weaknesses of the TRAI, especially when dealing with the DOT.

The new Appellate Tribunal would deal with all disputes and was a quasi-judicial body. It would have, as its chairperson, a retired or serving judge of the Supreme Court or a chief justice of a High Court. The chairperson and members would be appointed in consultation with the chief justice (of the Supreme Court) of India. This agency could adjudicate any dispute between the licensor (i.e., the government) and a licensee, between two or more SPs, or between an SP and a group of consumers. However, cases involving questions of monopoly and consumer grievance redress (by individual consumers) were outside this body's jurisdiction. Appeals against the decisions of the Appellate Tribunal could be made only to the Supreme Court. No civil courts, including High Courts, had any jurisdiction over the matters coming under the purview of the tribunal. The members of the tribunal could not be removed before the expiry of their terms except on certain grounds and only with the approval of the Supreme Court.

Splitting Up of DOT into DOT and DTS. In October 1999, the government separated the policy-making functions of DOT from the operational functions. It constituted a separate body, named the Department of Telecommunications Services (DTS)—now called Bharat Sanchar Nigam Ltd. (BSNL), which was corporatized on October 1, 2000—which would be responsible for the operation and maintenance of the system.   DOT would be responsible for policy formulation, licensing, international relations, promotion of private investments, and research and development.[51] However, since there was already an agency called the Telecommunications Commission to deal with policy issues, this bifurcation made limited sense, DOT having effectively become the Telecommunications Commission.

Opening Up of International Gateways. In August 1999, the government permitted private operators to set up and operate their own international gateways for their Internet and E-mail services. This ended VSNL's monopoly in this area. The gateways could be set up and operated only by licensed ISPs, and the gateways had to be within the areas of operation. Later, in March 2000, the government permitted any private company to set up gateways and sell bandwidth to ISPs.[52]

Opening Up of Long-Distance Telephony. On August 13, 2000, the government announced the opening up of domestic long-distance to the private sector. Thus, DOT's monopoly in this sector was ended. The long-distance operators could carry calls within and between circles; there were no restrictions on the number of players, although the calls within circles had to be with mutual agreement with the basic operators. There would be a onetime entry fee of Rs.1 billion and a revenue share with the government of 15% (DOT was exempted from the entry fee, but not from this revenue share).[53]

Tariff Restructuring. In May 1999, and again in August 2000, tariffs were restructured with lower rates for long-distance and higher rentals. The time slabs for reduced tariffs were also restructured and DOT increased the geographical area within which calls would be treated as local calls. On average, the changes in May 1999 probably cut the average tariffs by 20 percent, and the reduction in August 2000 by another 15%, though the exact reduction would vary with the nature and time of the calls made. Major as these reductions are, the long-distance charges in India are still among the highest in the world.

Quality and Coverage

The number of DEL lines in the country as on March 31, 1999 was 21.59 million,[54] and direct working connections, 27.7 million, giving a teledensity of around 3.03%.[55] The waiting list was 1.98 million,[56] less than six months (the rate of addition of new lines is around 4 million per year). The quality of services does not seem to have improved much; the phone fault rate per 100 stations per month continues to be around 16.4,[57] the same as in 1985. The call completion rate is still around 83%, and has not shown much improvement either. Fifty-six percent of the villages have been covered. Cellular services have been started in all four metros and in 18 circles. As of March 31, 1999, the number of cellular subscribers was 1.07 million[58] and rose to 2 million by October 2000, and the average airtime usage was about 400 minutes per month. 400 Internet service providers have been licensed, but only 85 have started service.[59] VSNL provides Internet service in Delhi, Mumbai, Calcutta, Chennai, Pune, and Bangalore; MTNL in Delhi and Mumbai; DOT in 258 other locations in the country. By end-2000, all secondary switching areas had Internet nodes of DOT from which users could connect at local call rates. The Internet subscriber base in the country is around 500,000.[60]

Private basic services have started in four states: Madhya Pradesh, Rajasthan, Maharashtra, and Andhra Pradesh. The total number of subscribers in the private line networks was 120,000 at the end of 2000 and 400,000 by the end of 2001, still a minuscule number compared to DOT's subscriber base.

COMPARISONS WITH MEXICO

Mexico's telecommunications sector in the late 1980s bears a striking resemblance to India's telecommunications sector of today. Its teledensity was 6.4 in 1990[61]; its services were of a notoriously poor quality; the waiting lists for new connections extended to seven or eight years; and the state monopoly, Telmex, was notoriously corrupt.[62] The drive for reforms was provided by:

- Mexico's intention to enter the General Agreement on Tariffs and Trade (GATT) and, later, the North American Free Trade Agreement (NAFTA);

- a change in the presidency; and

- increasing public criticism of the poor standards of service from Telmex.

The new president, Salenos de Gortari, first announced a general mandate to deregulate the economy and his plans to make Mexico a member of NAFTA. He built up public support for his moves and gained the support of unions through:

- announcing a 4.4% stock option scheme for the employees;

- offering loans to employees to enable them to purchase Telmex stock;

- announcing protection to Telmex's monopoly in long-distance till 1996.

He also gave certain targets to be fulfilled, with the possibility of withdrawal of some of the benefits if these were not achieved.[63]

Two new institutions were created in 1989: Dirección de Politicas y Normas de Communicación (DPNC) for policy and regulation, and Agency

Telecommunicaciónes de Mexico (Mexican Agency for Telecommunications) for operations. These were similar to the DTS-DOT bifurcation done in India.

This was followed by enacting a Mexican law on telecommunications that set: (1) the rules of competition in local and long-distance communications, radio, and satellite communications; (2) the rules for granting concessions; (3) the foreign equity to a maximum of 49% except in cellular, where this could be increased with the permission of the government; and (4) a rule that licenses could be given only to Mexican nationals and companies.[64] This was followed in 1996 by the creation of a regulatory authority, that was also charged with the function of promoting the sector.[65] Thus, the creation of institutions took place in step with the reforms processes, so that when Mexico entered into commitments with the World Trade Organization (WTO) in 1997, it had already in place strong institutions, especially for regulation and adjudication. The reforms were quite a success in that Mexico's line density increased to 11.2 by 1999, and cellular users increased from 64,000 in 1990 to 9.2 million by 1999.[66] Nevertheless, as Chapter 9 in this volume shows, the powers of the regulator, Cofetel, have been constrained by the courts, and Telmex has successfully fought attempts to control the exercise of its monopolistic powers.

Comparisons with China[67]

China's rapid progress in telecommunications rollout contrasts oddly with its slow progress in institutional and regulatory reform. In 1988, the numbers of fixed-line subscribers and mobile subscribers were 4.7 million and 10,000, respectively.[68] By 1999, the corresponding figures were 100 million and 57 million. Capital expenditure in telecom grew at 62% annually over this period, touching $18.1 billion in 1998 and declining to $14.5 billion in 1999.[69]

Unlike India's moves to create private sector provision of services, service provision has been a state function in China. The dominant carrier (China Telecom) was owned and controlled by the regulator, the Ministry of Posts and Telegraphs, until a new ministry designed to be the regulator of the communications industry was formed in 1998. This was the Ministry of Information Industry (MII). Only in March 2000 did the MII declare that it was independent of China Telecom, implying that it would be an impartial regulator between China Telecom and its state-owned competitors henceforth.

China's success in telecommunications has been attributed to competition within the state (see, e.g., Singh, 1999), primarily the entry of China Unicom into cellular services in 1994, with the support of the Ministry of Electronic Industry. But this appears to be only a minor part of the story. Even before China Unicom was established, telephone connections grew at 45% per annum between 1990 and 1995[70] (Yan and Pitt, p. 247). Further, the primary growth in teledensity has been through fixed-line connections.[71] But China Unicom did not compete with the dominant carrier, China Telecom, in fixed-line services until 2000. Even in cellular services, in 1999, China Unicom's cellular revenue of US$641 million [72] was only about a third of that of its primary cellular competitor, China Mobile's US$4.66 billion (51% owned by China Telecom).[73] The parent, China Telecom's, revenue in 1997 was USD$16.4 billion (Yan and Pitt, p. 254), while China Unicom's total 1997 revenue (including the Guoxin Paging unit that was transferred from China Telecom to it via the Ministry of Posts and Telecommunications (MPT) in 1999 and that had a revenue of US$878 million in 1997) was US$1.62 billion.[74] In 1998, China Unicom's profits of US$193 million was 1/112 of China Telecom (Gao and Lyytinen, p. 726) (all conversions from yuan at CNY 8.28 = 1 US$.)

If competition within the state is not the whole story, the addition of the loss-making postal service, under the MPT's umbrella, adds to the puzzle. According to reports quoted in Yan and Pitt, (p. 254), the postal service lost CNY 3 billion in 1994 and CNY 5 billion in 1995. The losses were made up by transfers from China Telecom's profits, a situation presumably no longer possible after the creation of the MII.

Until better explanations emerge, the answer to the question of how China succeeded in telecommunications must be the simple one: a unified monopoly under state control can do a very good job of spreading the network, even without competition. Subsequent to the successes up to the early 1990s, there have been moves to introduce competition (though within the state sector) now that the basic infrastructure, particularly the backbone network, is adequate. This makes sense inasmuch as the backbone network does not benefit much from competition, being a natural monopoly, while there are substantial efficiencies to be gained from competition in last-mile provision.

In March 2000, China Unicom won official approval to launch an international fixed-line service, after China Telecom agreed to allow the company to use its fixed-line network to offer long-distance calls. China Unicom now has licenses to operate local, domestic, and international long-distance phone services in competition with China Telecom. It has since gone ahead with plans to construct a parallel network, using fiber all the way to the home or office. It will thus bypass the existing toll transit network. A pilot covering 12 cities was completed by December 2000, and a 129-city network was under construction by March 2001.

All the major service providers, China Telecom, China Unicom, China Jitong, and China Netcom, are also investing in improving the Internet backbone. As a result of this, prepaid voice over Internet protocols (VoIP) telephony initially offered rates 70% below the standard market rates for fixed-line service when introduced two years ago, but the rates for circuit-switched phone calls have come down substantially since.

Figure 3.1
China's IP-Based Network

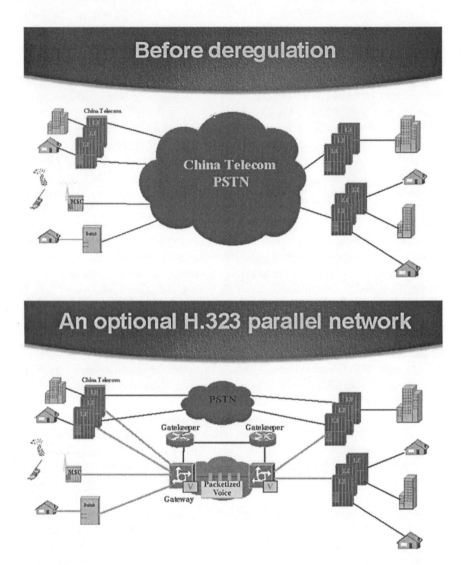

INSTITUTIONAL ANALYSIS

From an institutional perspective, the post-1999 moves by the government have led to stronger institutions. The functions of adjudication have been separated from the functions of recommending various technical and non-technical measures, laying down and monitoring standards, and suggesting improvements. The quasi-legal functions have been entrusted to a more specialized body. The powers of TRAI have been considerably enhanced, and so have the government's obligations. The government could do more to strengthen TRAI, such as by consulting outgoing members and the courts when it appoints new members and by giving TRAI greater resources to undertake research on markets and technology, but a good beginning has been made. There remain, however, some key issues:

1. The government should give up control on licensing in favor of TRAI. Presently, the government has the final power to issue the licenses under its own terms. We noted earlier that this is an arrogation of regulatory power for no obvious reason other than (perhaps) that of a defined transition. Now that TRAI's powers are clearly defined to ensure nondiscriminatory access and competition, it is counterproductive for DOT to allot licenses, given the conflict of interest due to its ownership of BSNL and the need for transparency in license allotment. Hence, instead of the present system, where DOT allots licenses after consulting with TRAI, the responsibility of licensing should transition over to TRAI. The Indian Telegraphs Act may have to be amended to give TRAI the powers to license and delicense providers.

2. An important issue of institutional structure is the concept of a circle as the basic license unit. Each circle is roughly congruent with a state and covers a large area. To obtain a license for fixed service provision, an applicant would have to demonstrate its financial capability to cover a large area. For example, Andhra Pradesh circle covers a population of over 70 million. It is likely that there would be only a small number of FSPs that could cover the whole state. This could lead to the neglect of less profitable areas until the new FSPs covered the more profitable areas. Up to March 2001, the government did not have a policy that would allow an access provider to cover only a small area, say, a few villages or a small town. Yet, this might be required if less profitable areas were to be covered. This strategy of small, independent providers is indeed how telephone service developed in the United States initially with high rural coverage.[75] An additional advantage is that small providers might be better able to compete with BSNL than might large providers with high upfront capital costs. Conversations with TRAI in February 2001[76] indicated that they were contemplating alternatives such as allowing FSPs to franchise areas (this has been enabled under NTP-1999) that they did not wish to directly cover.

    One of the fears that circle licensees will obviously express about the preceding is that increasing their competition will reduce their viability. We do not agree. Viability is a function of market share and the cost of capital. Given the low state of market penetration, acquiring the resources and managerial capability to cover even a small portion of the market effectively will take time. For example, in Mexico, due to its low initial teledensity of 6.4 at the start of reforms in 1990, even a decade of reform and the effects of a competitive market have not hindered the ability of service providers to raise capital for rollout.[77]

    If more initiatives for local-level access providers are not taken, there is likely instead to be a perverse outcome: that the private providers will neglect unserved areas in order to focus their attention on building market share among high value-added clients, such as commercial establishments in the big cities. They will neglect unserved areas because—even if potentially profitable–it makes sense to go for the most profitable areas first, especially since there is no threat of other providers coming into the fray in unserved or underserved areas. This already appears to be happening. Thus, the intention of policymakers–to license providers who will supplement BSNL's resources–will not be fulfilled in the short term.

3. Although TRAI is avowedly technology-neutral, an important technology, voice over Internet protocols (VoIP), is not permitted except for licensed FSPs. This means that competition for voice traffic using VoIP will not happen until FSPs begin offering services. By contrast, China has benefited greatly from allowing VoIP offered by ISPs with a reduction in costs up to 70% over circuit-switched calls.

4. One of the features of the current laws is that all providers are subject to the same ceiling price for their services. Essentially, this is a slab-based tariff, where low levels of usage are cheaper than high levels of usage. The objective is to enable affordability by lower-income users. This is a form of cross-subsidy between low- and high-volume users, since the costs of additional use are negligible. Hence, as TRAI gradually rebalances tariffs to reflect full costs, affordability will fall dramatically enough that there may be no increase in the number of existing connections. To see this, note that TRAI's estimates of costs per line are Rs.30,000 per line in urban areas and about 50% higher in rural areas.[78] Assuming that a 30% revenue realization is needed to cover depreciation and, financial and operating costs, this requires a revenue of Rs.9,000 per year from urban areas. Based on ITU estimates of emerging country populations spending between 5% and 10% of their income on telecommunications, this means, even at the higher level of 10%, that income must exceed Rs.90,000 per annum. There are 12 million households in India that qualify for a telephone at this level of income.[79] Since there are already 3 million rural users and 9 million urban households that have telephones (the rest of the installed DELs are commercial), there will be no change (other than normal economic growth) in the number of lines installed once full costs are charged.

Alternatives should be considered before writing off the possibility of providing basic services at economic costs. The first is to allow providers more freedom to charge the rates that they want to charge. They can be allowed to have different schemes or plans with varying access charges and call charges.[80] This approach would create a strong incentive for providers to search for new technologies or profitable methods of maximizing the use of their lines. For example, Telmex in Mexico recently introduced a very popular scheme called the Ladaphone scheme, whereby residents in apartment buildings can share lines through extensions that are separately billed (the "party line"). This has brought down the cost to users to less than half of the cost of a single line. Note that, if this happened in India, at the new qualifying income of Rs.45,000, the number of households that can afford telephony jumps from 12 million to 49 million. Another advantage of allowing flexible pricing is that private providers would be able to compete with BSNL by offering a range of higher-quality services at higher costs. It would also allow for a movement away from per-minute charges (that have no economic basis), to charging users a fixed monthly fee.

5. Restructuring BSNL: BSNL, recently created, is an institution in need of fixing, its inefficiency hidden by high monopoly profits. A key issue is overstaffing, as shown in the following table:

	Capital costs/line $	Number of lines/employee
DOT, India (3/98)	657.6	44
PLDT, Philippines	2951*	113
Telmex, Mexico	885	201
SBC, USA	781	351

* Includes revaluation reserve.
Figures as of December 1999, except where indicated.

In addition, the quality of BSNL's service is viewed as poor. This is particularly true in rural service. According to a TRAI report, only 7% of village public telephones (VPTs) offer STD service.[81]

BSNL's operations are vast, but it appears that profitability is primarily derived from a few high-volume commercial centers. BSNL will undoubtedly work hard to retain its market share in these centers in the face of competition from the private sector and will no doubt succeed to an extent and for a while. However, in the longer term, its inefficiency will be uncovered by the loss in long-distance revenues and loss of market share in premium accounts. Hence, it is important to restructure BSNL quickly while it still has value through strategic divestments or privatization through a substantial stock market listing.

CONCLUSION

In this chapter, we have highlighted the role that institutions and institutional structures play in determining the direction and pace of telecommunications reform. We have shown how institutional forces affect organizations' processes and decision making, leading to a consideration of the importance of regulation versus policy-making and the substitutability between them and between regulation and different market structures. These concepts have been applied to telecommunications reform in India to analyze whether the institutional structure that has been created by reform will fulfill the policymakers' objectives in terms of efficiency, levels of service, and investment. Our conclusion is that there has been significant progress, though significant institutional reform is still needed. There is a need to build up institutional capabilities within the regulator. The policymaker continues to undertake unnecessary regulatory functions that conflict with its role as a policymaker, preventing its ability to act fairly toward all market participants. Further, the basis on which telecommunications services are priced needs to change in order to improve levels of technology, investment, and coverage. Evidence suggests that this will significantly improve rural coverage. Finally, our analysis argues that the number of telecommunications providers needs to be substantially increased through new franchises at sub-circle levels.

Unfortunately, in many countries, especially developing ones, the need for building institutions is seldom appreciated. The result is much lost effort and wasted resources. The purpose of this chapter has been to point out the importance of institution building that will be needed to supplement other reforms.

NOTES

1.   DOT secretary Ghosh in interview with Dossani, September, 2000. Dossani, September 25, 2000. See also Chapter 1 in this volume.

2.   As defined by Clague (1997), Coase (1998), and North (1990).

3.   Scott (1995).

4.   Such may be the case for Indian telecommunications as well. The springboard for telecommunications reform in India came not from an ideological change of heart but from a resource crunch. As the New Telecom Policy 1999 (NTP-1999) states in the preamble: "NTP 1994 ... recognized that the required resources for achieving these targets would not be available only out of government sources and concluded that private investment and involvement of the private sector was required to bridge the resource gap."

5.   It is much more difficult to do this once defective policies create bad institutions, such as monopolies with strong lobbying powers to prevent further reform.

6.   SBC Communications market capitalization on October 18, 2000 was $180.3 billion, while AT&T's was $87.8 bn; in 1984, at the time of the breakup, AT&T was more valuable than SBC.

7.   This may be because the policymaker believes that these are activities in transition that will one day be awarded to the regulator, or, as seems to be the case, that it is worried about the political problems that will arise from the regulator's independent actions; but it does mean that the policymaker must build up capabilities, such as for determining financial stability, that are otherwise not needed and are more within the purview of the regulator's capabilities.

8.   In this case, the reason was an active regulator that was concerned at the lack of growth in venture capital, while the Department of Economic Affairs apparently did not have the necessary competence.

9.   India's reforms, in fact, date back to the early 1980s, when some steps were taken to free the economy from state control.

10. Dandekar (1992): 81–83.

11. Joshi and Little (1996): 171–218.

12. Ibid.

13. Ibid.

14. World Bank (1996): 9.

15. India, Ministry of Finance, Economic Division (S-37). The figure has been computed form the indices of industrial production for 1990–1991 (212.6) and 1998–1999 (332.0).

16. MTNL and VSNL were both monopolies in their respective spheres of operation.

17. NTP-1994, the section on "Revised Targets."

18. NTP-1994, the section on "Objectives."

19. Mokhariwale (2000): 4.

20. The total number of cellular subscribers in India as of April was in 1997: 368,114; 1998: 913,869; 1999: 1,213, 380; 2000: 1,962,787 (Sinha; 2000): 4.

21. Annual Reports of the Department of Telecommunications, Section on Performance Indicators 1985–1986 and 1998–1999.

22. This is the gross cost per line. It has been obtained by the gross capital investment in 1997–1998 (Rs.87335.7 million) divided by the number of DELs added (3.259 million) during the year (DOT's Annual Report, 1998—1999).

23. DOT presentations in San Jose, CA August 29, 2000.

24. Jain and Das (2000). Both figures include the cost of the last-mile connection, which is the dominant cost factor.

25. *The Telecom Regulatory Authority of India Act, 1997*, Section 4.

26. Ibid., Section 11.

27. Ibid., Section 12.

28. It appears the Delhi High Court went more by the legalities of provisions in the TRAI Act than by the broader purpose of the act itself.

29. Ibid., Section 11(2).

30. Ibid., Section 25.

31. *National Telecommunications Policy, 1999*, Section 2.0. These are not quotations verbatim.

32. Ibid., Section 3.5 for all the points in this paragraph.

33. Ibid., Section 3.6.

34. Ibid., Section 3.1.1.

35. Ibid.

36. Ibid.

37. "Revenue Share Fixed at 17%" (*Economic Times*, October 18, 2000).

38. Ibid., Section 3.1.1.

39. Ibid., Section 3.1.2 for all the points in this paragraph.

40. Ibid., Section 3.1.3 for all the points in this paragraph.

41. Ibid., Section 3.3 for all the points in this paragraph.

42. TRAI chairman M. S.Verma in interview with Dossani, September 26, 2000.

43. This is not a trivial ruling since DOT has fought TRAI in court earlier, as noted. However, the balance of public opinion is moving against such action, and we think that it is less likely that TRAI will be overruled in future.

44. Ibid., Section 4.0. Both these intentions have been carried out.

45. India, Ministry of Law and Justice, (2000).

46. *The Telecom Regulatory Authority of India (Amendment) Ordinance, 2000,* Section 5, amendment to old Section 4.

47. Ibid., Section 6, amendment to old Section 5 (2).

48. Ibid., Section 6, amendment to old Section 5 (3).

49. Ibid.,Section 9, amendment to old Section 11.

50. Ibid.

51. *Annual Report,* DOT, 1999—2000 p i,120-1.

52. "DOT to Permit Private Companies to Set Up Gateways," (*Economic Times* March 14, 2000).

53. "PM Keeps His Word, Opens Up long-distance Telephony," (*Economic Times* August 14, 2000); "Calling All Competitors," *Economic Times*, August 18, 2000.

54. *Annual Report*, DOT 1999—2000.

55. Mokhariwale (2000): 2

56. *Annual Report*, DOT 1999-2000, Section on "Performance Indicators."

57. Ibid.

58. Mokhariwale (2000): 4.

59. Sinha, op.cit, p.4-5.

60. Mokhariwale, op.cit, p 4.

61. Data from the official statistics on the Web site: http://www.cft.gob.mx/htm.

62. Gomez-Perez (2000).

63. Ibid., Griffith (2000).

64. Manikutty (2000): 10.

65. Ibid p 1—11.

66. Data from the official statistics on the Web site: http://www.cft.gob.mx/htm.

67. We are grateful to S. Kumaran of Cisco Systems for substantial input in this section.

68. India had 5.3 million fixed-line subscribers in 1988.

69. By comparison, India's capital expenditure in telecommunications was $6 billion for the fiscal year ending March 31, 2001.

70. There is evidence that the successes came at the cost of universal service provision. Singh (1999, p. 93), points out that 45% of China's telecom connections are in 7 coastal provinces. As of 1992 (He, 1997, p. 118), 18% of telephones were in rural areas compared with 72% of the population.

71. As of 1994, there were over 30 private networks run by about 20 ministries and state enterprises, with about 40% of the lines between them (He, 1997, p. 118), but not used for commercial purposes.

72. www.schwab.com, market guide/provestor plus company report on China Unicom, March 15, 2001.

73. Ibid.

74. Ibid.

75. Lipartito (1997).

76. TRAI chairman M. S.Verma, in interview with Dossani; February 22, 2001.

77. Accessing labor might be the bigger problem than accessing capital, especially after BSNL has offered its staff lifetime employment guarantees in return for agreeing to competition. The order of work, if the DOT's assumption on projected teledensities is to work out, is to add 15 million new lines a year for the next decade. Assuming that BSNL keeps up its pace of 4 million lines a year, this puts the burden of 11 million lines on the private sector. Assuming that efficiency levels match those of Telmex, this means that the private sector will need to add 55,000 new employees a year for the next 10 years.

78. TRAI (2000b).

79. Statistical Outline of India (1999—2000).

80. Already in India, cellular operators have such plans under which one can pay less fixed charges and more airtime charges, and vice versa.

81. Ibid.

BIBLIOGRAPHY

"Calling All Competitors." *Economic Times*, August 18, 2000.

Clague, C. *Institutions and Economic Development: Growth and Governance in Less-Developed and Post-Socialist Countries*. Baltimore: Johns Hopkins University Press, 1997.

Coase, R. "The New Institutional Economics." *American Economic Review* 88, no. 1 (1998).

Dandekar, V. M. "Forty years after Independence." *The Indian Economy: Problems and Prospects,* Bimal Jalan (ed.) Delhi: Penguin, 1992.

"DOT to Permit Private Companies to Set Up Gateways." *Economic Times*, March 14, 2000.

Gao, Ping, and Kalle Lyttinen. "Transformation of China's Telecommunications Sector: A Macro Perspective." *Telecommunications Policy* v.24, nos.8 and 9 (2000): 719–730.

Gomez-Perez, Alfredo. "Mexican Telecommunications: A Study of Privatization of the State Monopoly and Opening Up of the Market to Competition." Diss., McGill University, 2000.

Griffith, Kathleen A. "Telecommunications in Mexico." Available at the Web site http://www.vii.org/papers/mexi.htm.

India, Ministry of Communications, Department of Telecommunications. *National Telecommunications Policy, 1994*. Delhi: Ministry of Communications, Department of Telecommunications, 1994.

———. *The Telecom Regulatory Authority of India Act, 1997*. Delhi: Ministry of Communications, Department of Telecommunications, 1997.

———. *Annual Reports, 1985–1986* and *1998–1999*. Delhi: Ministry of Communications, 1986 and 1999.

———. *National Telecommunications Policy, 1999.* Delhi: Ministry of Communications, Department of Telecommunications, 1999.

———. *Annual Report, 1999–2000.* Delhi: Ministry of Communications, Department of Telecommunications, 2000.

India, Ministry of Communications, Telecom Regulatory Authority of India, *Consultation Paper on Licensing Issues Relating to Fixed Service Providers*, 2000a.

———. *Consultation Paper on Issues Relating to Universal Service Obligations*, 2000b.

India, Ministry of Finance, Economic Division. *Economic Survey, 1999–2000.*

India, Ministry of Law and Justice. *The Telecom Regulatory Authority of India (Amendment) Ordinance, 2000.* Gazette Extra-ordinary, January 24, 2000.

Jain, Rekha, and Pinaki Das. "Universal Service Obligations: Probing the Assumptions." Paper presented at the Workshop on 3G Reforms, Indian Institute of Management, Ahmedabad, October 13–14, 2000.

Jhunjhunwala, Ashok. "Towards Enabling India through Telecom and Internet Connections." Working Paper, IIT Madras, 2000.

Joshi, Vijay, and I.M.D Little. *India's Economic Reforms, 1991–2001.* Delhi: Oxford University Press, 1996.

Lipartito, K. "Cutthroat Competition, Corporate Strategy, and the Growth of Network Industries." *In Research on Technological Innovation, Management and Policy,* ed. R. Burgelman and R. Rosenbloom. Amsterdam: JAI Press, 1997.

Manikutty, S. "Who Needs Subsidy? A Study of Telephone Users in Gujarat." Paper presented at the Workshop in Telecommunications Policy: The Road Ahead, Indian Institute of Management, Ahmedabad, India, August 28–29, 1999.

———. "WTO: Opportunity or Constraint? Some Lessons from the Experiences of Mexico and China." Paper presented at the Workshop on 3G Reforms, Indian Institute of Management, Ahmedabad, October 13–14, 2000.

Mokhariwale, N. R. "Initiatives in Telecommunications Sector: An Overview." Paper presented at the Workshop on 3G Reforms, Indian Institute of Management, Ahmedabad, October 13–14, 2000.

North, D. *Institutions, Institutional Change and Economic Performance.* New York: Cambridge University Press, 1990.

"PM Keeps His Word, Opens Up Long-distance Telephony." *Economic Times*, August 14, 2000.

"Revenue Share Fixed at 17 Per Cent." *Economic Times*, October 18, 2000.

Scott, W. R. *Institutions and Organizations.* Thousand Oaks, CA: Sage, 1995.

Sinha, Sidharth. "Fixed-Mobile Interconnection in India." Paper presented at the Workshop on 3G Reforms, Indian Institute of Management, Ahmedabad, October 13–14, 2000.

Tata Services. *Statistical Outline of India, 1999–2000.* Mumbai, India

Wallsten, S. "An Econometric Analysis of Telecommunications Competition, Privatization and Regulation in Africa and Latin America." Working Paper, Stanford University, 2000.

Wellenius, B. "Telecommunications Reform—How to Succeed." Public Policy for the Private Sector," Note No. 130. World Bank, 1997.

World Bank. *India: Five Years of Stabilization and Reforms and the Challenges Ahead.* Washington, DC: World Bank, 1996.

Yan, Xu, and Douglas Pitt. "One Country, Two Systems: Contrasting Approaches to Telecommunications Deregulation in Hong Kong and China." *Telecommunications Policy*, v23, nos. 3 and 4 (1999): 245—260.

Chapter 4

Strategies for Rapid Telecommunications and Internet Growth

Ashok Jhunjhunwala

UNLEASHING TELECOMMUNICATIONS AND INTERNET IN INDIA

In 1990, India and China both had about 5 million telephone lines. A decade later, India had increased its connections to 30 million, while China crossed 160 million connections and was adding about 25 million connections every year. What are the policies that can make up the difference? This question is the subject of this chapter.

China's success began with a recognition among Chinese policymakers that providing telecommunications services was not a luxury but a necessity, especially with the growing use of the Internet. Indian policymakers, on the other hand, viewed telecommunications services as a luxury good until at least 1997, despite the importance of software services to the Indian economy from 1995 onward. In discussing the policy issues that made a difference, we assume that any telecommunications policy must include not just voice telephony but also Internet use, even for underprivileged users.

India in 2000 had about 30 million telephones and about 2 million Internet connections for its 1 billion people. The government's planners conservatively project a requirement of 175 million connections by the year 2010. We would argue for an even faster achievement of this important target. Looking at China's achievements in an era of technology that was far more costly and difficult compared with today's cost-effective wireless technology suggests that it is possible. In addition, India has at least one similar success story to its credit. This has been in the provision of cable television connections, where the numbers grew from 0 in 1992 to about 40 million households in 2000. What made this spectacular performance possible? Are there lessons to be learned here that enable expansion of telecommunications and Internet connections?

In this chapter, we look in detail at these lessons, examine bottlenecks in rapid telecommunications expansion, and suggest solutions; we look at some of the R&D efforts in the country, particularly the recent efforts of the Telecommunications and Computer Network Group (TeNeT) group at IIT Madras in developing technologies, that provide examples of what needs to be done; and we look at policies that need to be pursued toward this objective.

LEARNING FROM CABLE CONNECTIONS

Economic Issues

The most important lesson from the growth of cable TV connections in India is how to manage affordability. A cable connection in India costs from around $1.50[1] to $4 per month. This is affordable for almost 60% of the 180 million households in India, based on the assumption of cable spending not exceeding 5% of household disposable income.[2] Cable connections, which crossed 40 million in 2000, should, therefore, continue to grow at the same rate as in the past. The story of telecommunications and Internet is, however, very different.

In the United States, household monthly expenditure of US$30 on communications is affordable to well over 90% of its households, based on a spending of up to 5% of disposable household income. Thus, a telecommunications and Internet operator can expect a minimum of $360 per year of revenue from each household. If the operator invests $1,000 per line to set up the service—which is typical—the $360 per year gross revenue comfortably covers the finance charges, operation, maintenance, obsolescence cost, and normal profit of the service provider. Thus, a $1,000 investment per line is viable in the United States. Technologies are developed to provide the best service at this level of investment. As the service is affordable to well over 90% of households, lowering of per-line cost matters less than value-added services to businesses and wealthier individuals. The focus of U.S. research and development is, therefore, not on reducing per-line cost but instead on providing a larger basket of services at this fixed cost.

Developing countries like India, on the other hand, are very different. Assuming that a household is willing to spend up to 7% of its total income on communications, Table 4.1 shows the percentage of households in India that would be able to afford telecommunications service at various levels of cost. Thus, a revenue of over $350 (around $30 per month) is affordable to fewer than 1.6% of the households. If 30% of the households are to be provided service, the expected revenue has to decrease to around $10 to $12 per month. Further, the revenue expected must drop to around $5 per month to make telecommunications services affordable to 60% of India's 180 million households. Assuming again that 35% of initial investment is required as yearly revenue to pay for finance charges (which is as high as 15% in India), depreciation (around 10%), and operation and maintenance (around 10%), one needs to bring down the per-line network cost to about $300 to cater to 30% of Indian households and $200 per line to enable almost 60% of households to have telecommunications and Internet connections (as shown in Figure 4.1).

Table 4.1
Affordability of Telecommunications in India

Household Income (yearly)	% of Households	Affordable Expenditure on Communications (yearly)
> $5000	1.6%	> $350
$2500 - $5000	6.3%	$175- $350
$1000 - $2500	23.3%	$70 - $175
$500 - $1000	31.8%	$35 - $70

Source: Statistical Outline of India, 1999–2000, Tata Services, Ltd.

Unfortunately, in 2000 the cost of providing a telephone line in India was close to $800. While such a cost is affordable to most people in the West, it is affordable to only a few in India. From this point of view, the year 2000 teledensity of 3 represents a good achievement, as it already exceeds the affordability of telecommunications services at current costs and reflects, indeed, a large subsidy from other sectors in the economy.

Figure 4.1
Telecommunications Affordability for Indian Households

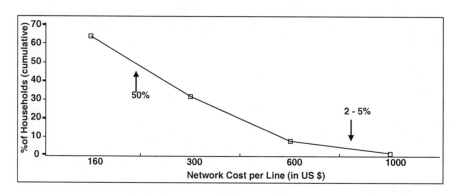

From a policy perspective, though, a teledensity of 3 is extremely low. Policymakers feel that it is imperative for India to raise its teledensity to 15 by 2010. But the unstated corollary of this is that the per-line network cost will have to fall by a factor of 3 to 4 for this to be affordable. While an attractive market awaits the firm that can offer such a low-cost service, we believe—given the R&D focus in the West, which is on value addition rather than on cost reduction—that this will not happen through normal commercial efforts in advanced countries. This, therefore, becomes the task of the Indian scientist and engineer to fulfill. The government's role should be that of an enabler, allowing competing firms to benefit from the fruits of such R&D initiatives.

Need to Focus on the Access Network. The telecommunications network today consists of a backbone network component (BN) and an access network component (referred to as access network, or AN). The BN consists of large switches and routers and interconnection of these exchanges and routers, including intercity connections and international connections. Fortunately, the cost of this part of the network has fallen rapidly over the last 15 years, driven by the R&D efforts in the West to provide higher and higher bandwidth on the backbone. It is already possible to lay high bandwidth fiber-optic networks at a cost of under $2,000 per kilometer (excluding rights-of-way). A careful design of the BN, even though very powerful, would not cost more than $100 per line, including the cost of switching equipment and rights-of-way (A. Jhunjhunwala, B. Ramamurthi, and T. A. Gonsalves, "The Role of Technology in Telecom Expansion in India," *IEEE Communications* 36; no. 11 (1998): 88—94).

The AN consists of the connection from the exchange (or Internet service provider [ISP] routers) to homes and offices, including an access switch. This part of the network is expensive to install, maintain, and upgrade with the latest technology; the installation cost of the AN is about 70% of the total per line cost, while the BN cost is one-third. In urban areas the AN cost exceeds $500 per line; this would be higher in rural areas. Besides, the access part of the telecommunications network requires maximum service and contributes most to the costs of operation. Since the technology for the BN does not admit to further economies, benefiting as it does from the same economies of scale as are applicable to all large installations, we believe that cost reduction is possible only in the AN. Such cost savings could come from bundling services, raising intensity of use from existing lines, and offering quality-price trade-offs.

Local Operation

The cable TV industry shows the value of focusing on the AN. Apart from low BN costs, the second important reason for the rapid growth of cable connection in India lies in the industrial organization of the cable industry. Driven by competition, the large suppliers of content over satellite have chosen to franchise the industry to small operators except in densely populated cities, where large players are more typical (a trend driven also by consolidation).

Typically, a cable TV operator in India installs a dish antenna and provides service to subscribers in a radius of about 700 meters. Installation is carried out by a self-employed person, typically with a couple of helpers. The operator then goes to each home selling the connection and visits every home every month to collect the charges. The service operator is available even on Sunday evenings to rectify any fault that may occur. Therefore, even though cable technology is significantly more complicated (because of taps, amplifier, and power feeding of amplifiers) as compared to twisted-pair-based telephone technology, cable service in India is superior to telephone services, providing Western levels of quality at a modest price. This is made possible by low operating costs at the franchise level.

Using local franchisees at the "last mile" is very common in labor-intensive, last-mile operations and is common, for example, to newspaper delivery everywhere in the world. Even in telecommunications in India, the success of the public call office (PCO), which generates about 20% of total telecommunications revenue for the state-owned provider, is the result of a franchise operation. It enables large sections of people in India to use telephones, providing an excellent example of how the telecommunications department has used the self-employed sector to expand service.

The obvious lesson for telecommunications and Internet is to franchise such local service providers (LSPs) to provide the access network for the subscribers. The access network, which is about 70% of the network cost and most difficult to maintain, should be owned and operated by such LSPs in a neighborhood. This implies that provision and maintenance of the last mile (including access switching), finding the subscriber, and installation of subscriber premise equipment, and bill collection should became the tasks of the LSP, which would run it as a small business. This, in addition, protects the telephone service provider from bearing the risks of default at the individual level, while, in turn, bearing the risk of the franchisee, which is significantly lower as well as being more easily collateralized. Costs at the level of the consumer can be controlled either by allowing multiple LSPs to operate in an area, even if served by a single BN owner, or by regulating prices (as is currently done for PCOs).

Regulation

The third reason for cable TV's success was that the sector grew in India in the absence of any regulations. The cable TV operator required no license and paid no license fees to the state. The user fees were kept low despite the backbone (the satellite beam) being provided by large firms. This was because these firms competed for providing service to the local operator. In most large towns, there is a choice of cable operators to connect to, and this prevents the local cable operator from behaving like a monopolist.

The obvious lesson for telecommunications is to make access network operation totally license-free. Just like cable, there are diseconomies of scale. An LSP should be able to start a service in a neighborhood or a small town by just registering itself as an operating company and connecting to the nearest backbone available. The access operator and the backbone operator could share revenue, say at 70% for the access operator and 30% for the backbone operator, reflecting the allocation of costs. Where there are multiple BN providers, the revenue share could be left to negotiation between the parties. In its absence, the regulator may be required to step in with an equitable determination of the revenue share. Such a policy enables a large number of LSPs to emerge all over the country and provide service in a local area.

Note that current telecommunications policy, which does not recognize licensees at the local level (except for PCOs) will have to be changed.

Internet Bottleneck

Internet access today, for the most part, uses a modem to connect a computer to a telephone line. One then dials an Internet service provider's telephone number and gets connected to an ISP router, which connects one to the Internet, as shown in Figure 4.2. This seemingly simple technique has a number of pitfalls. The most important pitfall is that Internet traffic passes through the telecommunications network. The telephone calls are of relatively short duration, and the telecommunications network is designed to handle only such traffic. The Internet is normally kept on for a much longer duration, and a large number of subscribers using the Internet would overload the telecommunications network, resulting in its collapse. It follows that Internet traffic networks should be designed not to pass through the telecommunications network but to bypass it. The access network must be designed to make this possible.

Figure 4.2
Internet Access Using Today's Telephone Network

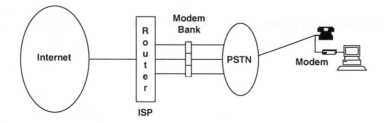

Future Access Network

A conceptual future access network is shown in Figure 4.3. Tomorrow's subscriber unit (SU) would provide direct interface to a telephone (or fax machine, cordless telephone, speakerphone, pay phone) as well as to a personal computer (PC) (via a serial port or Ethernet port) and would enable simultaneous voice and Internet communications. The subscriber units would be connected to an access unit (AU) using wired, wireless, fiber, digital subscriber line (DSL) on copper, coaxial cable, or even power line communications. A typical AU would serve anywhere from 200 to 2,000 subscribers. In urban areas, the AU would be deployed close to the subscribers, almost on street corners, making this last-hop link less than 800 meters. In rural areas, an AU could serve an area of 10-kilometer radius and sometimes even a 25-kilometer radius. The access unit separates voice traffic and Internet traffic. The voice traffic is switched to the telecommunications network (typically using a digital T1 [digital signal transfer speeds of 1.544 megabits per second] or E1 [digital signal transfer speeds of 2.048 megabits per second] connection to the telephone network and using standard access protocol). Internet traffic which typically arrives in bursts from a subscriber, followed by gaps, is statistically multiplexed before being carried to the Internet network. The ability to multiplex such "bursty" Internet traffic from multiple subscribers at AU enables one to overcome the bottleneck described earlier. It should be possible to carry voice traffic on Internet in the future when quality of service (QOS) on Internet permits this.

Figure 4.3
Future Access Network Consisting of Access Unit (AU) and Subscriber Unit (SU)

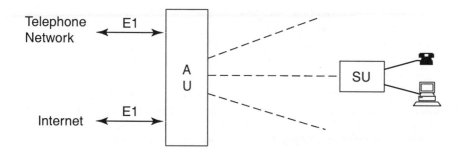

Such a conceptual access network solves the Internet tangle, as the Internet traffic does not enter the telephone network at all. The concentration of traffic at AU implies savings in backhaul bandwidth between AN and exchange/router. Besides, placing an AU close to the subscriber (at least in dense urban areas) implies lower cost for the last-hop.

SOME R&D EFFORTS

From the preceding tasks, it is clear that to enable Indians to access telecommunications and the Internet, one needs to provide 150 to 200 million telephones and Internet connections at the earliest time. It is also apparent that this is possible only by:

- significantly reducing the per-line cost of the telecommunications network with an ultimate target cost of around $200 per line; the key to such cost reduction today is to reduce the cost of the access network;

- conceptualizing and developing AN technology that is scalable and that would enable Internet data to be separated at AN, so that Internet traffic is not switched through the public switched telephone network (PSTN) at all.

With the current costs of the telecommunications network in India hovering around $800 per line, reducing cost to around $200 per line is indeed a difficult task. But then R&D tasks are not supposed to be easy; and a vision of enabling India through telecommunications and the Internet cannot be a simple task.

The task may be difficult but is achievable. This confidence emerged in the late 1980s; primarily due to the efforts of the Center for Development of Telematics (C-DOT), a telecommunications R&D organization set up by the Department of Telecommunications in the mid-1980s under the charismatic leadership of Sam Pitroda. C-DOT developed telecommunications switches, and these switches today connect 12 million of the total of 24 million telephones in India. The switches are rugged, work without air conditioning, and even today cost two-thirds of any imported switch. C-DOT has continued to upgrade the switch and has added integrated services digital network (ISDN) services, signaling system 7 (SS7), access protocols like V5.2, and even intelligent network (IN) functions.

But more important than the product itself, C-DOT generated confidence among Indian engineers that world-class design efforts can be undertaken in India. The large number of people whom it trained provided the basis for numerous design houses that emerged all over the country.

About 1996, TeNeT emerged at IIT Madras, Chennai. This group focused on developing a world-class, yet affordable, access network for India. It helped incubate a number of R&D companies formed by its alumni; Midas Communications, Banyan Networks, Vembu Systems (AdventNet Systems), Nilgiri Networks, and n-Logue Communications, thus formed, started working in partnership with IIT Madras to develop a wide range of access technologies. The products designed by this group today include fiber access network (optiMA), wireless-in-local-loop system (corDECT), direct Internet access system (DIAS), CygNet network management system (NMS), and a host of protocol stacks. The products are aimed at significant reduction in access cost and at the same time enable large-scale usage of the Internet. These products take into account that the future access network should separate the telecommunications and Internet traffic at the access unit (as shown in Figure 4.3) and that the connectivity from the AU to subscriber could use any of several media. A product summary follows.

corDECT WLL

The first access product developed is corDECT wireless-in-local-loop (WLL), shown in Figure 4.5. It consists of a subscriber unit called wallset with Internet port (WS-IP), located at the subscriber's premises. It has a U. S. standard telephone connection (RJ-11) interface for a telephone and a standard serial port (RS 232) to connect a PC (without use of a telephone modem). The system provides Internet at 35/70 kbps and simultaneous telephone conversation. The WS-IP is connected to a base station (CBS) on wireless, and the base station is connected to an access unit, which consists of a digital enhanced cordless telecommunications (DECT) interface unit (DIU) and an iKon remote access switch (RAS). The AU separates the voice traffic and switches it to the circuit-switched telecommunications network using E1 interface. The bursty Internet traffic from multiple subscribers is statistically multiplexed and connected to an Internet router using one or more E1 interfaces. A typical AU serves 200 to 1,000 subscribers. Figure 4.4 and Figure 4.6 show the pictures of WS-IP, CBS, and the DIU. The wallset-base station wireless link distance could be as large as 10 kilometers (using line-of-sight connection), though it is likely to be 1 to 2 kilometers in urban areas in order to reuse spectrum. To serve sparse rural areas, an area relay base station (ARBS) could be installed on a tower up to 25 kilometers away from a CBS and, in turn, serve subscribers in a 10 kilometer radius using a two-hop DECT link.

Figure 4.4
WS-IP: Wallset with Internet Port

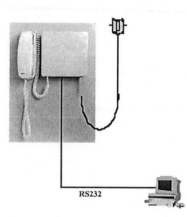

Figure 4.5
corDECT Wireless Local Loop

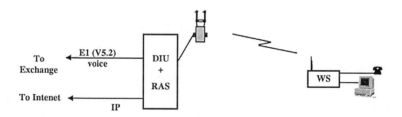

A multiple subscriber unit, referred to as multi-wallset (MWS), has been designed to serve four independent subscribers in the same building. The MWS brings down the per-line cost of corDECT by half.

Figure 4.6
DIU Base Station and WS-IP

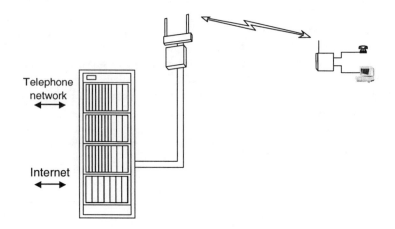

DIAS

The second access product, again modeled after the access unit of Figure 4.3, uses DSL-on-copper technology to provide access. As shown in Figure 4.7 and Figure 4.8, the direct Internet access system (DIAS) consists of a basic rate digital subscriber unit (BDSU) or high-bit rate digital subscriber unit (HDSU) at the subscriber's premises. The BDSU connects a telephone and provides an Ethernet interface for one or more computers. It is connected to an access unit referred to as Internet access unit (IAN) using twisted pair copper wires.

Figure 4.7
DIAS (DSL on Copper)

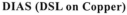
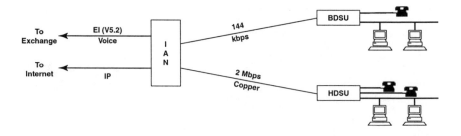

A typical distance is 800 meters, though 5 kilometers is possible using 0.4 millimeter twisted copper pair. The service provided is 144 kbps always-on Internet access, the rate of which drops down to 80 kbps when the telephone is being used. HDSU, designed for corporate subscribers, provides up to eight phones and an Ethernet connection for Internet. Up to 2 mbps always-on internet connectivity is possible with the copper distance being restricted to 3 kilometers. Figure 4.8 shows a picture of an IAN and a BDSU.

Figure 4.8
Direct Internet Access System

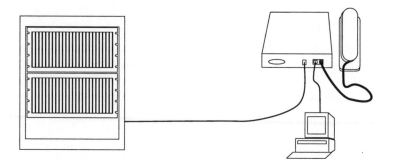

Access Center

The third access product designed by TeNet is a simple plain old telephone service (POTS) line connected to an access unit called versatile remote unit (VRU) located on a street corner.

This enables corDECT WLL, DIAS, and VRU to be combined into a single access center as shown in Figure 4.9. An access center could be located on a street corner in dense urban areas serving 200 to 2,000 subscribers in about a 800-meter radius. Alternatively, it could be located in a small town/village center and serve subscribers in a 10-kilometer radius or even a 25-kilometer radius.

The corporate and upper-middle-class subscribers are served using DSL and provided with always-on Internet connection. On the other hand, middle-class subscribers are provided service using either corDECT multi-wallset or POTS (using VRU). The AC can be made self-contained with a built-in power plant and battery backup. The ratio of DSL, WLL, and POTS subscribers could be varied depending upon the locality served and the subscriber profile.

Figure 4.9
Access Center (AC) Providing POTS, Wireless, and DSL Service

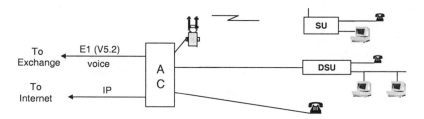

The access center provides one of the most versatile ways of providing telecommunications and Internet access. The total cost per line, including copper to an 800-meter radius, of providing service to about 250 DSL subscribers, 500 wireless subscribers (voice as well as Internet), and 250 subscribers with either MWS or POTS would work out to approximately $260 (the cost includes about 30% for local taxes).

Fiber in the Loop

A fiber-in-the-loop system is yet another product from TeNeT. A fiber D&I (drop-and-insert) backhaul system connects multiple access centers located on street corners (as discussed in the previous section), using plesiochronous data hierarchy (PDH) or a synchronous data hierarchy (SDH) ring network as shown in Figure 4.10.

Figure 4.10
Fiber Backhaul at 34/155 Mbps

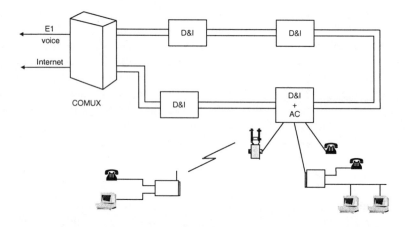

The voice and Internet traffic from each AC are taken to a central location in the city and handed over to the telecommunications switches and Internet routers, respectively. Alternately, if the AC is located remotely, where fiber may not be available, a point-to-point microwave radio (2 GHz / 7 GHz / 11 GHz / 13 GHz or 17 GHz) can be used to bring both the voice and Internet traffic to a town, as shown in Figure 4.11.

Finally, TeNeT has come up with an integrated network management system (CygNeT) to manage all these products as well as other telecommunications and network products. Integrating simple network management protocol (SNMP) and telecommunications management network (TMN) protocols, the CygNeT manages traffic configuration and health and enables a multi-tier operation.

Figure 4.11
Radio Backhaul

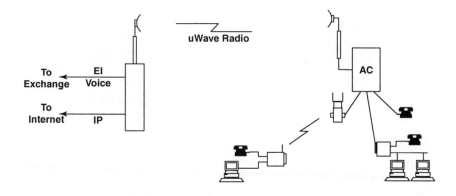

TeNeT's Future Products

TeNeT continues its innovations in adding features and services to its access network while bringing the cost down. Both corDECT wallset (WS) as well as digital subscriber unit (DSU) of DIAS system have been designed with built-in digital signal processing (DSP) with spare memory and computing power. Voice on Internet can thus be added to these systems when it is legally allowed and when QOS provisions on Internet enable its proper use. TeNeT is examining the possibility of developing a cable access system providing voice, video, and Internet, that could work in the adverse cable environment of India. The wireless connectivity on corDECT is being enhanced to provide 384 kbps packet-switched service on corDECT, and multilevel modulation is being examined to enhance the rate to one mbps. 3G radio interfaces are also being examined for use in the coming years. The DSL is being enhanced by addition of asymmetric digital subscriber line (ADSL) and very high data rate digital subscriber line (VDSL). Finally, the backbone interfaces of the AC are being enhanced to incorporate QOS.

Using the technologies developed by TeNeT, it is possible to set up a telecommunications network today at a total cost between $350 in urban areas and $400 per line in rural areas. This is still far away from $200 per line cost required to make telecommunications affordable to 60% of Indian households. However, TeNeT group's work over the past few years confirms that the target is reachable.

POLICY ISSUES AND TASKS

Implications of 150 to 200 Million Telecommunications and Internet Connection Targets

A goal of providing 150 million to 200 million telephone and Internet connections is not just a noble goal but has several implications. The large target implies that telecommunications and information technology (IT) can no longer be confined to large cities or among wealthier sections of the society but must reach each small town and rural area and all sections of people. This could enable rural youth to receive better education and train themselves to compete in this fast-changing world. It could result in software companies being set up in smaller towns and rural areas, initially as satellites to large software companies in the city (just as the Indian companies in the early 1980s attached themselves to software companies abroad), but slowly coming into their own. It could enable someone in a small town to set up a design house, carrying out the most complex designs of virtually anything, a task that was hitherto confined only to a few metros. Above all, this could create confidence among the youth in small towns and rural areas—the kind of confidence to deal with the world as equals, that we have started seeing in recent years in large cities of India. In fact, this goal of 150 to 200 million telephone and Internet connections opens up the possibility of comprehensive social development.

This does not imply that setting up Internet connections itself would automatically lead to all-round social development. These are mere possibilities, and active intervention would be required on various fronts to achieve this. The telecommunications and Internet connections, however, would open up the possibilities as a potent enabler.

Another implication of the goal of having 150–200 million telephone and Internet connections is that India would have to manufacture a large quantity of equipment, install and commission the lines, and maintain them. The numbers being very large, this in itself would create economic activity in the country that would be unparalleled. Even if we assume that $50 per year is required to service a connection, 200 million connections imply $10 billion of economic activity every year. This is by no means a small economic program.

Yet another implication emerges from the affordability issue discussed earlier, namely, that the cost of a telecommunications line needs to be reduced by a factor of 3 to 4. An effort to reduce cost by a factor of 3 to 4 of the internationally prevalent cost would propel the R&D in this sector to be the very best in the world. This, therefore, is not merely a program to expand telephony and Internet; *it is, in fact, a program to become a leader in technology in the world in this sector.*

Finally, a market size of 150 to 200 million (coupled with at least as large a market in other developing countries facing similar problems) is not small. Even at a cost of $250 per line, 200 million lines implies a market size of $50 billion.

The market size is comparable to the telecommunications market in the West. There is every reason for industry to view this opportunity with great interest.

India Has the Capability

As previously discussed, India has the capability to take up this challenging task of significant cost reduction. The efforts TeNeT (at IIT Madras), described earlier, indicate this. Even more important, India today has a large number of telecommunications and IT companies, that carry out major design and development tasks for the best products in the world. Bangalore, Chennai, Hyderabad, Pune, Mumbai, and several other cities are full of such companies. The problem is that most of these companies are carrying out development tasks today as service work for industries in the West. Not only are the products owned by companies in the West, but also the products are designed to primarily serve the markets of the West. The Indian companies are definitely capable of shouldering these challenging tasks, and without the efforts of many of them, no one C-DOT or TeNeT is capable of developing what is required for 150 to 200 million telecommunications and Internet connections.

The question is, why do these companies not work for the Indian market? The reason is that they do not have the confidence that this potential Indian market would really materialize. They do not believe that the government's policies would allow the opening of this market. They are afraid that bureaucratic decision making in India will not let them benefit from such a potential. They would rather continue service to the multinationals, where their returns are assured.

Policy Is Key

Therefore, a sound telecommunications policy is the key to generate such confidence in the Indian R&D community. The government not only has to come up with policies that enable Indian R&D to contribute toward India but also has to be *seen to promote this*. Indian telecommunications policies have been singularly lacking in this regard.

Even though DOT started privatization of telecommunications operations in 1994, with a view to liberalize the environment so that multiple players could use different technologies to help expand the telecommunications network, the process has been bogged down. Though the New Telecom Policy 1999 (NTP-1999) attempts to untangle the web, the policy does not display a basic understanding of the issues of affordability. That significant reduction of cost is imperative and that access networks need to be delicensed do not appear to have been considerations in the formulation of policies.

The privatization process of telecommunications allowed prospective operators to bid for the right to operate in a circle (whole state). States in India are large, and over $1 billion is required to build a telecommunications network for a state. Of course, only large corporate houses in India and multinationals could take up such a task. Furthermore, without an understanding of the ability to pay of the larger Indian population, these corporates have in the past bid very large amounts to obtain licenses. Unable to pay these amounts and faced with bankruptcy, they have prevailed upon the government to change the license fee payment to revenue sharing in NTP-99. NTP-99, formulated under this environment, did the best that was possible but is wanting as far as serious expansion of telecommunications and the Internet goes.

An important question is, why should privatization start with a statewide operation at all? Why cannot the access part of the network be opened up and operated by LSPs? This would enable tens of thousands of small operators to each put up a modest investment to provide services in a community (small area), much like the cable TV operations of today. Why has the privatization process not proceeded on these lines? If one also leaves it to the LSPs to choose their own technology and regulate only a revenue sharing and interconnect agreement, it would probably revolutionize deployment. An R&D company coming up with an innovative product has to get just a few of the thousands of LSPs to try out its product and not depend upon its acceptance by bureaucrats or basic service operators with multinational tie-ups. This single change of policy could get many of the Indian R&D companies to start looking inward.

Another problem that hampers the R&D efforts toward developing products for the Indian market is that the Indian design houses are not big enough to take on the might of the Motorolas and Alacatels of the world. This does not mean that their technology is not good enough; in fact, a reasonable part of the technologies of these multinational telecommunications giants is now being created in India. What they cannot match is the financial muscle of the multinationals. Statewide operators need large financing to carry out their operations and rely on vendor financing, where system vendors not only supply the equipment but also provide financing for this equipment. This is key to the purchase decision. Most multinationals are able to arrange financing from state-supported trade promotion (Exim) banks of their countries. The financing terms are extremely attractive—an interest rate corresponding to the London inter-bank offer rate (LIBOR) + 0.5% plus five years moratorium on payments is typical and might equal 6%. Operators are cash-starved in the first few years, and the five-year moratorium is extremely attractive. Coupled with an attractive interest rate (compared to about a 15% interest rate within India with no moratorium on payments), the financing terms are such that an operator is ready to buy an imported product at a 100% higher price as compared to a comparable indigenous product. Such a situation is a big barrier to Indian design houses designing for India.

Ultimately, the country loses on two counts. First, India uses a high-priced product for which payment has to be ultimately made, and the higher cost of the telecommunications network implies that telecommunications remains confined to a small percentage of India's population. Second, the Indian design house is discouraged from designing for India. Undoubtedly, the Indian policymakers have to pay serious attention to overcome this situation by designing attractive financing policies for indigenously designed products. What would help immensely is if they make the local service operation license free. This would create thousands of small operators who cannot all be financed by multinational vendors. These small operators depend much more on their own resources and try to minimize their costs. They are much more likely to adopt the indigenous, lower-cost products, to the ultimate benefit of the consumer.

Other Policy Initiatives

Another policy initiative, which is a must, is active encouragement for setting up telecommunications and Internet service in small towns and rural areas. A simple solution is to provide a higher revenue share (for the access franchisee) for operations in small towns and rural areas. Similarly, in order to encourage expansion of telecommunications and the Internet to the lower middle classes and poorer sections in the city, a higher revenue share can be provided to a franchise operator who provides connections in slums and houses of lower-income groups.

It is just not enough to encourage indigenous R&D; encouragement to indigenous manufacturing is equally necessary. It is simply not possible to import $50 billion worth of equipment. Indian manufacturing has to be strengthened and made world-class in order to achieve the policymakers' target. Clear policy initiatives encouraging indigenous manufacturing are required. For example, sales tax and excise duties have to be reduced.

Unfortunately, the government's budget deficit has led it to use telecommunications as a source of tax revenue, raising costs of service and further reducing affordability. An alternative would have been to encourage telecommunications growth by lower tax rates; the resulting larger volume would not only compensate for the lower tax rate but also propel more activity in this sector, bringing in indirect revenue to the government. Even though the large budget deficit clouds thinking in this direction, efforts have to be made to change mind-sets.

CONCLUSION

Providing 150 to 200 million telecommunications and Internet connections would empower the masses and transform India. The most important resource in this century is not going to be material resources but human resources. The expansion of the telecommunications and Internet network is the key if one has to convert India's large population into a large pool of human resources.

The expansion of the network, however, is not possible at the price point prevalent in the West. Significant cost reduction is required, and the efforts of C-DOT and TeNeT point out that this is indeed possible, but one needs to tap the large number of Indian electronics design houses to make this possible. Appropriate policies are necessary to make this possible. Opening up local service operation could be an important step in promoting such an effort.

Yet, all this would be only a beginning. The chapter has not dealt with several other concurrent actions that are necessary. First of all, the personal computer, as it exists today, is too costly and inappropriate to be used by hundreds of millions of people in India. Efforts to come up with a variety of low-cost access terminals and integrating these with communications devices are a must. Besides, today's PC consumes about 150 W of power. Providing back-up power in areas where a power cut can extend to 10 hours would be prohibitively expensive. The access terminal not only needs to be inexpensive but also should consume low power. Second, Internet access cannot reach millions without incorporating local language and local content in a massive way. Efforts so far in this direction have been rather poor. Similarly, expecting everyone to use a keyboard to access all information may limit the use of Internet. Voice-enabled Internet service (with Indian languages) must emerge soon. Finally, Internet in India requires Indian applications applications that emerge from the Indian way of life.

In spite of all the massive efforts required, this goal is very realizable. Its enunciation and analysis herein suggest that the outcomes are also feasible and may be converted to a reality.

NOTES

1. The dollar figures quoted in this chapter correspond to U.S. dollars.
2. Statistical Outline of India, 1999—2000, Tata Services, Ltd

Chapter 5

Privatization and Market Liberalization in Asia

J.P. Singh

THE INSTITUTIONAL ENVIRONMENT AND EFFECTS OF TELECOMMUNICATION PRIVATIZATION AND MARKET LIBERALIZATION IN ASIA

Are the privatization and market competition models resulting in the leveling of the playing field on the supply side of telecommunications services in Asia, and is growth demand-driven as expected? Quantitative indicators of network expansion and efficiency, as we argue, provide a partial and inconclusive picture. An evolutionary property rights framework results in a clearer picture. Examined in detail in this chapter are the institutional environments that lead to particular types of property rights, which, in turn, affect network expansion and efficiency. The chapter offers two conclusions: (1) introducing market competition is slow, messy, and difficult to manage, but, where present, it is better for growth than privatization alone, and (2) network expansion and efficiency are most noticeable where adequate property rights and enforcement mechanisms are in place. The chapter also conjectures that the "East Asia model" toward network expansion may not be easily generalizable, particularly for India.

In particular, this chapter evaluates the effects of privatization and market liberalization in telecommunications with respect to the creation and enforcement of property rights. The lesson is simple: property rights and markets thereof, which affect network expansion and efficiency, are only as effective as a particular country's political-economic environment allows them to be.

Why Asia? Most studies examining the effects of privatization on infrastructural expansion have looked at Latin America (Ros and Banerjee, 2000;

Molano, 1997; Ramamurthy, 1996), the reason being that (as Ros and Banerjee note), Latin America had 10 cases of private service provision between 1986 and 1995, while Asia had only two (Hong Kong and the Philippines). However, Asia is significant for three reasons. Privatization has now increased, and private provision is the norm for cellular and specialized services (see Table 5.1). Second, competition, even if among government providers, is significant, allowing us to observe its effects, too. Third, the high growth rates of service provision by government carriers in a couple of cases and, at times, low growth rates by private carriers make us look deeper into the mechanism of privatization to examine the institutional context in which it comes about. Third, recent studies like those by Levy and Spiller (1996), Melody (1997), and Singh (1999) note the differential effects of privatization rather than seeing it as a cure-all for service provision.

Table 5.1
Privatization and Market Liberalization Summary

	INCUMBENT PROVIDER	LOCAL	TOLL	INT'L	CELLULAR	VAS*	CPE
SINGAPORE	partial pvtn.*	R	R	R	C	C	C
SOUTH KOREA	partial pvtn.	C	C	C	C	C	C
MALAYSIA	partial pvtn.	M	C	C	C	C	C
INDIA*	govt. owned	P	P	M	C	C	C
CHINA	govt. owned	G	G	M	G	C	C
PHILIPPINES	private	C	C	C	C	C	C

R: recently liberalized; M: monopoly; P: partial competition; C: competitive; G: government providers' competition. *Includes Internet.
VAS [value added services]; pvtn [privatization]
A few categories are adapted and updated from Gary Hufbauer and Erika Wada eds. *Unfinished Business: Telecommunications after the Uruguay Round* p. 159 (Washington, DC: Institute for International Economics, 1997).

The cases examined are chosen carefully to account for variations in institutional environment, property rights, industry structure, and levels of development. The variations in environment, property rights, and industry structure are examined to see if they cause differences in network efficiency and expansion. The variations also allow us to examine the growth rates in countries with or without (and also, at times, before and after) privatization and market liberalization. Given the disparity in income levels of countries, three cases are those of low-income countries (China, India, and the Philippines), while three are mid- to high-income (Korea, Singapore, and Malaysia). Being sensitive to development levels means being cautious about the infrastructural expansion and historical development experiences of newly industrializing countries (NICs), like South Korea, Malaysia, and Singapore, which are often touted as "role models" for the developing world.[1]

Instead of evaluating network expansion and efficiency with a few "outcome" indicators only, a political economy framework suited toward examining the causes behind these outcomes—the evolution of property rights–is proposed in the next section. Second, the chapter outlines the way that property rights are evolving in each country with respect to the institutional environment of these countries. This environment, mostly focused on state structure and pressures on the state, is necessary to evaluate the path dependency of any country's economic growth. Finally, the newly created property rights are analyzed to conclude that (1) market competition is either slow to emerge or messy and difficult to manage, but, where present, it is better for growth than privatization alone, and (2) network expansion and efficiency are most noticeable where adequate property rights and enforcement mechanisms are in place. Moreover, while the dirigiste top-down "East Asia model" continues to break down, the liberal alternative of bottom-up pressures and service provision poses serious problems in terms of its evolution. On one end of the spectrum is the Philippines, with its messy and nepotistic industry history and liberalization program, and on the other end is Singapore, with its streamlined reforms, but now both enthused and challenged by liberalization prospects as they might challenge government control over information services provision and their content. Particular insights are drawn for India from the empirical evidence that is presented. A quote from Friedrich A. Hayek's (1994) seminal work *The Road to Serfdom* contextualizes the arguments made here:

The liberal argument is in favor of making the best possible use of the forces of competition as a means of coordinating human efforts, not an argument for leaving things just as they are. It is based on the conviction that, where effective competition can be created, it is a better way of guiding individual efforts than any other. It does not deny, but even emphasizes, that, in order that competition should work beneficially, a carefully thought-out legal framework is required and neither the existing nor the past legal rules are free from grave defects.

POLITICAL ECONOMY OF EVALUATING OUTCOMES

Telecommunications reforms are best evaluated via criteria rooted in dynamic institutional contexts, best understood with reference to new institutional economics (NIE). Both privatization and market liberalization as property rights are leading to creation of new institutions, often in macro political-economic environments undergoing radical change themselves. North (1990) says that neo-classical economic theory can tell us of resource allocations only at a given moment of time but fails when evaluating dynamic change. Olson and Kahkonen (2000) note that in evaluating dynamic contexts, it is important to realize that emerging markets' transactions are neither spontaneous nor self-enforcing and that both the creation and enforcement of property rights involve calculations of government power. For Williamson (2000), a bottom-up approach toward institutions examines the organizational environment in which particular rights arise rather than a top-down approach that solely examines the differential impact of emerging market norms.[2] Instead of evaluating the norms through the criteria of normative efficiency, Williamson proposes that we situate both markets and firms in the organizational constraints in which they are bound. This would force us to ask why particular organizational arrangements exist and if they are remediable, rather than merely "excoriate on politics" and politicians. Before calling for changes in the contractual environment, NIE first examines the origins and constraints embedded in this environment.

It is hard, in fact, to evaluate the outcomes of telecommunications market reform without reference to institutional contexts and property rights. First, growth rates in telecommunications in most countries, since telecommunications was made a priority in the 1980s, have been quite high compared to those of previous eras. Going by these growth rates alone would make us pronounce reform exercises to be a success story the world over. How should we examine the high growth rates of network expansion under state auspices in authoritarian countries like Myanmar, Laos, and China and compare them with low growth rates in more democratic and market-oriented circumstances? Thus, attributing change to reform is difficult without comparing countries temporally in terms of service provision and supply-side efficiencies before these reforms took place. A comparison with countries in which reforms have not taken place is also necessary. Second, reforms being a fairly new phenomenon, as in Asia, a time series on network outcomes is not available for the postreform period. Instead, property rights of some sort (which are supposed to generate these effects) are usually in place. A focus on property rights can then not only help us provide a conceptually rigorous way of measuring the effects of reform but, by their very nature, also point out the likely causes of the particular effects. Third, given the varying levels of reforms in different subsectors (See Tables 5.1 and 5.2), capturing precise effects of reform in sectorwide quantitative studies, which are usually carried out in this regard, remains a dubious proposition. Finally, given the noncomparable starting points for reform efforts, differences in levels of development and other cross-national variations, quantitative indicators may be too pithy to tell the precise story. For example, it is well known that countries with low teledensities can achieve much higher growth rates than those with high teledensities.

Table 5.2
Major Telecommunications Privatization and Liberalization Initiatives

SINGAPORE
Privatization began in 1990, with sale of 11% of stock (initial announcement was for 20—25%). Only 2% was sold to foreigners, 24% was sold by 2000.
Singapore Telecom monopoly on basic services until 2000. Cellular and paging privatized in 1997.
Market opening to foreigners by 2000 through World Trade Organization Telecom Accord. 49% foreign ownership.

Table 5.2 (continued)
Major Telecommunications Privatization and Liberalization Initiatives

SOUTH KOREA
Korea Telecom privatization began in 1991 with sale of 20% of stock (41% sold by 2000). It was corporatized in 1982 as Korea Telecom Authority (KTA).
Dacom was created in 1982 (33% owned by KTA until 1991). To compete with KTA, 100% privatized in 1994, started competing in long-distance in 1995.
KTA and Dacom compete in international and long-distance service.
KMTC (Korea Mobile Telecom Corporation), started in 1984, began privatizing in 1989, and was 100% privatized by 1994.
Liberalization of all services launched in 1998. Also, market access to foreigners allowed in all areas by 1998 under the WTO Telecom Accord.

MALAYSIA
Dominant carrier (Telekom Malaysia) privatization began in 1990 with sale of 25% stock, subsequently 34%. It became profitable by 1993. Earlier, corporatized in 1986 as Syarikat Telekom Malaysia.
Private cellular providers began to be commissioned in 1989. Celcom controlled 66% of the market by 2000. Eight providers in cellular, fixed-line, and satellite-based services by 1995, and 32 in paging by 1995.
Market access and foreign investment (limited to 30 percent) provided under the WTO Telecom Accord.
The Communication and Multimedia Act became effective 1999 and fosters convergence.

INDIA
1994 telecom policy divided country into 21 circles, allowing a private firm to compete with DOT (Department of Telecommunications, the state-owned provider at the time) in each circle for local and intracircle toll. Licenses given in 1996–1997, but most efforts stalled by licensing and interconnection disputes. Similar structure and problems in cellular. New Telecom Policy 1999 allows for revenue sharing.
Value-added services liberalized since 1992.
Mahanagar Telephone Nigam Ltd. (MTNL), a parastatal corporation, provides services for Delhi and Mumbai (Bombay).
Videsh Sanchar Nigam Ltd. (VSNL), another parastatal corporation, provides international and Internet services.
TRAI (the Telecom Regulatory Authority of India) came into being in 1997, TDSAT (Telecom Dispute Settlement and Arbitration Tribunal) in 2000.

CHINA
Basic service provision through China Telecom and its government competitor, China Unicom.
Privatization of specialized services began in 1995. Foreign firms involved in building infrastructure. First cellular license sale in late 1997 for China Telecom (only in Guangdong and Zhejiang Provinces).
Competitive provision of services by two other state-owned providers (China Unicom since 1992 and Jitong since 1994).
Ministry of Information Industry formed in 1998.

Table 5.2 (continued)
Major Telecommunications Privatization and Liberalization Initiatives

PHILIPPINES
Dominant provider was Philippines Long-Distance Telephone Company (PLDT). During 1990s liberalization, PLDT lost 25% market share from a high of 94%. Eight government providers service rural areas with a 10% national market share.
Industry now features several local (cellular and terrestrial) operators and nine international operators.

While quantitative indicators tell a partial and/or inconclusive story by themselves, their analysis is nonetheless important to point out a few broad trends, and thus it helps to count them as dependent variables affected by property rights and institutional environments. They are also able to show us growth rates and cost efficiencies (penetration and productivity indicators) during particular periods even if they tell only a partial story about the underlying causes. The empirical evidence examined in this chapter (see Tables 5.3 and 5.4) also paints inconclusive results about telecommunications reform: for every success, there's a puzzle or contradictory evidence.

Table 5.3
Network Efficiency Indicators

	YEARS	SINGAPORE	S.KOREA	MALAYSIA	INDIA	CHINA	PHILIPPINES
Main Lines Per Employee (CAGR%)	1985-90	10.4	11.86	11.6	5.5	14.95	-1.43
	1990-95	16.63	4.58	15.38	16.03	44.42	15.83
	1995-98	-3.4	3.4	11.9	21.1	32.3	34.9
Telecom Revenues Per Main Line (CAGR)	1985-90	15.43	5.8	0	8.45	3.01	12.11
	1990-95	12.12	4.18	0.95	-8.46	1.31	-4.58
	1995-98	-2.66	4.36	-3.43	-4.1	-11.06	-5.79
Rates Of Changes In Service Costs (1996–97)*	Home	-39	-21	-13	+2	-23	+14
	Business	-31	-26	-5	+29	-23	+5

Source: International Telecommunication Union, *World Telecommunications Indicators,* on diskette; Gary Clyde Hufbauer and Erika Wada, eds., (*Unfinished Business: Telecommunications after the Uruguay Round* (Washington, DC-Institute for International Economics), 1998), p. 185.

CAGR — compound average growth rate

"Home" and "business" include initial costs and local calls for terrestrial and cellular networks. It also includes toll and international calls for terrestrial telephony. All calculations, except in the last two rows, are those of the author.

Table 5.4
Network Expansion Indicators

	YEARS	SINGAPORE	S. KOREA	MALAYSIA	INDIA	CHINA	PHILIPPINES
Main Lines (per 100 population)	1980	21.68	7.34	2.95	0.3	0.2	0.9
	1985	30.96	16.1	6.11	0.39	0.3	0.9
	1990	39.96	30.97	8.97	0.6	0.6	1.0
	1995	47.85	41.47	16.56	1.29	3.35	2.09
	1998	56.2	43.3	19.8	2.2	7.0	3.7
Compound Annual Growth Rates (%)	1985-90	4.7	13.97	7.98	9.0	14.86	2.12
	1990-95	4.2	6.0	13.0	16.5	41.1	15.86
	1995-98	5.5	1.45	6.13	19.47	27.84	20.97
Waiting List (000)	1980	4	604	133	447	164	--
	1985	0.05	280	183	839	274	173
	1990	0.07	0.7	82	1961	689	567
	1995	0.02	0	122	2227	1620	900
	1998	0	0	160	2705	7400	900.2
Tele-accessibility (residential main lines as percent of total)	1980	73.9	62.8	58	--	--	--
	1990	67	82	72	--	28	61
	1995	61	79	72	--	71	64
	1997	60.4	78.3	72.3	--	77.7	--
Cellular Mobile Subscribers (per 100 population)	1990	2.0	0.19	0.5	0	0.0016	0.06
	1995	10.6	3.69	5.1	0.008	0.3	0.73
	1998	34.6	30.2	9.9	0.1	1.9	2.2

Source: International Telecommunication Union, *World Telecommunications Indicators,* on diskette; Gary Clyde Hufbauer and Erika Wada, eds., (*Unfinished Business: Telecommunications after the Uruguay Round* (Washington, DC-Institute for International Economics), 1998), p. 185.

The clear success story seems to be cellular with its rapid diffusion, but here, again, China's "success" with government-led terrestrial telephony makes one wonder if market liberalization is the likely cause of this success (Table 5.4). The lesson seems to be reinforced by the two NICs, South Korea and Singapore, that have eliminated their waiting lists and, boast very high teledensities and falling costs for services. Korea, which has had some form of competition (among government carriers) since the mid-1980s, can be seen to have an efficient sector, too, and is the only country in the 1995–1998 period with a positive growth rate for revenues per main line. However, most of the increases in teledensity, the entire elimination of waiting lists, and many of the cost efficiencies came about under state auspices for countries like Singapore and South Korea. Privatization and liberalization being relatively new in these countries, the degree to which the infrastructural growth and efficiency indicators can be attributed to them is not clear.

While Malaysia and India are not comparable in terms of their levels of development, they offer interesting parallels in terms of their reform experience. Their main-line growth rates during the 1990–1995 and 1995–1998 periods are clearly high during the time period when, in Malaysia's case, privatization and market competition are in place or, in India's case, there are sufficiently high competitive pressures on the monopoly basic service provider while the rest of the market is being liberalized. (Given the economic downturn in East Asia, the lower 1995–1998 growth rates for Malaysia are understandable.) Both also show increases in growth rates for main lines per employee. Beyond this, the efficacy of reform in these countries is called to question on the following grounds: waiting lists begin to increase during the reform period, and revenue efficiencies are low for Malaysia and negative for India.[3]

At this point, contrasts with China and the Philippines offer a sobering picture for all the cases. China offers the highest growth rates—under state control. The Philippines offers the lowest growth rates during 1980–1990, with a private provider (and some degree of market liberalization). Second, China's revenue and employee efficiency indicators do well in spite of the high levels of employment (which is an important social objective in China). Lastly, China's contrast with India is particularly telling, too. Both are at similar levels of development, and both started off with similar teledensities in 1980, but China is now far ahead. Like Korea in the 1980s, China now has government-sanctioned and government-led competitive providers. It seems to indicate that government bodies competing with each other maximize welfare better than private ones! This would even be supported by the evidence of government-owned MTNL (with its high rates of growth) in Mumbai (Bombay) and Delhi, which sees India's Department of Telecommunications Services (DTS) as its competitor.

In sum, while growth seems to be the order of the day in the cases examined, it is not clear if the variation is due to, or in spite of, reform efforts. Second, it seems that growth rates are particularly high (and, as shown later, reforms more streamlined) in catalytic states such as Singapore and South Korea.[4] They are also high for the 1990s for countries like Malaysia, the Philippines, and India, moving toward market reform. How should we arbitrate between the two types of cases?

It is the thesis of this chapter that outcomes posited by quantitative indicators are misleading only if we refuse to check them against the property rights and institutional contexts that are important for explaining the variations and inconsistencies told by these indicators. While the property rights literature in telecommunications literature is still developing, it does provide a few clues to the kind of property rights most likely to lead to industry's making credible commitments toward network expansion and efficiency under market-oriented circumstances. Thus, the essential features of efficient property rights in terms of policies, regulations, and market structure of telecommunications sectors are noted later, building on similar concerns noted by Levy and Spiller (1996), Dokeniya (1999), Garcia (2000), Melody (1999), and Singh (1999). This list is not exhaustive but gives most of the commonly mentioned property rights issues. The rationale behind such emerging property rights can be summarized as follows: avoidance of capture by the government's internal prerogatives, streamlining the regulatory process so it does not become messy or nepotistic, and efforts to rule out rent-seeking by the industry. In other words, property rights must be impartial, inclusive, transparent, and enforceable.

Policy

For property rights to be demand-driven, civil society, as well as private businesses, must be involved or included in policy/law formation, the state's internal prerogatives must be lessened, and checks must be placed on executive and/or legislative discretion. A competitive party system and political institutions (including a capable bureaucracy) designed to deal with pluralism are usually most effective in designing and implementing efficient policies. The states must be able to make credible commitments toward enforcing property rights. Policy making must involve experts who can work toward realizing the society's objectives in the long run.

Regulation

A truly autonomous agency, free from everyday government influence, with sufficient human and financial resources, can help with efficient enforcement, but many other things matter as well. Regulations must be transparent and safeguards against regulatory indiscretion and incumbent power must be built in. The presence of an independent judiciary and legislative/executive checks on regulatory authority are also useful. The regulatory authority can also help effect a separation of powers by intervening between the government and the industry.

Market Structure/ Industry Performance and Operations

Given the scope for positive externalities in telecommunications, rules governing network architecture, pricing, and interconnection must be transparent (some of these things may very well be regulatory issues). Cost-based pricing scenarios have greater welfare benefits. The industry must be free of influences from politicians and government officials; thus, management needs to be insulated from these pressures. Rules governing private property and competition, if enforceable, can also alter the incentive structure in favor of network expansion and efficiency.

Three basic observations taken from institutional economics provide the theoretical backdrop for evaluating the property rights criteria previously noted vis-à-vis their demand and supply. The first proposition is that creation and enforcement of efficient property rights are path-dependent, which is the "key to an analytical understanding of long-run economic change" (North, 1990). Thus, a brief foray into the reform "history" of each country examined is necessary to evaluate the current shape of property rights. The second proposition concerns the encompassing interest of even autocrats to provide public goods either for regime legitimacy or for maximizing their revenues and taxes. Therefore, even special interest-driven states can act in a responsible fashion, though Olson (1993) notes that this encompassing interest in providing such public goods can seldom be sustained beyond a generation. The third proposition concerns the ability of some user groups to do better than others because of their ability to overcome their collective action problems and gain access to the state (Olson, 1982). All three propositions are rooted in the historical and institutional environment to which the rest of this chapter is devoted in terms of the cases examined.

The progress made by each case in this chapter, in terms of property rights, is examined by focusing on the institutional history and environment of these countries. Such a focus also resolves the apparent paradox of high growth rates in many of the East Asian societies under state control and the low growth rates followed by high growth rates in many of the market-oriented cases examined here.

SINGAPORE

Singapore's telecommunications reform is streamlined and shaped by the powerful Singaporean state, which plays a key role in shaping societal preferences and intervenes directly in the economy. The role played by the state is so central to Singapore's economy that it is possible to discount the demands that the state faces. The role of the state, however, provides the macro backdrop against which the preference given to multi-national corporations (MNCs) and the current international strategy of Singapore Telecom (SingTel) need to be traced. Nonetheless, the state makes sure that all of its population receives telecommunications services, in turn ensuring the legitimacy of the state. Singaporean property rights in telecommunications have now moved beyond positing telecommunications as a public good, thus allowing private competition.

Singapore's telecommunications has gone through three phases. In the first phase, lasting until the late 1970s, telecommunications responded to business and societal needs via an expansion of its infrastructure. This phase was characterized by service enhancement and reduction of waiting lists for telephone connections. State legitimacy in Singapore rests ultimately in being able to deliver a high standard of living to its citizens. The two groups at the microlevel that matter to the state in terms of telecommunications include the Singapore society and international business groups. The latter are often the only actors emphasized in examination of Singapore's telecommunications, but it is important to remember that Singapore's waiting list for telephones of two years in 1972 (which included society at large) was brought down to less than two weeks in 1979. By 1980, Singapore had the highest teledensity in the developing world (while now its penetration rates are comparable to those of any in the developed world). Similarly, in the 1980s, the benefits of integrated services digital network (ISDN) or broadband networks in Singapore, when provided, were universal.

During the second phase, the 1980s, telecommunications became part of the state's pro-active strategy to carve out a competitive advantage for the city-state. Services such as banking, financial services, and tourism were emphasized, and a new drive was launched to attract MNCs. (There are over 650 MNCs in

Singapore, many of them with regional headquarters.) These MNCs played a key role in shaping Singapore's international competitiveness. The National Information Technology Plan (NITP) was started in 1986 with the aim of making Singapore an information society. By the time of NITP's announcement in 1986, an "information communication infrastructure" was recognized as vital for Singapore's information society strategy. Earlier plans were given a renewed thrust and easily implemented, given the coordination among ministries of finance, trade and industry, and communications and the powerful Economic Development Board. By 1989, Singapore could boast of 100% ISDN coverage. Cellular service was introduced in 1982, and by 1990 the city had 52,000 mobile telephone subscribers (cellular teledensity was 34.6 in 1998). Data network facilities were extended to Singapore's bureaucracy and commercial facilities. Private networks emerged for important services and industries.

The third phase of Singapore's telecommunications strategy, starting in the late 1980s, may be identified as enhancing the state's international role, partial liberalization of state monopoly in telecommunications, and drafting and implementing an ambitious plan (IT 2000) to encourage new multimedia services. Presenting Singapore Telecom as a corporate and commercial entity was necessitated by this role. Only partial privatization was necessary to send the right signal to international markets. A carefully orchestrated privatization of around 11% of the stock (down from the initial announcement of 20–25%) took place in 1993, though 24% of the stock had been sold by 2000. The trade media dubbed it as "the most prestigious international equity deal of the year" (*Euromoney,* April 1993). Only about 2% of the stock was allowed to be held by foreigners. Competition was also introduced in local and international telephony by April 2000, two years ahead of schedule. However, the 76% state ownership of SingTel marred its moves to acquire or hookup with providers in neighboring markets.

The comprehensive, state-led vision for telecommunications in Singapore continues with an aggressive push into multimedia services. Its cable service, launched in 1997, is already considered one of the best in the region (Jussawalla, 1999) and the firm is positioning itself to be a regional hub for broadcasting, too. Its Internet strategy, through private competitive provision, seems to be paying off, both ensuring aggressive expansion as well as getting the population to go along with content regulations in the name of social stability (Wang, 1999).

Singapore's comprehensive program in telecommunications has been shaped by a catalytic state that has to respond directly to only a few cohesive external pressures. While MNCs have direct access to the state, and societal pressures are more indirect, the state does respond to both in providing basic services and can remain sufficiently autonomous in doing so. In boasting of its present and future communication services, Singapore increasingly speaks of itself as "an intelligent island." A 100% fiber-optic network is expected to be available by 2005. But, as with large users elsewhere, 30% of the users account for nearly three-fourths of all telecommunications traffic, while only about 2% of the traffic comes from the bottom 30% users (Bruce and Cunard, 1994). It is also undeniable that foreign firms operating in Singapore are slated to receive the best of telecommunications services, with all other user groups coming second in terms of priority. The exception might be the interactive services program Singapore One, leading to convergence between cable and phone networks, which is aimed at all business, state, and residential consumers (though it has had problems attracting customers and is criticized as being a "field of dreams"). Finally, even with an MNC-oriented coalition in Singapore, the state's working is made easy by the fact that it faces no opposing pressures (political opposition is itself quite weak and marginalized).

A state-led development strategy, in which the state could concentrate in meeting the demands of particular groups, has worked well in Singapore's context. In the 1990s, Singapore's liberalization program was driven more by SingTel's desire to play an aggressive regional and international role than by any kind of inability to meet demands at home. It was becoming clear by 2000 that three-fourths ownership of SingTel by government was hampering its international ambitions. Furthermore, while the public support for the state's Internet strategy has been noted, as Singapore moves toward providing the latest generation of interactive services, it poses a problem for the state, which has traditionally regulated information flows in the country. One scholar (Sisodia, 1992) noted the "irony" a decade ago that "there is an inherent conflict between the democratization of information creation and access and the state's long-standing determination to control closely the information citizens receive."

SOUTH KOREA

The emerging property rights in South Korea are heavily influenced (and biased toward) powerful business conglomerates (*Chaebols*) and, as in Singapore, shaped by a powerful state. But universal service became a political priority for regime survival in the 1980s. While it is tempting to attribute South Korea's superior infrastructure expansion to privatization and a liberalized marketplace in the 1990s, the expansion that took place in the 1980s is momentous and overshadows that of the 1990s (see Table 5.4).

The powerful South Korean state, whose buildup of administrative capacity can be traced to the beginnings of the Yi dynasty in 1392, has played a catalytic role in the telecommunications infrastructure. The centralization and increasing authoritarianism of the state are particularly important in the case of President Park Chung Hee (1961–1979), whose assassination was a direct result of widespread dissatisfaction with elite domination, and the post assassination period was marked by serious civil unrest. In the 1980s, the South Korean state, therefore, became more conscious of providing services (including telecommunications) to its growing ranks of middle-income consumers. While the corporatization of Korea Telecom Authority (KTA) and the creation of Dacom and Korea Mobile Telecom Corporation (KMTC) were also due to pressures from domestic business, it is nonetheless important to view the elimination of waiting lists by 1987 (which exceeded 5 million in 1982) in light of the political legitimacy of the state.

Domestic business demands, especially those coming from its top 30 *chaebol,* which produce 15% of the GNP, have mattered the most in terms of reform. Other significant pressures come from the top 108 corporations (less than 1% of the total exporters), which account for two-thirds of the exports, and from the country's well-developed electronics industry. Of late, the pressures from foreign providers, equipment manufacturers, and MNCs have also been particularly intense. Bilateral negotiations with the United States and the WTO multilateral negotiations have been specifically important in opening the Korean telecommunications market (Hyun and Lent, 1999).

Korea is thus caught among many pressures for reform purposes. The state hedges between pressures from its *chaebol*, international pressures, and pressures from its increasingly affluent consumers. Another element making the state cautious is pressure from Korean workers. In fact, plans to privatize the main telephone carrier, Korea Telecom (KT), in 1995 were met with strikes by the workers (KT has almost 60,000 workers). President Kim Young Sam described it as equivalent to "an attempt to overthrow the state," itself indicative of how seriously the state views these pressures (*The Economist*, June 10, 1995).

While the 1980s was marked by a steady and streamlined expansion of telecommunications services, the Korean state initially found itself in an increasingly unenviable position in the 1990s with its liberalization and privatization program. Charges of nepotism for awarding telecommunications licenses (especially in cellular) to influential *chaebol* by the previous administrations came under intense public and judicial scrutiny in South Korea. As Table 5.4 shows, South Korea's cellular penetration was below that of Malaysia in 1995, though it shot up exponentially after that. The privatization of KT (and Dacom) was held up at times by worker protests and at others by the unwillingness of the state to make the firms' affairs public.

The liberalization program since the late 1990s has gone more smoothly. The state gained some autonomy, first, from domestic pressures opposed to liberalization by streamlining of the ministries and raising the stature of the Ministry of Information and Communications (MIC) in 1994 (Hong, 1998) and, second, from the financial crisis in 1997, which allowed foreign agencies to exert more power. It is now undeniable that South Korea offers a glimpse into a steadily privatized, liberalized, and up-to-date marketplace. KT is reinventing itself as a multimedia high-tech-type company, heavily prodded by the Internet-driven business in Korea. KT privatization has been allowed to proceed, even though worker pressures remain, with the state's owning only 59% of the stock (as of March 2001), which is expected to be reduced further. The foreign ownership limit was also raised to 49% from 33% (although the actual ownership was only 18%) in March 2001. While charges of policy nontransparency and control of KT (like government control of SingTel) continue, the country as a whole is seen as more liberalized and accessible than Singapore. Both countries have, in fact, now liberalized their telecommunications sectors ahead of schedule. Like Singapore, comprehensive policies to introduce an information society have been introduced and implemented in South Korea. Internet and cellular growth rates have both boomed, with nearly 28 million cellular subscribers by April 2000.

Korean property rights, shaped decisively by the state, are surely dividing common property in telecommunications among private hands, but in the Korean scheme of things, domestic investors come first, foreign ones second (though a shift occurred between 1997 and 2000), and medium-scale and small-scale businesses after that, followed by the middle-income groups in the country. Policy and regulatory functions are controlled (sometimes opaquely) by MIC. Korea also has an ambitious program in place for bringing about a universal "information society" and has allowed privatization and competition. But the effectiveness of these new property rights and future outcomes is dependent upon the birth of an institutional structure that can safeguard against policy, regulatory, and industry excesses. The alternative, a rebirth of the erstwhile authoritative or catalytic state (as in Singapore), seems increasingly unlikely.

MALAYSIA

Malaysia represents the case of a strong state more or less pushing through its telecommunications reforms with its administrative clout but nonetheless having to satisfy disparate constituencies in all phases of its telecommunications reform. Demand pressures on the Malaysian state come from its socio-economic cleavages, which include Malaysia's multiethnic society, rural–urban divisions, and, to some extent, federalist or regional breakdowns. These divisions make it hard for the Malaysian state to implement emerging property rights effectively. Malaysian pluralism often makes telecommunications reforms difficult and, at times, biased in favor of politically powerful groups.

The dominant carrier's corporatization and partial privatization in 1990 were accompanied by the liberalization of the Malaysian telecommunications market as a whole (see Table 5.2). Twenty-five percent of Telekom Malaysia's stock was initially privatized (34% by 2000), and while the corporation still has problems meeting waiting list demands, it had become a profitable entity by 1993. The opposition to restructuring the dominant provider diminished by the time of privatization, and most of the energies of user and other interest groups in the 1990s were focused on the liberalizing market structure.[5]

The market liberalization exercise was marked both by trying to satisfy the potential providers of telecommunications (and favoring the native Malay Bumiputeras, who dominate state policy) and by also trying to appease the various user groups. The biggest challenge was meeting the service demands of rural users for whom provision costs are high while marginal revenues are low. Rural users are important for the Malaysian state, as the rural population accounts for 46% of the total in contrast to an average of 27% for upper-middle-income countries. Also, Bumiputeras are concentrated in rural areas. Thus, Malaysia's official policy, in its rhetoric at least, displays a rural bias, even though it is not always borne out by numbers. For example, rural teledensity was 3.8 in 1994 against a national total of 14.9 (Telekom Malaysia Berhad, *Operational Review* [1995]). On the other hand, while Kuala Lumpur accounts for less than one-sixth of the total main lines in the country, it attests to the diffusion of telephones in the country as a whole. Most significantly, over 60% of households in Malaysia have access to a main line. Even if exaggerated, this number shows the importance to the Malaysian state of building its legitimacy widely.

Overall, in spite of service enhancement, Malaysia's waiting list for telephones, which decreased in the 1980s, increased again in the 1990s, from 82,000 in 1990, to 160,000 in 1998 (Table 5.4). Finally, Telekom Malaysia, as could be expected from a dominant incumbent provider, indulged in a number of practices that made matters difficult for new entrants. Interconnection with Telekom's network and high charges were a major problem.

The liberalization of the cellular industry, in particular, is illustrative in terms of Malaysian property rights. The state sought to leapfrog the technological frontier and assured rural areas that cost-effective cellular service would soon be available to them. The next step was to license cellular service providers that would then compete with Telekom's own cellular service provider ATUR (introduced in 1985). The first provider to be commissioned was Celcom, a Bumiputera concern, in 1989 (which by 2000 controlled over two-thirds of the cellular market). But by 1995, seven licenses had been issued for mobile telephony alone, leading observers to term it a case of "privatization run amok" (*Far Eastern Economic Review*, [June 15, 1995[). Even by 2000, Telekom Malaysia's own cellular concern had not turned a profit, mostly due to low subscriber bases. The case of overlicensing extended beyond cellular. TRI (the holding company for Celcom) geared itself for providing international service (a Telekom Malaysia monopoly) to its customers. Binariang, another cellular provider (with a 20% share by U.S. West and 33.3% by British Telecom), was to provide domestic and international services, too. In addition, Time Communications was licensed to lay out a 1,000-kilometer fiber-optic network for local service and hoped to provide international services. All in all, there were eight providers for cellular, fixed-line, and satellite-based services. The state had also licensed 32 paging providers. "The stampede for licenses seems to have overwhelmed the state. Having dispensed permits freely, in some cases to political favorites, ministers appear to have realized belatedly how big a problem they had created for themselves" (*Far Eastern Economic Review*, [June 15, 1995]). Another former official admitted: "Licensing appears to be a political process to please all masters" (interview, July 1995). By mid-1995, Prime Minister Mahathir Mohamad personally intervened in the overcrowded telecommunications market, declaring that the state would like to see mergers or consortia develop. A similar action was taken in April 1999 by the minister for energy, communications, and multimedia, who froze issuing of new licenses because of the excessive number of players.

The Malaysian state continues to play a strong and effective role in its society, but it faces pluralistic pressures and the difficulty with arbitrating those pressures given its current institutional constraints. Beginning in July 1997, the state's legitimacy (built on economic foundations since the 1969 riots and subsequent policies) faced a strong challenge from the currency devaluation and financial crisis. However, it seems to have weathered the crisis well, especially in terms of going ahead with its comprehensive plans for information technologies. The Communications and Multimedia Act 1998 became effective April 1999, merging telecommunications, broadcasting, and computer ministries and creating an independent regulator (Malaysian Communications and Multimedia Commission). The act is especially meant to encourage projects such as the Multimedia Super Corridor (MSC), a 30-mile facility with state-of-the-art computing and information capabilities.

INDIA

Indian telecommunications liberalization in the 1990s was driven by a state that saw its capacity and consensus fritter away over the last 50 years under the weight of pluralistic pressures and personalistic rule (such as under the so-called Nehru–Gandhi dynasty). While the present Bharatiya Janata Party (BJP)–led government comes with a pro-business tilt, it must hedge among domestic industrialists and politicians encouraging the concept of *swadeshi* (indigenization), international pressures wanting liberalization, and antiliberalization pressures from government and trade union employees.

Indian reform efforts in the 1980s were halting and nepotistic, even though demands from businesses, urban residential users, and government administrations continued to grow. India was pushed toward further telecommunications liberalization after a severe fiscal and balance-of-payments crisis in 1991 that weakened the status quo constituencies in the country and empowered many businesses to demand liberalization. Specialized services, including cellular, were liberalized between 1991 and 1994, and basic telephone service was liberalized after the announcement of the National Telecom Policy in 1994 (NTP-1994). The 1994 policy announced ambitious goals for provision of telephones (20 million lines by 2000) and also liberalized the telecommunications sector further. The state-owned monopoly, then called the Department of Telecommunications (DOT), could not be corporatized or privatized due to resistance from its 480,000 workers (tacitly supported by 18 million employees in other state-owned enterprises). DOT was to compete with a private player in each of the 21 regions (known as telecom circles) announced by the state, but the complex licensing procedures, marred by government corruption and resistance from DOT, led to marginal service provision in only 6 of the 21 circles operated by 2000. The BJP government announced a New Telecom Policy in 1999 (NTP-1999), which tried to streamline the licensing process and free prospective operators of heavy license fee burdens by allowing revenue-sharing arrangements. The operators were still shy of investment, given lack of autonomous and transparent regulatory clout. In particular, foreign investment in telecommunications had slowed to a trickle by 2000. NTP-1999 also divided DOT into a policy-making body (named DOT) and a service provider, Department of Telecommunications Services (DTS). NTP-1999 renewed plans for corporatization of DTS, which was effected in October 2000 as the newly formed Bharat Sanchar Nigam Ltd. (BSNL), despite union pressure. Similar pressures have also staved off long-planned privatizations of MTNL (the government service provider in Mumbai and Delhi) and the international carrier VSNL. DOT also remains opposed to liberalization of domestic toll services, but by July 2000 it seemed to be losing on this front.

Each stage of the liberalization process in India has been marked by awarding of contracts and licenses to those with most access to the state's decision-making processes along with many court battles and scandals. Unlike the Chinese state, to which India is frequently compared, a single liberalization "coalition" has not emerged, given India's more democratic environment and plurality of actors. The many things going on simultaneously in the Indian telecommunications landscape reveal the many influences at work on the Indian state. The most powerful liberalization coalition includes international and domestic businesses supported by foreign states and international organizations. Urban users have exerted pressures through the media and other agencies, but so far they are not formally part of the business coalition. The opposing coalition includes trade unions and politicians (who may be supported by domestic businesses continuing to benefit from the past or extant inward-oriented policies and with a stake in keeping MNCs out of the market). The Indian state's juggling between these interest groups (including constituencies within the state-owned monopoly) is producing one of the most complex liberalization programs ever undertaken. While many groups with high demands for services (large businesses, exporters, urban users) continue to be denied services, the state must also hedge between providing services to these groups and providing them to rural areas, where more than two-thirds of Indian voters live but where the teledensity is only 0.4. All of India's 650,000 villages were to have connectivity by 1996, according to NTP-1994, but by 2000 not even half of them did.

The creation and sustenance of the regulatory authority, the Telecom Regulatory Authority of India (TRAI), was damaged by opposition from the DOT, which was loath to give up its authority. From 1994 to 1997, the state hedged on TRAI's creation, and even after it came into being, its decisions were publicly challenged and not implemented by the DOT. Because of the weak mandate given to TRAI, its willingness to play an aggressive role against the DOT after 1997 was marred by judgments against its authority in the Indian courts. BJP moved toward strengthening TRAI's authority in March 2000 and also sought to create an independent Telecom Dispute Settlement and Appellate Tribunal (TDSAT) to arbitrate between operators and government, but the effectiveness of these bodies cannot be judged as of March 2001. While a tug-of-war on defining the features of regulatory authority continues, the Indian government is also getting set to merge the ministries of telecommunications, information, and broadcasting to encourage convergence. Plans call for making TRAI a "superregulator," but whether such a union of powerful turfs can be effected yielding to a superregulator, remains a politically challenging and moot proposition.

India thus offers the interesting case of a state facing pluralistic pressures that has liberalized its marketplace, but safeguards and checks against unrestrained authority are few. Political institutions have long succumbed to the party in power (analogous to the Philippines, examined later), usually driven by special interests, and only recently have opposition parties started playing a significant role.

CHINA

Although Chinese infrastructure is impressive, the Chinese state is also primarily driven by awarding of favors to groups with the most access to state decision making. These personalistic favors and defining telecommunications as a public good shape the emerging property rights in telecommunications. While privatization has not taken place, state-led competition is being credited for phenomenal growth in main lines and cellular subscribers.

China might at first seem to be an odd choice for a special-interest-dominated state for telecommunications, because the state seems so insular. However, its highly authoritarian and centralized decision-making procedures reveal the influence of powerful groups that account for everything from awarding of lucrative economic contracts to widespread corruption within the state. In telecommunications, the challenge to the traditional telecommunications monopoly, the Ministry of Posts and Telecommunications (MPT), came from other powerful ministries within the state and politically powerful groups of domestic and international large users. In China's centralized context, where channels to the elite decision making are limited, the challenge to MPT coalesced around the two newly formed interministerial service providers known as Liantong (China Unicom) and Jitong. China Unicom is more powerful, with its shareholders coming from the influential electronics, railways, and power ministries, and was poised to become China's second carrier. Jitong is owned by 26 state institutions and sought to provide a variety of specialized services. Provincial administrations are also being given more power to provide telecommunications services. While not providing services, MNCs led by Alcatel, American Telephone and Telegraph (AT&T), and Motorola are selling a lot of equipment to a country that has one of the most ambitious service enhancement programs in the world.

Competition in China comes in the form of governmental rivalries, and many steps have been taken to check incumbent power. However, the competition is also becoming so diversified and complex that it is making streamlining of regulation difficult. MPT was merged with that of electronics in 1998 and later with broadcasting, film, and television to create a "super-ministry, the Ministry of Information Industry (MII). In order to hasten competition, MII was asked to give up its operational role of China Telecom, the dominant incumbent provider. While its rival China Unicom is still struggling, it is nonetheless credited for bringing effective competition and pressures for network expansion" (Yan and Pitt, 1999). There are now plans to break up China Telecom into three different types of service providers. Provincial bodies are also gearing up to provide telecommunications, and although broadcasters and Internet providers are officially barred from telephony services, many are planning to do or have found ways to do so already.

While decision making is not as transparent as in other developing countries, two things nonetheless stand out in China's context. First, a coalition for reforming telecommunications with access to the state's decision making exists. "The reform coalition consists of a powerful group which includes the major manufacturing and user ministries, large national users, local states and interest groups and international equipment suppliers and service operators" (Tan, 1994). The insulated nature of Chinese politics accounts for the narrowness as well as the existence of a "reform coalition" among its privileged groups. (A small number of privileged groups would find it easy to form a coalition.) Second, reform has, in turn, mostly benefited the coalition partners, in which incumbents like China Telecom have gained more than others. This is also evident from the networks available to powerful ministries, equipment deals for MNCs, and availability of advanced services for users in export-oriented areas such as Guangdong and Fujian.

Chinese reform continues the devolution of power to provincial bodies and alternative providers. Privatization of a few telephony services is being allowed, as witnessed in the sale of cellular licenses beginning in 1997. Apart from the networks built by large users, provincial autonomy in building networks is important. It accounts for the accelerated deployment of services along the eastern and coastal areas. Many of the provinces even took the lead in collaborating with foreign providers such as with Cable and Wireless in Shenzen starting in 1984. In the mid-1990s, AT&T and Singapore Telecom planned on building business user and fixed-line networks in Shanghai. But the seemingly centrifugal nature of the network is, in fact, not quite so, given its hierarchical structure and the ultimate controls through Beijing's elite, central, decision-making bodies like the State Council. MII might also be seen as further centralization of state functions while at the same time it streamlines regulation and policy (Tan, 1999). Foreign providers have actually been kept quite disciplined by Beijing, and there are a few widely known legal cases brought by the government on foreign contracts.

The tightly controlled telecommunications reform in China, however, may become difficult in the future as its political system adjusts to the post-Deng and post-1997 Hong Kong eras, along with successive international pressures (such as China's pending application for membership with the WTO) and those generated internally. Given the diversity of China's telecommunications industry and the impending liberalization with its entry into WTO, the MII was, in fact, preparing new regulatory rules by July 2000. Government rivalries are also making it difficult to introduce streamlined regulation. Nonetheless, China has by far the most ambitious service enhancement program in the world. Apart from a teledensity of 7 in 1998, China in 2000 could boast of 56 million mobile subscribers, over 15 million pagers, and 6 million Internet users. But whether or not China can reach its targets in the future depends on how well it controls its political pressures. The neat ordering of its "reform coalition" can break down with China's inability to control its provincial or reformist pressures and as international manufacturers and providers get aggressive. Summing up China's development experience with special reference to telecommunications, Mueller (1994) noted that China's "development is thus driven by a jarring dialectical tension between economic freedom and political authoritarianism, between decentralization and centralization, between capitalist practice and socialist ideology."

THE PHILIPPINES

The dominant, historically stagnant, and privately owned telecommunications provider in the Philippines, the Philippines Long-Distance Telephone Company (PLDT), has served as the example for many arguments. Most authors note that the industry structure historically approximates that of the United States. But its actual performance is that of a predatory firm surviving in an equally predatory political environment. PLDT is also used to illustrate the case of how private industry (especially when foreign-controlled) remains essentially exploitative (Wolf and Sussman, 1995) or to show how, without efficient property rights in place, even private provision or competition does not work (Esfahani, 1996). The following assessment concurs mostly with the latter in showing how PLDT did not deliver under the predatory and uncertain institutional environment until the late 1980s and how the pace of telecommunications growth picked up pace in the country in the 1990s, when a modicum of institutionalized rule-making and stability ensued. The 2.12% growth rate of main lines prior to 1990, as opposed to high double-digit growth rates after that, is just one indicator of this (see Table 5.4).

The political-economic context of the Philippines is provided by centuries of colonial rule (first by the Spanish for three centuries, followed by the United States for over 50 years). The colonial rule set in place an executive authority revolving around a tiny, but very competitive, elite. Not only were the boundaries between the elite and the ruling groups quite porous, but whichever elite groups dominated the political scenario received all the rent-seeking favors economically. Ownership of industry remained private, including in telecommunications, because "[p]ublic ownership of an enterprise meant the total loss of the associated surplus once the ruling group was out of power" (Esfahani, 1996). The dominance of the executive, reaching a pinnacle under President Marcos' martial-law years (1972–1986), marginalized the importance of the legislature and the judiciary, both of which were set up in emulation of the

United States model but worked differently due to the historical-societal context. Centralization of authority, often encouraged by the United States, was also seen to be for containing ethnic and left-wing strife.

Telecommunications came to Manila in 1905, and the PLDT itself came into being in 1928 after getting a 50-year franchise. PLDT's majority ownership passed into an American firm's, GTE, hands in 1956, which remained its dominant shareholder until the late 1970s. The period 1956 to 1990 featured inimical growth rates due mostly to two reasons. First, PLDT catered to the elite, both domestic and foreign, and limited itself mostly to Manila. In 1987, one year after Marcos was deposed, the teledensity for the country was 1.31, but that of metro Manila was 7.37, giving a teledensity of 0.31 for the rest of the country (Aquino, 1994), but during the 1970s PLDT was able to meet registered demand for telephones. In fact, PLDT brought the waiting list for main lines from 60% of total service down to about 12% in 1974. This was not surprising given that even with high growth rates, wealth accrued to only a few, and the demand thus came from the elite. Second, PLDT's patronage rested on privileged rule-making from the regime, which ensured its good fortune during periods of political stability and made it hesitant to invest during political uncertainty (as in the period from late 1970s onward, when Marcos' health and political fortunes became suspect). With its access to power, PLDT was also able to keep effective competition out. Thus, the Department of Transport and Communication (DOTC) and the National Telecommunications Commission (NTC), created in 1979 to provide policy guidance and regulatory supervision, were both effectively captured by PLDT instead (Esfahani, 1996).

After Marcos, President Cory Aquino did promulgate a new constitution aimed at redemocratization, but the elite families, including the Cojuangco family, which controlled PLDT by then, stood in the way. The family moved to weaken regulatory control on itself by, for example, replacing the anti-PLDT secretary of transport and communications with one favorable to PLDT interests (Wolf and Sussman, 1995), and it stalled state policies in areas that would have affected its interest adversely. It stifled competition with interconnection bottlenecks and got injunctions against license sales to competitors. Thus, even though there were more than 60 licensed providers in telecommunications in the 1980s, PLDT controlled 94% of the market share.

With the growing middle-income and worker groups in the Philippines and the political discontent following the Marcos and Aquino administrations, the need for a more responsive political-economic structure has strengthened. While the Ramos administration, too, was answerable to many in the ruling elite, it did pass critical deregulatory legislation in 1993 in such a way as to fortify the rules in telecommunications. The two most important developments were mandatory interconnection and licensing of private providers with guarantees that the cellular providers would install 400,000 main lines and that international gateway operators would install 300,000 main lines within five years. By 2000, PLDT met effective competition from Globe Telecom in both terrestrial and cellular telephony and Bayan Tel in cellular telephony. The differences in growth rates in 1985–1990 versus the 1990–1995 and 1995–1998 periods are especially striking. A teledensity of 18 is planned by 2015. The newly licensed operators themselves consist of elite family groups aligned with powerful telecommunications service providers from abroad. For example, Globe's shareholders include 28% each held by SingTel and Deutsche Telekom. The growth indicators run counter to the cost and revenues ones (Table 5.3), but that may be due to the decreases in cross-subsidies and political rents. In fact, service costs, especially for international calls, ran quite high and are used to subsidize domestic telephony. NTC has keenly audited the new providers for main lines installed, but it has been less successful in enforcing interconnection and pricing regulations.

The Philippines case, more than perhaps any other in this chapter, demonstrates the effectiveness of efficient property rights. While the Philippines' institutional environment still remains weak and unresponsive to public interest, given the evidence of the 1990s (and a contrast with other cases), the Philippines case may be more illustrative of the malfunctioning of markets in a vitiated political environment prior to the 1990s than of any inherent weakness of markets themselves.

COMPARATIVE ANALYSIS OF DEMAND AND SUPPLY

The supply side focuses on the special-interest-driven nature of most Asian states. However, in the case of three of the East Asian states examined (South Korea, China, and Singapore), the state was strong enough to contain all pressures and (in South Korea and Singapore) to build its legitimacy through universal service provision. The impressive growth of the infrastructure until the early 1990s is a testimony to the effectiveness of this model. It seems that private property rights are not necessary for infrastructural expansion in the "East Asia model," but as economic and political liberalism makes an entrance in East Asia, it is hard to predict if its current institutions will be able to enforce the property rights as effectively as they have done in the past. Singapore so far has done a better job of containing these pressures than South Korea. Not only are the property rights in the latter biased toward the *chaebol*, but their implementation is continually challenged by workers and the civil society in general, which is at odds with the elite underpinnings of the state. Singapore state's continuing catalytic role can be seen in the March 1998 streamlined auction for a local and long-distance provider ending Singapore Telecom's monopoly in the year 2000. However, whether the state can remain so monolithic in its task as its boundaries become increasingly seamless with information technologies is a moot point.

In the case of India and Malaysia, where the states, while being special-interest-driven, cannot contain pluralistic pressures, privatization and liberalization measures become messy. Malaysia represents the special case of a semi-catalytic state becoming quite dysfunctional. Its corporatization, privatization, and liberalization program can be viewed as success stories (inasmuch as the transitions were relatively smooth and opposition-contained).

But by the mid-1990s the evolving property rights had resulted in nepotism and negative externalities from a crowded marketplace. Legislative and regulatory safeguards were also not forthcoming. The mess of liberalization and privatization in India from the supply side also points to the danger of bringing in market competition before political checks and balances and a regulatory framework are in place. With state capacity in Malaysia, the state was at least able to start streamlining the reform process in 1995, but the Indian scenario, which features a weak and inept state, continues to suffer from an anarchic liberalization program. The formation of a semiautonomous regulatory authority and the emergence of competitive politics in India may change the course of institutional evolution, but it is too early to tell if that would be the case.

The Philippines case is analogous to that of Malaysia and India in the inability of the state to go beyond powerful (elite) pressures on it, but its example is instructive for another reason. Unlike Malaysia and India, the Philippines does not feature broad-based reform coalitions, although middle-class pressures (especially in urban areas) were quite intense in the 1990s. Second, its private provider and slow liberalizations featured poorly during the 1980s political environment, but during the 1990s the reform was strengthened. This is revealed in the increase in infrastructural growth rates and worker productivity from 1990—1998.

The supply-side lesson is clear: efficient property rights take a long time to evolve and to be implemented and enforced. *For economic growth, efficient property rights must include criteria of impartiality, inclusiveness, transparency, and enforceability.* This is a tall order, which cannot be fulfilled even by sophisticated pluralistic systems like the United States, best suited for creating and enforcing private property rights. It would be unrealistic to expect Asian states to evolve and implement such property rights in a decade or so. North (1990) sums up the issue well: "When there is radical change in the formal rules that makes them inconsistent with the existing informal constraints, there is an unresolved tension between them that will lead to long-run political instability."

Turning now to the demand side, collective action (or alliance formation) is easier for privileged groups in a society with small numbers and difficult for larger groups with fewer resources. For this reason most influential reform coalitions in Asian countries have an elite nature, usually including influential business users, equipment manufacturers, international organizations like the World Bank and WTO, and foreign governments. But while it may be difficult for other groups to form coalitions, other entrenched coalitions (often representative of erstwhile economic strategies), opposed to reform, may exist. Not only is reform partly a result of the interplay among these coalitional interests, but the problem gets even more complicated when there is not one or two but several coalitions. Only countries like China have the ability to showcase a cohesive coalition in favor of infrastructural expansion.

With multiple coalitions, reforms may be slow and piecemeal, but there is also a positive side to the story. Articulated coalitional demands, especially plural ones, are forms of restraints on political systems. Inasmuch as political systems now begin to respond to wider demand pressures, they are moving away from exclusive considerations rooted in the supply-driven integrated post, telephone and telegraph (PTT) model, even when the change is slow and piecemeal (as in India and the Philippines). Second, these coalitions are often part of other nationwide processes and might in the long run turn out to be not so elitist at all.

LESSONS FOR INDIA

Two types of lessons for India may be culled from the preceding discussion. These deal either with broad caveats about strategies that may be observed *across* cases or with specific insights that India may learn from *particular* cases discussed earlier.

In terms of broad lessons, two themes are relevant. First, the so-called East Asia model is not particularly generalizable to India. This model is predicated on tremendous state capacity or resources that can be called upon to deal with a limited number of pressures. Both features are problematic in the Indian context. The Indian state might still possess great bureaucratic and material resources, but its capacity to employ these resources gainfully toward development tasks has continued to fritter away, especially since Indira Gandhi's time, as the state has hedged among various crises of legitimacy that it has faced. The Indian state just does not convey the sense of purpose about economic growth that states like Singapore and South Korea do. Atul Kohli (1990) sums up the situation aptly: "The irony of India's political-economic situation is tragic: the state is highly centralized and omnipotent, but the leverage of its leaders to initiate meaningful change has diminished." Furthermore, unlike many of the East Asian countries, the Indian state must deal with pluralistic pressures in a democratic context. It just does not have the luxury of systems as in China, Singapore, and South Korea to marginalize many societal pressures. This produces further gridlock in government decision making. Witness the difficulties that India has had in implementing several well-intentioned telecommunications policy incentives in the 1990s that fell apart, among other things, due to pluralistic pressures and state ineffectiveness in dealing responsibly with them. Thus, India needs to stop flirting with the notion of an East Asia grand strategy for itself, although microelements within the East Asia model may still be relevant. It cannot be, nor should it try to be, another China or South Korea.

A second broad lesson, which has already been well spelled out, is that competition and privatization work if the political checks and balances are in place. Both India and Malaysia have seen pro-competition measures fall apart because the checks and balances were not in place. Indian policymakers are particularly fond of announcing big and bold measures and then scurrying to put the institutional structure in place. Institutions and micromeasures often follow on the heels of policy announcements, even in countries like Britain and the United States, but the gap is seldom as grave as delays in announcing a regulatory authority itself (as was the case with TRAI) or taking several years to sort out important policy implications (as was the case with NTP-1994). The fate of the recently announced convergence bill in India might be similar unless the Indian state *figures out in advance how* it would create and institutionalize the kind of interministerial cooperation that is necessary for the bill to be effective. Remember that such cooperation needs to be institutionalized for it to be effective and not enforced as a fiat from the prime minister's office or decreed by the courts.

In terms of particular cases, India may learn the following from those examined in this chapter:

- The state can increase its legitimacy by creating effective policies for universal service. This is apparent from the Singapore, South Korea, and Malaysia cases.

- The Indian state needs room to maneuver in arbitrating the pluralistic claims that it faces. Countries like South Korea show that such autonomy can often be created through the merging of several ministries, as was the case with its Ministry of Information Industries. Singapore, Malaysia, and China have tried similar experiments with creation of MIIs.

- The Chinese case illustrates that even competition among government providers can lead to better service. This is also borne out historically in India when one observes the rivalries among VSNL, MTNL, and DTS (now BSNL).

- The case of the Philippines is perhaps the most relevant for India. It shows that when effective property rights are in place, competition and privatization lead to network expansion and efficiency.

CONCLUSION

The scenarios focusing on the effectiveness of privatization and liberalization need to account for the role that politics plays in these efforts. Efficient property rights can be expected only in rare circumstances when the polity has a highly developed civil society, and existing institutions produce restraint. Of special importance here is the symbiotic relationship between property rights and the institutions for their enforcement. This chapter shows that in terms of supply, sequencing and the fit between domestic institutions and the degree of privatization and liberalization are important. From the demand side, well-organized, large user groups are clear winners from reforms, but universal service in countries like South Korea and Singapore resulted from state prerogatives. To make the beneficiaries of reforms less dependent on powerful user groups or the state's internal prerogatives, we need an appreciation of the internal mechanisms of states and their interaction with civil society to understand how societal preferences are articulated and arbitrated to shape property rights.

NOTES

1.   An article in *Telecommunications Policy*, for example, noted that South Korea is "an ideal model for many developing countries because of success in implementing its national telecommunications infrastructure in a short period of time" (Hyun and Lent, 1999, p. 390).

2.   In the context of telecommunications literature, a bottom-up approach is employed by Levy and Spiller (1996), while a top-down approach is employed by Ros and Banerjee (2000). Beyond noting that privatization alters the incentive structure faced by firms, the latter authors do not examine the environment in which these property rights arise as Lavy and Spiller do.

3.   Privatization and market competition often entail phasing out subsidies and lowering service costs, and thus it is hard to define efficiency in terms of revenues per main line. This is especially true of the 1995–1998 period in Table 5.4, where five of the six cases posit negative growth rates.

4.   Catalytic states possess a great deal of administrative capacity and other resources, can stay sufficiently autonomous in their decision making, and historically may inherit a pro-development agenda. See Singh (1999).

5.   This does not mean that privatization went smoothly. For example, the country's ethnic Indian minister for energy, telecommunications, and posts who headed Telekom Malaysia's privatization effort came under investigation in 1992 for offering 9 million shares to three companies owned by other ethnic Indians (*Far Eastern Economic Review* [July 16, 1992]: 56).

BIBLIOGRAPHY

Aquino, T. G. (1994). "The Philippines." In E. Noam, S. Komatsuzaki, and D. A. Conn (Eds.), *Telecommunications in the Pacific Basin: An Evolutionary Approach*. New York: Oxford University Press.

Bruce, R., and Cunard, J. (1994). "Reform the Telecommunications Sector in Asia: An Overview of Approaches and Options." In Bjorn Wellenius and Peter A. Stern (Eds.), *Implementing Reforms in the Telecommunications Sector: Lessons from Experience*. Washington, DC: World Bank.

Dokeniya, A (1999). "Re-forming the State: Telecom Liberalization in India." *Telecommunications Policy* 23 (2): 105—128.

Esfahani, H. S. (1996). "The Political Economy of the Telecommunications Sector in the Philippines." In B. Levy and P. Spiller (Eds.), *Regulations, Institutions, and Commitment: Comparative Studies of Telecommunications*. Cambridge: Cambridge University Press.

Garcia, L. G. (September 2000). "Networks and the Evolution of Property Rights in the Global, Knowledge-Based Economy." Presented at the Telecommunications Policy Research Conference.

Hayek, F. A. (1994). *The Road to Serfdom*. Chicago: University of Chicago Press.

Hong, S. G. (1998). "The Political Economy of the Korean Telecommunications Reform." *Telecommunications Policy* 22 (8): 697—711.

Hyun, D., and Lent, J. A. (1999). "Korean Telecom Policy in Global Competition: Implications for Developing Countries." *Telecommunications Policy* 23 (5): 389—401.

Jussawalla, M. (1999). "The Impact of ICT Convergence on Development in the Asian Region." *Telecommunications Policy* 23 (3-4): 217—234

Kohli, A. (1990). *Democracy and Discontent: India's Growing Crisis of Ungovernability.* Cambridge: Cambridge University Press.

Levy, B., and Spiller, P. (Eds.). (1996). *Regulations, Institutions, and Commitment: Comparative Studies of Telecommunications.* Cambridge: Cambridge University Press.

Melody, W. H. (1999). "Telecom Reform: Progress and Prospects." *Telecommunications Policy* 23 (1): 7—34.

Melody, W. H. (Ed.). (1997). *Telecom Reform: Principles, Policies and Regulatory Practices.* Lyngby: Technical University of Denmark.

Molano, W. (1997). *The Logic of Privatization: The Case of Telecommunications in the Southern Cone of Latin America.* Westport, CT: Greenwood Press.

Mueller, M. (1994). "China: Still the Enigmatic Giant." *Telecommunications Policy* 18.

North, D. C. (1990). *Institutions, Institutional Change and Economic Performance.* Cambridge: Cambridge University Press.

Olson, M. (1993). "Dictatorship, Democracy, and Development." *American Political Science Review* 87: 5567-576.

Olson, M. (1982). *The Rise and Decline of Nations: Economic Growth, Stagflation, and Social Rigidities.* New Haven, CT: Yale University Press.

Olson, M., and Kahkonen, S. (Eds.). (2000). *A Not-So-Dismal Science: A Broader View of Economies and Societies.* Oxford: Oxford University Press.

Ramamurthy, R. (Ed.). (1996). *Privatizing Monopolies: Lessons from the Telecommunications and Transport Sectors in Latin America.* Baltimore: Johns Hopkins University Press.

Ros, A., and Banerjee, A. (2000). "Telecommunications Privatization and Tariff Rebalancing: Evidence from Latin America." *Telecommunications Policy* 24 (3): 233—252

Singh, J. P. (1999). *Leapfrogging Development? The Political Economy of Telecommunications Restructuring.* Albany, NY: SUNY Press.

Sisodia, R. S. (May-June 1992). "Singapore Invests in the Nation-Corporation." *Harvard Business Review: 40-47.*

Tan, Z. (1999). "Regulating China's Internet: Convergence Toward a Coherent Regulatory Regime." *Telecommunications Policy* 23 (3-4): 261—276.

Tan, Z. (April 1994). "Challenges to the MPT's Monopoly." *Telecommunications Policy* 18.

Wang, G. (1999). "Regulating Network Communication in Asia: A Different Balancing Act?" *Telecommunications Policy* 23 (3-4): 277—287.

Williamson, O. E. (2000). "Economic Institutions and Development: A View from the Bottom." In M. Olson, and S. Kahkonen (Eds.), *A Not-So-Dismal Science: A Broader View of Economies and Societies: 92-118.* Oxford: Oxford University Press.

Wolf, A. B., and Sussman, G. (1995). "Privatization of Telecommunications: Lessons From the Philippines." In B. Mody, J. Bauer, and J. Straubhaar (Eds.), *Telecommunications Politics: Ownership and Control of the Information Highway in Developing Countries.* Mahwah, NJ: Lawrence Erlbaum Associates.

The World Bank. (1997). *World Development Report 1997: The State in a Changing World*, Washington DC: World Bank.

Yan, X., and Pitt, D. C. (1999). "One Country, Two Systems: Contrasting Approaches to Telecommunications Deregulation in Hong Kong and China." *Telecommunications Policy* 2323 (3-4): 245—260.

Chapter 6

A New Approach to Service Provision

Vinod Khosla

Technology offers India the opportunity of engaging the most talented of its citizens in the development of their country. These citizens are distributed throughout India, and the challenge is to access their talents. The potential benefits are large. When one looks at the impact of technology on agriculture, health care, communications, and transportation in the Western world, there emerges the expectation that technology can lead to such "increasing returns to scale" in India as well. Through the use of technology, it may, therefore, be possible to achieve substantial development in India as well. The first area to focus on is telecommunications, because it enables human interaction more efficiently than any other medium; and human interaction is the enabler of India's greatest resource its human capital and entrepreneurial energy.

The following section presents an approach for India that accounts for these concerns and yet offers a path that can afford India the benefits of using its human capital efficiently and with entrepreneurial flair. It is based on several assumptions; first, that shared knowledge can be the driver of wealth creation in any economy regardless of its stage of development. This is not a trivial assumption except in the sense that, without any sharing of knowledge, a nation's output reflects the level of knowledge of its isolated citizenry, and this cannot be as good as the level of knowledge that is possible through the sharing of information. North Korea and some countries in Africa, such as Uganda, are examples of countries where isolation has reduced growth to negative numbers. By contrast, the United States is the world's champion of shared knowledge and economic growth, and there seems little doubt that the two are related and that technology drives U.S. economic growth. (See Chapter 8 in this volume; also

Jipp [1963]; Norton [1992].) The successful countries (other than the United States) that have used knowledge to drive growth are the countries of Western Europe, Israel, and the Tigers of East Asia. By contrast, China's growth is based on subcontracting its labor off-site to manufacturing companies and not on sharing knowledge. That may be why, despite China's prowess in manufacturing, there do not exist too many branded products that are made in China. Mexico, Indonesia, and other countries that are nearer to India's stage of development than the developed nations of the West face situations similar to that of China.

There are some reasons to believe that India can follow the Western path of knowledge-driven growth. If one identifies the generic requirements for success in the knowledge economy, an inclusive list will probably be egalitarianism, capitalism and competition, fluidity of resource allocation/application, availability of education and knowledge capital, low costs, low barriers, a wide range of educational opportunities, Internet-enabled public access to worldwide resources, lifelong learning models, reverence for research, and the establishment of role models. India lacks several of these requirements, but, more crucially, it possesses some of those that are most difficult to acquire, such as the competitive spirit, a legal and regulatory framework that encourages egalitarianism and competition, low costs and barriers, a reverence for research, lifelong learning models, and respect for role models.

Hence, the proposition that shared knowledge can drive wealth creation in India is taken as an assumption of some importance for this analysis, yet a reasonable one.

Yet, we argue that—successful though it has been in developing its own talents—the U.S. model of telecommunications-based technological development is only indirectly applicable to India. That model engaged its citizenry with the technological revolution through the use of an already developed access infrastructure. What was overlaid on this infrastructure was simply the introduction of competition into the telecommunications industry through the passage of the Telecommunications Act of 1996. Competition spurred the Internet revolution as providers of infrastructure and services sought to more efficiently span an already bridged "last mile."

The Indian model has to be different because universal service is too costly at this time for a country in which the majority of the people cannot afford the individual costs of connection. In the next two decades, the goal of giving all Indians access to telecommunications is unrealistic. Many countries that have been in India's current position have tried at one time or other to provide telecommunications services to everyone and have failed. China is the most recent example,[1] but over the twentieth century, the developed countries of Europe and Japan also went through this route unsuccessfully. Each ended up putting its limited resources in the big cities.

Different though it must be, the appropriate approach for India relies heavily on markets. Opening up the telecommunications infrastructure and services to the markets is an idea whose time has come since it has been demonstrated that the economies of scale in telecommunications are far offset by the benefits of entrepreneurship at the last mile. But it is still an idea that, by itself, will not lead to a high teledensity in India. The reason is that competition will go first where the returns are highest, which are the heavily developed urban areas. This is the same outcome as in other industries and services that is leading India to a divided population, mega slums parading as cities, broken family structures, and poorly utilized critical resources.

The second assumption of this analysis is that an efficient telecom infrastructure used by those best able to use it (which might be a small proportion of the total population) will generate externalities that will be large enough to impact agriculture, health care, and other social requirements on a national scale. The underlying sub-assumptions are that (1) the highest levels of knowledge can be made available remotely using an efficient telecom infrastructure, and (2) a national impact can be had even if the knowledge is used by a small proportion of the population, provided the population is chosen correctly. Indeed, to keep costs affordable, it is essential that the proportion be small. Further, given the inherently egalitarian nature of ideas, choosing the population correctly is critical. It cannot be assumed that the population in a metropolis, for example, contains the needed human capital. Even if one put in place incentives to attract the best people to the big cities, the offsetting costs of large-scale movement, cultural discontinuities, and so on will mean that the best will not come.

Put differently, this assumption implies that if the productivity of a small proportion that uses an affordable telecom infrastructure is high enough to look after the economic needs of the country, and if this population is diffused throughout the country, then a strategy that makes telecommunications accessible to this proportion is a better strategy than trying to build either a telecom infrastructure that is universally accessible or one that is concentrated in big cities. The analogy is with that of agriculture: if, as in the United States, less than 5% of the country's population can efficiently produce enough food for the country, the best national policy for food production is to create an environment in which those 5% (or less) can do the best possible job in various parts of the country. Hence, the role of the state should primarily be to support agriculture with activities that have high externalities, such as agricultural extension services, in selected areas throughout the country.

The third assumption is self-selection. If the right infrastructure is put in place, it is assumed that it will attract those best able to use it. For this to happen, the role of the state has to be minimized in selecting those who will use the infrastructure. Instead, the state needs to tackle an important externality: if human capital is equally spread all over the country, and if the last mile solution is impossibly costly, then the efficient solution is to place infrastructure where the average cost of accessing it is the lowest. This means that infrastructure cannot be placed in the metropolises, which is what will happen if pure competition is to hold sway.

A NEW APPROACH TO UNIVERSAL COMMUNICATIONS

There are 600,000 villages in India. The state-owned provider, BSNL, run by the Department of Telecommunications, had managed to cover about 60% of them with public call offices by the year 2000. BSNL's approach is to provide a thin pipe from a town to nearby villages chosen in order of population density. Over time, a larger number of such connections are provided. This, by itself, is an inferior design. (See Chapter 12 in this volume.) However, for purposes of this analysis, its problem is its unaffordability on a large-enough scale for providing high-enough bandwidth for knowledge sharing.

Suppose, starting ab initio, that one draws 5,000 circles on a map of India, each with an indicated radius of 40 kilometers, to cover the whole country. Each circle would, on average, cover 120 villages with an average population of 150,000 people. Note that both a rail infrastructure and a trunk fiber backbone are already in place in each such circle in India. Our proposal is that the state should build 5,000 communications centers or "work centers" and link these to the rail and fiber infrastructure.

In fact, this geography is roughly where India is going in any case. There were already 3768 urban areas in 1991, up 12% from 1981. 29% of India's population was urban in 2000 and expected to rise to 34% in 2016 (Statistical Outline of India, p.51)

In the proposed work center approach, not every Indian family is targeted to get a telephone at home, but every citizen can access a telephone, the Internet, health care, and education if he or she has the motivation, the drive, the willingness to work hard, good ideas, and entrepreneurial energy. People stay within the traditional semirural or rural infrastructure, within their "circle," rather than moving away from their families to the overcrowded cities. On average, people would travel 20 kilometers per day (or less, given the falling density away from the work center), with a maximum movement of 40 kilometers for those currently living in the most remote areas.

Over time, undoubtedly, some of these people would move permanently closer to their work centers, creating 5,000 small cities over, say, the next 25 years, rather than a dozen metropolises, each with populations of 15–30 million residents, as is likely to otherwise happen.

The cost of making such centers happen is affordable. As noted earlier, the trunk fiber backbone already exists. What is needed is to extend it to a nearby railway center and install a shell infrastructure. Other than that, the state needs to make sure that its regulatory structure allows private firms to bid for, and supply, any range of telecommunications services that they wish to supply. Such a regulatory structure is already in place and merely needs to be enabled for the purpose. (See Chapter 2 in this volume.)

An upper limit of the state's cost is $1million per center to enable a T-1 or better quality of line to be available at each workcenter. This can be funded in several ways:

- The firms that bid to supply services at the workcenter could pay a portion of their revenue, say, 5%.

- Large, state-level franchisees that have a universal service obligation (USO) should be allowed to transfer the budget for their USO obligation to providing service in these work centers.

- The USO fee of 5% on revenue that is currently levied on large licensees should be allowed to be used for financing the work centers.

However, we do not recommend that the state ask providers at the work centers to pay up-front costs for access to the backbone since this would have to be recovered through charges to users and will raise costs. (See Chapter 3 in this volume.) Neither should the state-owned provider, BSNL, participate in service provision at these centers. The job of BSNL in universal service should be to continue to use its universal service resources to provide public call offices at villages.

The preceding approach will lead to other benefits in addition to the direct ones just outlined:

- A telecommunications structure has two parts, static and dynamic. The static part, which is the backbone, should be shared in a resource-starved country such as India. Normally, the price of the static parts would reflect this. For example, the costs of rights-of-way ought to be very high in Indian cities. In practice, this has not happened for three reasons: (1) because the state owns the roads and wants to encourage the growth of backbone, there is almost no charge for rights-of-way for laying fiber in Indian cities; (2) the state governments have no stake in the centrally owned telecommunications provider, BSNL, and see the entry of newcomers as a source of state revenue; hence, they would like to encourage them even if it means the overuse of rights-of-way; and (3) the incumbent has tried to exclude newcomers from sharing its backbone (despite excess capacity) through high user charges.

The proposed plan forces the incumbent to yield all uses of its backbone at the work center to newcomers, thus leading to a sharing of static costs.

The dynamic part of the backbone is the technology that goes on the backbone. It is also the most costly part of an infrastructure. Since, in the work centers, private entrants will choose the technology that suits them, this ensures that the effective cost of telecommunications continues its downward trend.

- Technology will be appropriate to affordability. For example, it is irrational to build a public switched telephone network (PSTN) infrastructure in India when voice over Internet protocols (VoIP) is cheaper by at least 70%. India does not need a telecom infrastructure that offers 99.999% reliability in call completion. A VoIP system offers 98% + reliability at a cost of less than a third of the PSTN infrastructure. (See Chapter 4 in this volume.) China Unicom, China's newest long-distance service provider, has already chosen the cheaper option of VoIP over the circuit-switched network. (See Chapter 3 in this volume.) Even in the United

States, if the telecom infrastructure was being designed from scratch, it would be heavily biased toward Internet protocol (IP) because of data needs.

- India and China have much in common, and these two countries should cooperate in setting standards. U.S. standards were set in the context of their legacy infrastructures and power bases. The 1990s trend toward ATM (asynchronous transfer mode) in the United States was driven not by economics or by the best technology but by the Regional Bell Operating Companies' need to preserve their legacy business model. The work center developments will allow India to develop IP-based standards in cooperation with China.

CONCLUSION

So far, the approaches to building a telecom infrastructure that have been proposed in the public policy literature for poor countries such as India attempt to resolve, but do not succeed in resolving, the problem of unaffordability. Simply put, the problem in a poor country is that the substantial majority of the population cannot afford to pay the capital cost (or its annualized equivalent) of $800 to $1,000 per line. Hence, the widely recommended policies of creating a universal service fund, decentralizing service provision, and encouraging competition to bring down costs will not by themselves bring about a telecom infrastructure of acceptable quality to the bulk of the population for several years.

The government of India recognizes the futility of its current approach but does not seem to have a solution to this problem through policy initiatives. Some of its approaches work in a perverse fashion. For example, although a universal service fund tax of 5% on revenue is levied on service providers, the government takes a much larger share of revenue as an up-front sales tax (it varies between 8% and 12%) in order to fund its other social service programs, such as health and education.

We argue that telecommunications is the modern means to delivering all kinds of services and encouraging entrepreneurship, but we recognize that expecting the government of a poor country like India to deliver telecommunications services to the whole population in a short time frame is unrealistic. Expecting the private sector to do so in the current environment and providing incentives to do so will, at best, drive private investment to the overcrowded cities.

This chapter argues that a different approach is needed and provides such an approach. It calls for the state to play a role in developing work centers spread out across India. The state's role should be to locate the work centers near rail centers and ensure that its state-owned incumbent provide access to already developed trunk fiber. The private sector, through appropriate regulatory design and competition, will take care of the rest in a way that is affordable and yet, will have a national impact on the country's development.

NOTE

1.   According to He (1997), 46% of China's telephone lines are in seven coastal provinces, and the ratio of rural phones to the total is only 18%.

BIBLIOGRAPHY

He, B. "Democracy, Transnational Problems, and the Boundary Question: Challenge for China — An Interview with David Held." *Social Alternative* 16, no. 4 (1997): 33–37.

Jipp, A. "Wealth of Nations and Telephone Density." *Telecommunications Journal* (July 1963): 199—201.

North, D. C. (1990). "Institutions, Institutional Change and Economic Performance." Cambridge: Cambridge University Press.

Statistical Outline of India, 1999—2000. Mumbai, India: Tata Services Ltd.

Chapter 7

Lessons in Telecommunications Policy and Practice

Heather E. Hudson

TOWARD AN INDIAN INFORMATION ECONOMY

The purpose of this chapter is to identify lessons learned from various experiences around the world in restructuring of the telecommunications sector and efforts to extend service to unserved or underserved populations that appear relevant to the Indian context. Issues identified are relevant to the goals of telecommunications development in India, particularly as set out in the New Telecom Policy of 1999 (NTP-1999). Each lesson is documented with cases and examples, with a particular focus on developing countries, but examples from the United States, Canada, and other Organization for Economic Corporation and Development (OECD) countries are included where relevant. Special attention is given to the goals of providing access to poor, rural, and disadvantaged populations.

The intent is to suggest not that solutions elsewhere are necessarily right for India but that certain principles and strategies are generalizable. Certainly, India presents daunting challenges, with its population exceeding 1 billion, 24 languages spoken by more than 1 million people, and more than 600,000 villages. Year 2001 teledensity in India is estimated at 3.3 lines per 100; in rural areas it is only 0.4, or 4 lines per 1,000.

TELECOMMUNICATIONS AND DEVELOPMENT

Information Is Critical to Development

The theoretical underpinning of research on the impact of information and communications technologies in general is that information is critical to the social and economic activities that constitute the development process. Information is obviously central to activities that have come to be known as the information sector, including education and research, media and publishing, information equipment and software, and information-intensive services such as financial services, consulting, and trade. But information is also critical to other economic activities ranging from manufacturing, to agriculture and resource extraction, to management, logistics, marketing, and other functions. Information is also important to the delivery of health care and public services. If information is critical to development, then information and communications technologies, as means of accessing, processing, and sharing information, are links in the chain of the development process itself.[1]

In general, the ability to access and share information can contribute to the development process by improving:

- *efficiency,* or the ratio of output to cost (e.g., through use of just-in-time manufacturing and inventory systems and, through use of information on weather and soil content to improve agricultural yields);

- *effectiveness,* or the quality of products and services (such as improving health care through telemedicine);

- *reach*, or the ability to contact new customers or clients (e.g., crafts people reaching global markets on the Internet and educators reaching students at work or at home);

- *equity*, or the distribution of development benefits throughout the society (such as to rural and remote areas, and to minorities and disabled populations).[2]

Some of the pioneering research on the role of telecommunications in development has been done in India. S.N. Kaul[3] estimated the value of rural telecommunications to villagers, based on the cost of transport and time away. Research on the SITE project showed how satellite communications could be used for village education and community development. Recent projects and research on telecenters are providing insights on how Internet access can provide new outlets and higher prices for village products.

Telecommunications Is Necessary but Not Sufficient for Development

The results of numerous studies have shown that telecommunications is *necessary but not sufficient* for development.[4] The reality is that many other factors contribute to economic development, including:

- other infrastructure, particularly electrification and transport

- a skilled workforce

- cost of operations including facilities and labor

Regions with all of these advantages may well be able to attract new jobs by encouraging investment in modern and competitively priced telecommunications. Nebraska in the United States and New Brunswick in Canada have attracted a thriving call center industry because of their combination of a reliable and relatively low-cost workforce and high-quality telecommunications. Western Ireland has become the back office for many United States companies, building on its assets of a well-educated and comparatively low-cost labor force and high-quality infrastructure, including telecommunications. Indian software developers have sold their services overseas by contracting to write computer code, which is transmitted to overseas high-technology companies, typically via dedicated satellite networks.

One policy implication is that where other favorable conditions exist, creating incentives for upgrading and competitive pricing of telecommunications may be an important development strategy. A second implication is that agencies that support provision of access through facilities such as telecenters (which may be called public tele-info centers—PTICs—in India) and other similar initiatives should carefully consider the preceding factors in identifying sites for these facilities. (Typically, a telecenter includes information and communication technologies such as telephone, fax, computer with modem, telephone circuits, and Internet access installed in a community center, library, school, post office, coffeehouse, or other accessible community location.) For the telecenter to contribute to local development, other infrastructure such as electricity must be available, as well as resource people with technical skills and local service agencies and entrepreneurial activities such as women's cooperatives, commercial agriculture, or small businesses that could benefit from increased opportunities to access or share information.[5]

The Larger the Network, the Greater Its Value

A basic rule of connectivity known as Metcalfe's law is that the number of connections and thus the potential value of a network increase almost as the square of its users. Theodore Vail, the early visionary president of American Telephone and Telegraph (AT&T), understood this principle and realized that the Bell System could be much more than a connection for the nation's elite if it extended access at affordable prices throughout the society. The expanding network would generate more value for customers and more revenue for AT&T. (In contrast, many integrated post, telephone and telegraph (PTT) systems have grown slowly, keeping rates relatively high. They offered a service that elites could afford but did not provide the greater access that could have contributed to national economic growth as well as revenue for the PTT.)

Metcalfe's law has relevance for policy as well, because it, in conjunction with the evidence of the role of telecommunications in socioeconomic development, suggests that the policymakers' top priority should be ensuring availability and affordability of networks so that anyone who wants to use them can do so. Strategies designed to increase access rather than to protect incumbent operators are likely to contribute more to economic growth.

PLANNING AND POLICY

Separate the Goals from the Means

Policymakers and regulators have a tendency to confuse the goals with the means. The role of the government should be to set goals and not to dictate how they should be achieved. For example, the Federal Communications Commission (FCC) initially tried to dictate the size and technology to be used in two-way very small aperture terminals (VSATs), in order to minimize interference. Innovative engineers were able to convince the FCC to set the technical specifications and let the industry determine how to meet them. The result was smaller and cheaper terminals than would otherwise have been developed.

An Indian example would be that the state require the upgrade of village public call offices (PCOs) for data communications. Perhaps the goal should be stated as providing access to E-mail and the Internet in every village. The means may range from upgrading PCOs for data communications, to establishing public access in schools or community buildings or in privately run business centers or tea shops.

Telecommunications Planning Should Not Be Done in Isolation

Telecommunications planning should be done in conjunction with ministries responsible for other sectors and in consultation with relevant agencies at the state and local level to establish priorities. For example, an East African country had a policy of rolling out PCOs according to the government's administrative hierarchy, from province, to region, to district, to village. On paper in the capital this plan seemed rational, but in practice it missed what should have been higher priorities. For example, there was no access to telecommunications at an intersection of two major national highways, which was the most important transport junction in the country. The intersection had no phone because it had a very small permanent population, yet every day truckers asked if there was a phone they could use to find out where to deliver their loads, notify agents that they were delayed, or order spare parts that were not available at the truck stop. A neighboring country had no provision in its national plan to extend telecommunications services to game lodges, although tourism had become the top foreign exchange earner for the country. Tour operators and travel agents had no way to call the lodges to book space, and the lodges had no way to notify the travel agencies of vacancies.

It would appear that transition to a market-driven telecommunications sector would solve such problems in that facilities would be installed where there was predicted to be significant revenue, such as truck stops, guest houses, and other businesses. Yet, operators themselves may assume that too little revenue is at stake in rural and impoverished areas to make it worth consulting locally about demand and placement of facilities. This appears to have been the case in South Africa, where fixed and wireless operators are required to install a quota of lines in disadvantaged areas. Often they did not consult with local people, instead putting phones in locations that were considered inaccessible or providing no outlets for sale of the phone cards needed to use the phones. The result was not only lack of as much access as the license requirement was designed to provide but a self-fulfilling prophecy of low revenue.

Start with Thirsty Horses

In India, national information infrastructure plans call for availability of Internet access in every community. However, not all communities may have identified needs for these services. Given limited resources, it may be best to start with pilot projects that would test out both the technologies and techniques for putting them to use. Communities that have requested access and can demonstrate their commitment, for example, by donating space for the equipment or nominating candidates to be trained as outreach staff, should receive priority. This approach of identifying potential innovators and early adopters may be called looking for thirsty horses (as in the saying "You can lead a horse to water, but you can't make it drink").

REGULATION

Assuring Independence of the Regulator May Be Difficult

The common wisdom is that regulators must be independent both of the industry and of the political process. In countries that began with the PTT model, the goal is to make the regulator independent from the PTT to avoid conflict of interest between operator and regulator, a necessity in a competitive environment where equitable rules must be set and enforced for all operators. However, a problem with this approach is that, typically, employees who once worked for the PTT now work for the regulator, making it inherently difficult to avoid bias in assumptions or decisions.

In India, while the division between the Department of Telecommunications (DOT) and Department of Telecommunications Services (DTS/Bharat Sanchar

Nigam Ltd. (BSNL) may address the legal separation between policy and operation, it is likely to be far more difficult to eliminate bias, whether intentional or not, of DOT employees toward their former employer. It may be possible to guard against explicit bias favoring the BSNL, but perhaps a more significant danger is that DOT employees will start with assumptions of what is feasible and practicable based on their BSNL experience. Strategies that could address this problem would be to include professional staff such as economists from other ministries in the DOT, use external consultants without ties to the old DOT, and request public filings and comments so that all relevant views may be considered.

Independence may also be interpreted as being at least at arm's length from the political process. For example, the appointment process and length of terms of commissioners or other regulatory officials indicate how tied the regulator is to the current political leadership. The appeals process may also indicate how independent the regulator really is. In the United States, for example, FCC decisions that are appealed go to the federal courts. On the other hand, in Canada, the Canadian Radio-television and Telecommunications Commission (CRTC's) decisions are appealed to the cabinet, which may vary or overturn a CRTC decision on political grounds.

If The Government Is Slow to Act, Regulation Becomes Policy

A distinction is often made between policy making, typically carried out through a government ministry or department with responsibilities for telecommunications, and regulation, to be carried out by an independent body, (i.e., not related to the operator or directly responsible to a minister). However, in telecommunications, the distinction between regulation and policy quickly becomes blurred, because of the pace of technological change and market pressures in the communications industry. For example, some Canadian entrepreneurs requested permission from the CRTC to establish direct broadcast by satellite (DBS) in Canada. Industry Canada, the responsible ministry, stated that it was working on a policy for direct satellite transmission that it anticipated introducing in about five years. However, the CRTC needed to make a decision much sooner, as direct broadcast by satellite (DBS) signals were already available in parts of Canada from U.S. satellites. By dealing with the DBS application and setting the ground rules so that Canadian DBS could be introduced, the CRTC effectively made Canadian DBS policy. In the United States, the FCC has made decisions on such issues as high-definition television (HDTV), wireless standards and auctioning spectrum that are de facto policies.

It appears that India has made a different functional distinction in placing much more limited responsibility in TRAI as an adjudicator and arbitrator, while retaining responsibility for licensing as well as policy making within the DOT.[6] Although perhaps attractive conceptually, a danger of this approach is that the government will not respond in a timely manner, so that the Indian telecommunications industry will lag behind foreign industries or lose opportunities to enter new markets. One strategy to avoid this problem is to set firm, enforceable deadlines for decisions on license applications and other time-sensitive matters. This approach was used in the U.S. Telecommunications Act of 1996, which set specific deadlines for the FCC to complete various rule makings and directives required to implement the act.

Effective Regulation Requires Participation

It is often thought that the issues in telecommunications policy and regulation are so technical and arcane that most people would have nothing useful to contribute to the decision-making process and that public participation would add little of value. However, all regulatory agencies are overworked and understaffed and cannot find or analyze all the data that would be useful to guide decision making. Major users are likely to have well-thought-out views on the impact of proposed regulations or the need for reforms that would enable the telecommunications sector to better serve their industries. The ability of small users and consumers to contribute may seem less likely; it may take some time for their representatives to get up to speed on telecommunications technology and economics. However, the contribution of such groups may also provide perspectives that might otherwise be overlooked.

A problem for consumer groups is the cost of tracking the issues and preparing testimony or other interventions. In order to ensure that such consumer perspectives are represented, in Canada the CRTC pays the costs of participation in hearings by consumer organizations that contribute evidence that would not otherwise be available.

Old Distinctions May No Longer Be Relevant

Classifications and distinctions that once were useful may no longer be relevant. For example, telecommunications services have been classified by the International Telecommunication Union (ITU) and its members into fixed, mobile, and broadcasting. Regulators typically issue separate licenses and approve separate tariff structures for fixed and mobile services, yet these distinctions have become blurred. Mobile telephone service was designed for communication while in vehicles; however, modern cellular and personal communications systems (PCS) are used for personal communications and can often be considered a substitute for fixed network connections. In many developing countries, wireless has become the first and only service for many customers who never before had access to a telephone.

Long Periods of Exclusivity Do Not Serve the Public Interest

In a liberalized environment, the length and terms of operator licenses can impact the pace of growth of networks and services. Regulators typically face choices concerning how long to protect incumbents to enable them to prepare for competition and how long to grant periods of exclusivity or other concessions to new operators to minimize investment risk. Yet exclusivity and long time periods may be the wrong variables to focus on if the goal is to increase availability and affordability of telecommunications services. Instead, a transparent regulatory environment with a level playing field for all competitors and enforcement of the rules is cited by investors as key to their assessment of risk.

A few countries have granted licenses with as much as 25 years of exclusivity, although 10 years or less seems more common. Even 5 to 10 years seems like a lifetime given the rapid pace of technological change, with Internet time measured in dog years (seven to a calendar year). Some jurisdictions such as Hong Kong and Singapore have negotiated terminations of exclusivity periods with monopoly operators in order to enable their economies to benefit from competition in the telecommunications sector. India's retention of its international telecommunications monopoly within Videsh Sanchar Nigam Ltd. (VSNL), which is state-controlled (and majority-owned by the state, although some shares are in private hands and it is listed on the international stock exchanges) until at least 2004 appeared to be placing an unnecessary burden on Indian businesses that must compete in an increasingly global economy. However, this monopoly period was revised to end on March 31, 2002, in return for some benefits to shareholders of the firm.

Users Will Find a Way

Protecting dominant carriers that continue to charge prices far above those for comparable services in other countries not only penalizes users, as previously noted, but drives the more agile to find alternatives. The users' response to unaffordable prices is increasingly to bypass the network. People with telephones in most developing countries can access callback services to make international calls at a fraction of the price charged by their own international operators.

Many monopoly operators claim that callback is siphoning off revenues that they need to expand their networks, which would also probably create more jobs. However, the relationship is not so simple. For example, an Internet service provider (ISP) from a small West African country pointed out that without callback, he would not be in business. He needs a relatively inexpensive international connection to the Internet in order to provide affordable Internet access for his customers. By using bypass, he is creating new jobs in value-added services as an Internet provider, as well as providing an important information resource for economic development of the country.[7] The Office of the Telecommunications Authority (OFTA), the Hong Kong regulator, negotiated an early termination to Hong Kong Telecom's monopoly on international services, which was to last until 2006. Before the termination of the monopoly, OFTA effectively introduced international competition by licensing competitive local companies that offered callback access. In fact, the Hong Kong government even encouraged its departments to use callback to save money.

Oversight with Enforcement Will Be Needed

The marketplace is generally the best mechanism for bringing innovative and affordable services to most users, including the majority in rural areas. However, there will be an ongoing need for oversight to monitor progress toward meeting targets, to enforce compliance with performance standards, and to review and revise benchmarks. For example, there will be a need for monitoring to determine whether there are disparities in access, quality of services, or pricing that need to be addressed. Otherwise, operators may not meet targets that are conditions of their licenses in areas that they think will not be profitable or install facilities but not maintain them adequately if they assume that the revenue-generating potential is low. For example, in South Africa quality of service for lines installed as a requirement of licenses was often much below service quality in more profitable areas.[8]

Operators must also be held to their license conditions if licensing is to be an effective means of extending access. It appears that this has not been the case for village phones required to be installed by new fixed-service providers (FSPs) in India. Telecom Regulatory Authority of India (TRAI) notes that only 12 village public telephones (VPTs) had been installed by three FSPs in the first 24 months, while a total of 42,841 VPTs were required under the terms of the licenses.[9]

EXTENDING ACCESS

Fixed Lines Close Large Gaps Too Slowly

In developing countries without sufficient wire-line infrastructure, wireless personal networks can be used for primary service. In China, there are more than 50 million wireless customers. In Uganda, within one year of licensing a second cellular operator, attractive pricing and aggressive marketing of prepaid service using rechargeable phone cards have resulted in there now being more cellular customers than fixed lines in the country. For most of the new subscribers, their cell phone is their first and only telephone.[10] Other developing countries where wireless is used as a primary service include Colombia, Lebanon, Malaysia, the Philippines, South Africa, Sri Lanka, Thailand, and Venezuela.[11] Table 7.1 shows Asian developing countries where wireless mobile lines contribute significantly to teledensity, providing 25% or more of all subscriber connections. The ratio in India is only 6.6%.

Cellular operators in South Africa were required to install 30,000 wireless pay phones within five years as a condition of their license.[12] This policy, plus rollout requirements placed on Telkom South Africa, the monopoly fixed operator, contributed to a significant improvement in access to telephone service. By 1998, 85% of South Africans, including 75% of those living in rural areas, said that they had access to a telephone. In townships and rural areas, access typically meant an available pay phone within a short walk.

Table 7.1
Mobile Phones as Percentage of All Telephone Lines: Selected Asian Countries

Country	Mobile Phones/All Lines
Cambodia	76.3%
Philippines	48.1
Malaysia	40.3
Thailand	31.0
China	28.5
Indonesia	26.8
Bangladesh	25.6
Mongolia	25.1

Source: ITU, World Telecommunication Development Report, (2000).

Resale Is an Effective Means to Increase Access

Authorization of resale of local as well as long-distance and other services can create incentives to meet pent-up demand even if network competition has not yet been introduced. Franchised pay phones have been introduced in Indonesia, India, Bangladesh, and other countries in order to involve entrepreneurs where the operator has not yet been privatized and/or liberalized. Indonesia's franchised call offices known as Wartels (Warung Telekomunikasi), operated by small entrepreneurs, generate more than $9,000 per line, about 10 times more than Indonesia Telkom's average revenue per line.[13]

Franchised telephone booths operate in several Francophone African countries; in Senegal, private phone shops average four times the revenue of those operated by the national carrier.[14] In Bangladesh, Grameen Phone has rented cell phones to rural women who provide portable pay phone service on foot or bicycle to their communities.

Resale of network services can also reduce prices to customers. Most interexchange carriers in the United States are actually resellers that lease capacity in bulk from facilities-based providers and repackage for individual and business customers, offering discounts based on calling volume, communities of interest, time of day, and other calling variables. Competition in domestic long-distance is now authorized in India; however, the market for international traffic will not be liberalized until 2002. International resale could bring the benefits of lower prices to users and, in turn, to the Indian economy much sooner.

Universal Access Goals Must Be Moving Targets

Universality has been defined in various countries in terms of population density, distance, and time. Some set targets of public telephones within a radius of a few kilometers in rural areas; others aim to serve every community or settlement. China, India, Mexico, Nepal, and Thailand, for example, aim for at least one telephone per village or settlement.[15] The ITU's Maitland Commission called for a telephone within an hour's walk throughout the developing world. These targets are likely to change over time.[16]

The concept of universal access continues to evolve, in terms of both services that should be universally included and our understanding of access, which includes *availability, affordability,* and *reliability.* Universal access should, therefore, be considered a dynamic concept with a set of moving targets. Rapid technological change dictates that the definitions of basic and advanced or enhanced services will change over time, while the unit of analysis for accessibility may be the household, the village, municipality, or even institutions such as schools and health centers. Thus, for example, a multi-tiered definition of access could be proposed, identifying requirements within households, within communities, and for education and social service providers. For example:

Level One: community access (e.g., through kiosks, libraries, post offices, community centers, telecenters)

Level Two: institutional access (schools, hospitals, clinics)

Level Three: household access

In North America and Europe, the goal has been to provide basic telephone service to every household, with the assumption that businesses and organizations could all afford access to at least this grade of service. However, for Internet access, the United States is applying community and institutional access models. The U.S. Telecommunications Act of 1996 specifies that advanced services should be provided at a discount to schools, libraries, and rural health centers.[17] Advanced services are currently interpreted as Internet access. In the future, it is likely that advanced services will be redefined, perhaps to include access to new generations of services available through the Internet or its successors. It should also be noted that industrialized countries such as the United States and Canada have extended the concept of basic service beyond quality adequate for voice to include single-party service and circuits capable of supporting the capacity of current modems, with the assumption that people will want to communicate electronically from their homes.[18] These criteria are also likely to be revised over time to keep pace with demands of the evolving information economy.

In developing regions, the need for services besides basic voice is now spreading beyond urban areas, businesses, and organizations, to small entrepreneurs, NGOs (nongovernmental organizations), and students, driven by demand for access to E-mail and the Internet. E-mail is growing in popularity because it is much faster than the postal service and cheaper than facsimile transmission or telephone calls. For example, a message of 2,000 words takes 10 minutes to read over a telephone, 2 minutes to send by fax, and about 4 seconds to transmit via 28.8 kbps modem.[19] Such services can be valuable even for illiterates. A member of Parliament from Uganda stated that his father sent many telegrams during his lifetime but could neither read nor write. Local scribes wrote down his messages and read the replies to him. Similarly, information brokers ranging from librarians to telecenter staff can help people with limited education to send and access electronic information.

Telecenters equipped with personal computers linked to the Internet enable artisans, farmers, and other small entrepreneurs to set up shop in the global marketplace.[20] South Africa is funding the installation of telecenters equipped with phone lines, facsimile, and computers with Internet access through a Universal Service Fund; South Africa now plans to provide Internet access to government information and electronic commerce services through post offices. Many other countries are extending public access to the Internet through telecenters, libraries, post offices, and kiosks. Initiatives to support public Internet access through community telecenters are being supported by many development agencies such as the International Telecommunication Union (ITU), United Nations Educational, Scientific, and Cultural Organization (UNESCO), United Nations Development Program (UNDP), Canada's International Development Research center (IDRC), the U.S. Agency for International Development (USAID), and the World Bank.

A Carrier of Last Resort May Not Be the Best Way to Guarantee Universal Service

Many countries include a universal service obligation (USO) as a condition of the license. The cost of USOs may vary depending on geography and population density. In Mexico, the privatized monopoly operator, Telefonos de Mexico (TelMex), was to provide service to all communities with at least 500 population by the year 2000. In the Philippines, local exchange obligations are bundled with cellular and international gateway licenses; licensees were required to install up to 300,000 access lines in previously unserved areas within three years.[21]

Some countries require the dominant operator to act as a "carrier of last resort," with the obligation to provide rural service if no other carrier has done so. Typically, the dominant carrier is entitled to a subsidy to provide the service based on its cost estimates. However, this approach can be flawed if there is no incentive for the carrier with the universal service obligation to use the most appropriate and inexpensive technology and to operate it efficiently. It can also serve as a justification for the dominant carrier to be protected from competition because it has additional costs and obligations not required of new entrants. If subsidies are provided to serve high-cost areas, they should be made available to *any* operator willing to provide them.

Rather than designating a single carrier of last resort, some countries are introducing bidding schemes for subsidies. In Chile, a development fund was established in 1994 to increase access for the approximately 10% of the population in communities without telephone access. The regulator estimated the required subsidies, distinguishing between commercially viable and commercially unviable, and put them out to competitive tender. There were 62 bids for 42 of the 46 projects. Surprisingly, 16 projects were awarded to bids of zero subsidy; as a result of preparing for the bidding process, operators were able to document demand and willingness to pay in many communities. Once completed, these projects will provide service to about 460,000 people, about one-third of the Chilean population previously without access.[22] Peru is introducing a similar program.

While proxy models can be used to judge whether carriers of last resort are overestimating costs of providing rural service, wherever possible, rural service should be provided by operators who see it as a valid commercial proposition and thus have their own incentives to be efficient and to stimulate demand through affordable pricing and innovative services.

If Subsidies Are Needed, They Must Be Targeted

The traditional means of ensuring provision of service to unprofitable areas or customers has been through cross-subsidies, such as from international or interexchange to local services. However, technological changes and the liberalization of the telecommunications sector now make it impracticable to rely on internal cross-subsidies. As noted earlier, customers may bypass high-priced services by using callback services or Internet telephony.

In a competitive environment, new entrants cannot survive if their competitors are subsidized. Therefore, if subsidies are required, they must be made explicit and targeted at specific classes of customers or locations such as:

High-cost areas: Carriers may be subsidized to serve locations that are isolated and/or have very low population density so that they are significantly more expensive to serve than other locations. This approach is used in the United States and has recently been mandated in Canada.

Disadvantaged customers: Subsidies may target economically disadvantaged groups that could not afford typical prices for installation and usage. Some operators may offer interest-free loans or extended payment periods to assist new subscribers to connect to the network. In the United States, the Lifeline program subsidizes basic monthly services charges for low-income subscribers. The subsidy funds come from a combination of carrier contributions and surcharges on subscriber bills. Some 4.4 million households receive Lifeline assistance. Also in the United States, the Linkup program subsidizes connection to the network for low income households.

Funds for subsidies may be generated from several sources such as contributions required from all carriers, for example, a percentage of revenues, a tax on revenues, or a surcharge on customer bills. Subsidies may also come from general tax revenues or other government sources. Some countries with many carriers rely on settlement and repayment pooling schemes among operators to transfer payments to carriers with high operating costs. For example, the U.S. Universal Service Fund is mandated by the Federal Communications Commission (FCC) but administered by the carriers through the National

Exchange Carriers Association (NECA) and transfers funds to subsidize access lines to carriers whose costs are above 115% of the national average.[23]

In Poland, over 7,885 localities were connected between 1992 and 1996 with funding of US$20 million from the state budget.[24] In 1994, Peru established a rural telecommunications investment fund, FITEL (Fondo de Inversion de Telecomunicaciones), which is financed by a 1% tax on revenues of all telecommunications providers, ranging from the country's newly privatized monopoly operator, Telefonica/ENTEL, to cable TV operators. Since established, it has generated an average of US$450,000 per month, growing by US$12 million annually.[25] Private sector operators may apply to FITEL for financing.[26]

RURAL ISSUES

Rural Demand May Be Much Greater Than Assumed

In designing networks and projecting revenues, planners often assume that there is little demand for telecommunications in rural areas. Similarly, telecommunications service providers may be reluctant to extend services to poorer populations that are assumed to have insufficient demand to cover the cost of providing the facilities and services. Their forecasts are typically based solely on the lower population densities than are found in urban areas, coupled with a "one size fits all" fallacy that assumes that all rural residents are likely to have lower incomes and therefore lower demand for telecommunications than urban residents.

Rural residents may need telecommunications to order parts and supplies, check on international prices, and arrange transport of their produce to foreign markets. Egyptian farmers in poor Nile delta villages use the telephone to fill orders for vegetables from markets in Alexandria and Cairo. Tuna fishermen in poor, primarily rural provinces of the Philippines use cell phones to arrange cargo space on aircraft to get their catch to Tokyo. In rural North America and Australia, the service sector is a major component of the rural economy, largely due to the provision of government services. In developing countries, governments are often assisted by NGOs. Thus, in addition to commercial activities, there may be significant demand from government agencies and NGOs operating in rural areas to administer health care services, schools, other social services, and development projects.

A study for the World Bank estimates that rural users in developing countries are able collectively to pay 1% to 1.5% of their gross *community* income for telecommunications services.[27] The ITU uses an estimate of 5% of *household* income as an affordability threshold.[28] Using a conservative estimate, 20% of households in low-income countries such as India could afford a telephone.[29] This estimate exceeds the Indian New Telecom Policy's target of a national teledensity of 15 by 2010 (the target for rural areas is just 4 lines per 100).

Just as income may not fully explain demand for information technologies and services, lack of access to telephone service cannot necessarily be attributed to lack of demand or purchasing power. For example, in many developing countries, television sets are much more prevalent than telephones. In industrialized countries, both TV sets and telephone lines are almost universally available. However, in middle-income countries there are twice as many TV sets as telephone lines, while in low-income countries, there are more than 5 times as many TV sets as telephone lines (see Table 7.2). In India there were about 3.3 times as many TV sets as telephone lines in 1999.

Table 7.2
Access to Telephone Lines and Television Sets

Country Classification	Tel Lines / 100	TV Sets / 100	Ratio: TV Sets/Tel lines
High Income	54.1	61.9	1.1
Upper Middle Income	13.4	26.3	2.0
Lower Middle Income	9.7	22.7	2.3
Low Income	2.5	13.1	5.2

Source: Derived from ITU, World Telecommunications Development Report, (1998).

It appears that where television is available, a significant percentage of families will find the money to buy TV sets. Thus, even in the poorest countries, there may be much more disposable income available than per capita gross domestic product (GDP) data would indicate, and there may be significant demand for other information services.

Other approaches may also be used to gauge demand for information services. For example, the presence of video shops indicates significant disposable income available for television sets, video cassette players, and cassette rentals. Telephone service resellers (such as in Indonesia, Senegal, and Bangladesh), local cable television operators (common in India), and small satellite dishes on rural homesteads and urban flats (common in Eastern Europe and many Asian countries) also signal demand and ability to pay for information services.

Revenues from rural telephones may also be greater than expected, especially if incoming traffic as well as outgoing traffic are included. For example, it is important to anticipate the influence of family ties on calling patterns. Communities where many people have left to seek work in the city or overseas may have high volumes of incoming traffic. For example, Filipina domestic workers call home from Hong Kong, Singapore, and Malaysia; Indians and Pakistanis call home from the Middle East; and miners in South Africa call their families in other parts of South Africa or neighboring countries such as Mozambique and Zimbabwe. There may also be extensive calling among family members scattered in villages throughout a rural region.

The significance of rural toll traffic seems particularly important in estimating rural revenues in India, where revenues from village phones with STD (subscriber trunk dialing or long-distance service) are apparently nearly 50 times as high as revenues from VPTs without STD.[30]

Rural Areas May Not Be as Expensive to Serve As Is Often Assumed

It is typically assumed by both operators and regulators that the costs of providing telecommunications in rural areas are unavoidably high and, coupled with low demand, render rural services necessarily unprofitable. While costs per line are bound to be higher than in urban areas, creative strategies for design and implementation may reduce costs.

Topography and climate are important considerations in system design. A microwave network may be an appropriate solution for plains and valleys, but it is extremely costly to site and maintain microwave towers in mountainous regions and in very remote areas, where satellite service is likely to be more suitable. Designing for such conditions as well as for available transportation facilities and labor can also reduce costs. For example, the Alaskan carrier General Communications Incorporated (GCI) specified that VSATs built for operation in Alaska villages must be designed to be flown into villages in Cessna Caravan aircraft, as there are no roads to most villages. Maintenance and troubleshooting are to be done by bush pilots who regularly fly into the villages. Bell Canada trains local technicians to do basic telephone installation and troubleshooting in northern Canadian communities. Such policies may not only reduce downtime but also cut costs of sending in company technicians from regional centers. Other strategies such as the use of prepaid stored-value telephone cards can save time and money by eliminating the need to collect coins from pay phones (while also preventing pilferage).

Modular design that allows for adding capacity when required will also reduce costs of upgrading service. Demand may increase not only with population growth but also if there are changes in the economy or demands for new service. A digital microwave system installed in the Australian Outback reached capacity much earlier than expected not only because of its design (which required remote switching for village-to-village traffic) but also because of unanticipated demand for fax and then Internet access. Upgrading the network required a complete overbuild. In the Marquesas in the South Pacific, satellite earth stations have been installed for telephone service and TV reception, but circuit capacity is very limited. When asked whether additional capacity was possible if demand increased (e.g., for Internet access for schools), a site engineer said, "There will never be more demand here."[31] Never assume never.

Rural Benchmarks Need Not Be Set Lower than Urban Benchmarks

A persistent assumption that "something is better than nothing" often underlies policy for rural areas. However, a corollary of the preceding lessons, that revenues in rural areas may often be higher and costs lower than assumed, is that it is no longer technically or economically justifiable to set rural benchmarks lower than urban benchmarks for access both to basic telecommunications and to the Internet.

For example, the U.S. Telecommunications Act of 1996 sets a standard of reasonable comparability: rural services and prices are to be *reasonably comparable* to those in urban areas. While the United States and other industrialized countries must upgrade outdated wireline networks and analog exchanges in rural areas, developing countries can leapfrog old technologies and install fully digital wireless networks. Thus, developing-country regulators can also adopt rural comparability standards to avoid penalizing rural services and businesses in access to information services. For example, in the Philippines, after extensive discussion, both government and industry representatives agreed on rural benchmarks, including digital switching, single-party service, and line quality sufficient for facsimile and data communications. The industry representatives stated that the new digital networks that they were installing in rural areas met those specifications and that older networks should be brought up to those standards.[32]

Some Rural Areas May Be Viable for Commercial Franchises

Some countries grant monopoly franchises to rural operators. For example, Bangladesh has licensed two rural monopoly operators; they are allowed to prioritize the most financially attractive customers and charge a substantial up-front subscriber connection fee. The Bangladesh Rural Telecommunications Authority (BRTA) is profitable, even though it has to provide at least one public call office (PCO) in each village that requests one.[33]

Although in most countries a single carrier provides both local and long-distance services, it is also possible to delineate territories that can be served by local entities. In the United States, the model of rural cooperatives fostered through the Rural Utilities Service (RUS, formerly Rural Electrification Administration) has been used to bring telephone service to areas ignored by the large carriers. As noted earlier, wireless technologies could change the economics of providing rural services, making rural franchises much more attractive to investors. As a result of availability of funds from the RUS for upgrading networks, rural cooperatives in the United States typically provide more modern facilities and better Internet access than provided by large telephone companies serving rural areas.

Other countries are opening up rural areas to competition as part of national liberalization policies. Argentina allows rural operators to compete with the two privatized monopolies, Telecom and Telefonica. Some 135 rural cooperatives have been formed to provide telecommunications services in communities with fewer than 300 people.[34] Finland's association of telephone companies has created several jointly owned entities that provide a range of rural, local, and long-distance services in their concession areas, in competition with the national operator.[35] In Alaska, a second carrier, GCI, competes with AT&T Alascom to provide long-distance services in rural and remote areas. This competition has benefited Alaskan schools in gaining access to the Internet. GCI has assisted school districts in applying for E-rate subsidies for Internet access, apparently viewing this initiative as a win-win opportunity for both schools and the telephone company.

Applying These Lessons in the Indian Context

Status and Goals

As already noted, year 2000 overall teledensity in India is about 3 lines per 100 population and only about 0.4 lines per 1,000 in rural areas. The New Telecom Policy 1999 (NTP-1999) has set targets of national teledensity of 7 per 100 by the year 2005 and 15 per 100 by 2010. Further, it has specified the following universal service objectives:

- provide voice and low-speed data service to all the villages in the country by 2002

- achieve Internet access for all district headquarters by 2000

- achieve telephone on demand in urban and rural areas by 2002[36]

In the year 2000, there were about 28 million DELs (direct exchange lines). To achieve teledensity targets of 15 lines per 100 in urban areas and 4 lines per 100 in rural areas by 2010 will require an additional 148 million lines, or about 5.7 times as many lines as existed in the country in 2000.[37] In addition, in 1999, there was still a waiting list of about 4 million, which was not expected to diminish in the next few years, despite increased investment, because of increased demand stimulated by lower prices as well as because of population growth.

Of India's 607,491 villages, 374,605 or about 62% had village public telephones (VPTs) as of April 2000, leaving an additional 232,886 to be served in less than two years to meet the NTP's goal of serving all villages by 2002. Three competitive fixed-service providers were required to install a total of 42,841 village pay phones in their first 24 months of operation. However, they had installed a total of only 12.[38]

Based on an analysis of a large sample, TRAI estimates that the average annual revenue per line of VPTs with direct-dial long distance (STD) at Rs.35,472 (about $760) and only Rs.744 (about $16) for VPTs without STD. However, the STD village phones, which generate almost 50 times as much revenue, account for only 7% of all village pay phones at present. TRAI notes that some of the factors contributing to the low ratio of STD to non-STD phones are:

- lack of reliable transmission media

- lack of availability of STD facilities in all rural exchanges

- high security deposit required from the franchisee to provide the STD facility

- high cost of call loggers (people to record calling information)

- technological limitations of some analog radio systems that result in poor call completion rates[39]

TRAI estimates installation costs of village pay phones at approximately Rs.75,000 (about US$1,600). Using their high estimate of a 24% annual cost recovery and midrange estimate of 10% annual operating expenditures, the annual cost per VPT is about Rs.25,500 (about $550). TRAI does not state what percentage of the STD revenues is retained by the VPT. However, it appears that STD village phones would actually have a positive cash flow.

Teledensity Targets

It seems unlikely that the existing fixed-service operators will be able to finance and rollout fixed-line networks on a scale to meet these targets despite the huge, pent-up demand for service. To meet the NPT's goals will take innovative strategies and incentives that have not been tried before. Indian policymakers will have to think creatively to create an environment where these and other goals can be accomplished. For example, the distinction between fixed and mobile from a planning perspective should be ignored. The teledensity goal should be achieved by whatever technological means is appropriate. This is likely to mean that for many people, their first and only network access will be by cellular (wireless) phone. To take maximum advantage of wireless, cellular operators must have incentives to extend coverage and to offer a variety of pricing packages (using prepayment, smart cards, resale, bundled and unbundled services, etc.).

Other innovative strategies should be explored to take advantage of existing infrastructure and entrepreneurship. For example, cable operators could be licensed to provide local services, with interconnection to the national network.

Village Access

To achieve the village teledensity goals, new approaches are also clearly required, as it seems highly unlikely that the operators will meet these targets based on experience to date. To provide public pay phones to all remaining villages:

- All new village phones should provide STD (necessary both to generate revenue and to provide villagers with access to the national network and to Internet/data services).

- Cellular operators should also be required to provide wireless VPTs to villages covered by their networks. (This has happened in some places as a market-driven outcome because of the definition of a long-distance call. In some submarine and rural areas, a cellular call to the nearest city is charged, per the regulator's instructions, as a local call, whereas the same call made through wires is charged as a long-distance call.)

- Other operators should be allowed to provide village services through resale.

In addition, to increase the revenue from all VPTs and provide access to data and voice in all villages, existing VPTs should be upgraded to STD. To accomplish this goal:

- Rural switches should be upgraded to provide STD.

- Where rural switches have not yet been upgraded, VPT circuits should be routed to switches that provide STD.

- The franchisee deposit requirement for STD should be lowered, or an alternative scheme devised that would minimize risk to the service provider while being financially feasible for the franchisee to obtain and offer the service. For example, prepaid phone cards (that could be rented to customers) could reduce the risk of lost revenue while providing affordable access for customers.

Data Services

The principle of moving targets should be applied. It is probably realistic to interpret slow-speed access by year 2000 standards as 56 kbps, which can be delivered over a reliable dial-up network using a modem. As demand for higher bandwidth grows, policies to facilitate higher-speed access, such as to businesses, government offices, and community access centers, should be developed. Such services could be provided via the existing telephone network (e.g., integrated services digital network [ISDN] or digital subscribers line [DSL]), over cable TV networks, or by wireless or satellite. Access to affordable broadband will require further opening of the network to competition so that all of these (and other) options could be offered, depending on location and demand.

Internet Availability

The FSPs should be required to provide connectivity, leaving it up to district governments or other agencies to figure out where to provide Internet access and how to provide local facilities such as a personal computer (PC), simple terminal, or net appliance. The Center for Development of Telematics (C-DOT) could be asked to develop a community access package, or a competition could be held to design a community access package suitable for villages. The package might include such features as low capital and operating costs, rugged design to cope with heat and dust, modular design for simple installation and maintenance, solar power, and so on.

Implementation should probably be done on a phased basis, beginning with villages that have requested Internet access (the thirsty-horse principle). Each village could be asked to demonstrate its commitment to getting access by designating a location for the equipment and two persons to be trained in operation and troubleshooting (a variation of the technology plan required for schools to participate in the E-rate program in the United States). Installation, training, and support could be contracted out to NGOs, small businesses, or others that could demonstrate the competence to provide these services.

CONCLUSION: IMPLEMENTING THE VISION

This chapter places telecommunications policy within the context of development policy. It assumes a broadening of information infrastructure issues to include rural as well as urban access, a range of levels and targets for services, and pricing to ensure affordability of access to a range of telecommunications services, including access to the Internet. A conclusion that can be drawn from the preceding analysis is that changing the policy environment to create incentives to serve previously ignored and underserved populations is likely to be the fastest and most equitable means of achieving the goal of universal access to telecommunications and information technologies and services throughout India.

NOTES

1.   See Hudson (1984, 1995); Saunders, Warford, and Wellenius (1994).

2.   Hudson (1997b).

3.   See Hudson (1984); also Harris, Roger (1999).

4.   Hudson (1997).

5.   Hudson, Heather E. Telecentre Evaluation: Issues and Strategies. *Telecentre Handbook.* Commonwealth of Learning: Vancouver, Canada, in press.

6.   Department of Telecommunications. New Telecom Policy 1999-2000 Details. www.DOTindia.com/flash/NewTelPo_Details.htm.

7.   Personal communication, July 1997.

8.   Unpublished data collected by the Universal Service Agency of South Africa, 1999.

9.   Telecom Regulatory Authority of India. Consultation Paper on Issues Relating to Universal Service Obligations. TRAI, New Delhi, July 3, 2000, p. 22.

10. Personal interview, Uganda Communications Commission, Kampala, November 1999.

11. ITU (1998), p. 49.

12. Ibid., p. 50.

13. Ibid., 1998, p. 77.

14. Ibid., 1998, pp. 77—78.

15. Ibid., 1998, p. 69.

16. In fact, the cover of the Maitland Report featured two rotary-dial telephones; although digital switching and tone dialing existed in 1983, it was widely assumed that the most basic services and technologies were all that was necessary or appropriate to extend access in developing regions.

17. Telecommunications Act of 1996 (1996).

18. See Canadian Radio Television and Telecommunications Commission Hearing on Telecom Public Notice CRTC 97-42, Service to High-cost Serving Areas, 1998. (www.crtc.gc.ca)

19. M. Hegener, quoted in ITU (1998, p. 80).

20. Petzinger (1998, p. B1).

21. Hudson (1997a).

22. ITU (1998, p. 79).

23. See www.neca.org, and information on the Universal Service Fund on the FCC's website, www.fcc.gov.

24. ITU (1998, p. 78).

25. Ibid., p. 79.

26. Kayani and Dymond (1997, pp. 63—64).

27. Ibid.

28. ITU (1998, p. 35).

29. Ibid., p. 37. It should be noted that this calculation appears to assume even distribution of income throughout the society at higher income levels, which is not necessarily true.

30. TRAI (2000, p. 49).

31. Personal interview, December 1996.

32. Meeting at Department of Transport and Communications attended by the author, Manila, January 1998.

33. Kayani and Dymond, p. 18.

34. Ibid.

35. Ibid., p. 19.

36. Department of Telecommunications, p. 10.

37. TRAI, p. 19.

38. Ibid., p. 22.

39. Ibid., p. 48.

BIBLIOGRAPHY

Cronin, Francis J., Elisabeth K. Colleran, Paul L. Herbert, and Steven Lewitzky. "Telecommunications and Growth: The Contribution of Telecommunications Infrastructure Investment to Aggregate and Sectoral Productivity." *Telecommunications Policy* 17, no. 9 (1993): 677–690.

Cronin, Francis J., Edwin B. Parker, Elisabeth K. Colleran, and Mark A. Gold. "Telecommunications Infrastructure and Economic Development." *Telecommunications Policy* 17, no. 6 (August 1993): pp. 415—430.

Department of Telecommunications, Department of Telecom Services. New Telecom Policy 1999—2000. Details.www.DOTindia.com/flash/NewTelPo_Details.htm.

Hardy, Andrew P. "The Role of the Telephone in Economic Development." *Telecommunications Policy* 4, no. 4 (December, 1980): 278—286.

Harris, Roger. "Success Stories of Rural ICTs in a Developing Country." Unpublished manuscript. Kuching: University of Malaysia, Sarawak, 1999.

Henry, David, et al. *The Emerging Digital Economy II.* Washington, DC: U.S. Department of Commerce, 1999.

Hobbs, Vicki M., and John Blodgett. "The Rural Differential: An Analysis of Population Demographics in Areas Served by Rural Telephone Companies." Paper presented at the Telecommunications Policy Research Conference, September 1999. See also www.rupri.org.

Hudson, Heather E. *When Telephones Reach the Village: The Role of Telecommunications in Rural Development.* Norwood, NJ: Ablex, 1984.

———. *Communication Satellites: Their Development and Impact.* New York: Free Press, 1990.

———. "Universal Service in the Information Age." *Telecommunications Policy* (November 1994).

———. *Economic and Social Benefits of Rural Telecommunications: A Report to the World Bank.* Washington, DC: World Bank, 1995.

———. "Converging Technologies and Changing Realities: Toward Universal Access to Telecommunications in the Developing World." *Telecom Reform: Principles, Policies, and Regulatory Practices.* Lyngby, Denmark: Technical University of Denmark, 1997a.

———. *Global Connections: International Telecommunications Infrastructure and Policy.* New York: Wiley, 1997b.

———. "African Information Infrastructure: The Development Connection." *Proceedings of Africa Telecom 98.* Geneva: International Telecommunication Union, 1998a.

———. "The Significance of Telecommunications for Canadian Rural Development." Testimony on Behalf of the Public Interest Advocacy Center, et. al., Canadian Radio Television and Telecommunications Commission Hearing on Telecom Public Notice CRTC 97-42, Service to High-cost Serving Areas, 1998b.

———. "Beyond Infrastructure: A Critical Assessment of GII Initiatives. Competition, Regulation, and Convergence: Selected Papers from the 1998 Telecommunications Policy Research Conference." Ed. Ingo Vogelsang. Mahwah, NJ: LEA, 1999.

———. "Telecentre Evaluation: Issues and Strategies." *Telecentre Handbook.* Vancouver, Canada: Commonwealth of Learning in press.

Industry Canada. *The Canadian Information Highway.* Ottawa: Industry Canada, April 1994.

Information Highway Advisory Council. *Canada's Information Highway: Providing New Dimensions for Learning, Creativity and Entrepreneurship.* Ottawa: Industry Canada, November 1994.

International Commission for Worldwide Telecommunications Development (Maitland Commission). *The Missing Link.* Geneva: International Telecommunication Union, December 1984.

International Telecommunication Union. *World Telecommunication Development Report 1998.* Geneva: ITU, 1998.

———. *World Telecommunication Development Report 1998.* Geneva: ITU, 1998.

————. *Challenges to the Network: Internet for Development.* Geneva: ITU, 1999a.

————. *World Telecommunication Development Report 1999.* Geneva: ITU, 1999b.

————. *World Telecommunication Development Report,* 2000. www.itu.int/ti.

Jordan, Miriam. "It Takes a Cell Phone: Nokia Phone Transforms a Village in Bangladesh." *Wall Street Journal,* June 25, 1999.

Kayani, Rogati, and Andrew Dymond. *Options for Rural Telecommunications Development.* Washington, DC: World Bank, 1999.

Lankester, Chuck, and Richard Labelle. "The Sustainable Development Networking Programme (SDNP): 1992–1997." UNDP: New York, June 1997. Paper presented at the Global Knowledge Conference, Toronto, June 22–26, 1997.

Margherio, Lynn, et al. *The Emerging Digital Economy.* Washington, DC: U.S. Department of Commerce, 1998.

Mayo, John K., Gary R. Heald, and Steven J. Klees. "Commercial Satellite Telecommunications and National Development: Lessons from Peru." *Telecommunications Policy* 16, no. 1 (1992): 67–79.

McConnaughey, James W., et al. *Falling through the Net: Defining the Digital Divide.* Washington, DC: National Telecommunications and Information Administration, 1998.

National Telecommunications and Information Administration. *20/20 Visions.* Washington, DC: U.S. Department of Commerce, 1994.

Siochru, Sean. *Telecommunications and Universal Service: International Experience in the Context of South African Telecommunications Reform.* Ottawa: International Development Research center, 1996.

Parker, Edwin B., and Heather E. Hudson. *Electronic Byways: State Policies for Rural Development through Telecommunications.* 2d ed. Washington, DC: Aspen Institute, 1995.

Parker, Edwin B., Heather E. Hudson, Don A. Dillman, and Andrew D. Roscoe. *Rural America in the Information Age: Telecommunications Policy for Rural Development.* Lanham, MD: University Press of America, 1989.

Petzinger, Thomas Jr. "Monique Maddy Uses Wireless pay phones to Battle Poverty." *Wall Street Journal,* September 25, 1998, p. B1.

Rogers, Everett. *Diffusion of Innovations,* 4th ed. New York: Free Press, 1995.

Saunders, Robert, Jeremy Warford, and Bjorn Wellenius. *Telecommunications and Economic Development,* 2d ed. Baltimore: Johns Hopkins University Press, 1994.

Telecommunications Act of 1996. U.S. Congress. Public Law 104-104, February 8, 1996.

Telecom Regulatory Authority of India. "Consultation Paper on Issues Relating to Universal Service Obligations." TRAI, New Delhi, July 3, 2000.

United Nations Administrative Committee on Coordination (ACC). "Statement on Universal Access to Basic Communication and Information Services." April 1997. Quoted in ITU (1998, p. 10).

U.S. Department of Commerce. *Digital Economy 2000.* Washington, DC: Department of Commerce, June 2000.

World Information Technology and Services Alliance (WITSA). *Digital Planet: The Global Information Economy.* Washington, DC: WITSA, 1998.

Web Sites

Alaska Public Utilities Commission: www.state.ak.us/local/akpages/COMMERCE/apuc.htm

Aloha Networks: www.alohanet.com

Canadian Radio Television and Telecommunications Commission (CRTC): www.crtc.gc.ca

Department of Commerce: www.ecommerce.gov/ece/

Federal Communications Commission: www.fcc.gov

General Communications Inc. (GCI): www.gci.com

Healthnet: www.healthnet.org

InfoDev: www.worldbank.org/html/fpd/infodev/infodev.html

International Development Research center: www.idrc.org

Leland Initiative: www.info.usaid.gov/regions/afr/leland

MagicNet: www.magicnet.mn

Soros Foundation: www.soros.org

National Exchange Carriers Association: www.neca.org

National Telecommunications and Information Administration: www.ntia.doc.gov

Rural Utilities Service:www.rus.usda.gov

Sustainable Development Networking Programme: www.undp.org

Vitacom Inc.: www.vitacom.com

Chapter 8

Universal Service, Competition, and Economic Growth

Gregory L. Rosston and Bradley S. Wimmer

THE CASE OF THE HIDDEN SUBSIDY

Several countries have undertaken telecommunications reform over the past two decades. As a result of their experiences, many other countries are re-thinking their own approaches to telecommunications regulation. Generally, countries are moving toward market-based approaches, privatizing formerly nationalized monopolies, and, subsequently, relaxing entry conditions. Such movements, it is hoped, will not only improve the performance of the telecommunications sector will also enhance the country's overall economic performance. Recent research has shown that improvements in telecommunications infrastructure are correlated with increases in economic growth rates.

India is an example of a country following the path of privatization and liberalization. As countries move toward competitive markets, they will be required to confront issues associated with universal service, which consists of policies whose intent is to increase the number of subscribers. Historically, universal service programs have been funded through distortionary pricing systems that keep the price of some services artificially high in order to subsidize others. While such policies are sustainable under government-owned or -sanctioned monopoly systems, competitive pressures force regulators to address such economically irrational pricing structures.

The current situation in the United States, where subscription rates are high, telephone companies are privately held, and competition exists in many sectors of the industry, differs from that of countries in the process of liberalizing their industries. There are, however, several important lessons that can be taken from the United States' experience. First, implicit subsidies are untenable in competitive markets. Second, competitive entrants respond to profit incentives. As a result, the presence of implicit subsidies affects how competition develops. (De)regulators in other countries should be cognizant of these lessons as well as the political economy that leads interest groups to support inefficient solutions.

The telecommunications system in the United States has had relatively high penetration rates for a long time. The passage of the Telecommunications Act of 1996 and subsequent changes in regulations set the stage for the introduction of competition to every sector of the market in the United States. We provide evidence that the web of implicit subsidies put in place over the many years of monopoly regulation in the United States has yet to be addressed adequately by regulators. Further, this web of implicit subsidies is affecting the development of competition.

The U.S. experience, at both the national and state levels, shows that economically irrational policies lead to undesirable outcomes. Once such policies are put in place, their removal requires that some rates be increased, while others be allowed to fall. Changing rates leads those who would be hurt by rate increases to protest any rate change that affects them, even when the change improves overall efficiency. While theoretically possible, it is very difficult or impossible to implement the type of side payments that would result in Pareto improvements. As a result, interest groups tend to influence the process, making change difficult.

In this chapter, we draw upon the universal service and competition experience in the United States to highlight important issues for policymakers in countries where telephone penetration rates are relatively low. We do this by relating universal-service programs to the literature addressing the effect that improvements in telecommunications infrastructure have on economic growth rates. This analysis shows that universal-service programs that increase the cost of using the network attenuate the benefits that investment in telecommunications infrastructure bring to an economy and impede the development of competitive markets. This means that policymakers need to carefully analyze universal service and competition policies, especially when trying to implement hidden or uneconomic subsidies.

The chapter is outlined as follows. We examine the relationship between telecommunications investment, competition, and economic growth; provide background information on universal service in the United States; provide evidence that implicit subsidies remain in local rates in the United States; examine how the presence of these implicit subsidies is affecting the development of competition; and give concluding remarks.

TELECOMMUNICATIONS INVESTMENT AND GROWTH

Improvements in telecommunications infrastructure improve economic efficiency by improving the flow of information and reducing transaction costs. Telecommunications services are an input to many important sectors of the economy. For example, in India, the developing high-technology sector is very dependent on telecommunications services.

Investments in telecommunications have been shown to yield improvements in the overall growth rate of economies. Jipp (1963), Norton (1992), and others show that a positive correlation exists between measures of telecommunications infrastructure investment and economic growth.[1] Greenstein and Spiller (1995) find that a positive correlation exists between investments in telecommunications in the United States and improvements in the performance of information-intensive industries, such as finance. Overall, because improvements in telecommunications infrastructure affect the manner in which firms and consumers interact, its benefits are not limited to any one sector.

In a related literature, Madden and Savage (1998) show that increased telecommunications infrastructure investment, by itself, is not the source of economic growth. Rather, it is the intensity with which the infrastructure is used that is important. Using data on a cross-section of Asia-Pacific countries, they show that a positive and statistically significant relationship exists between the growth in telecommunications service exports (i.e., international calling volume) and economic growth. This result is important because it shows that, as expected, many of the benefits of telecommunications infrastructure investment are not realized when regulators reduce calling volume by holding usage rates artificially high. Thus, while such cross-subsidies may improve penetration rates, the full benefits of telecommunications investment are not fully realized when regulator-imposed high rates impede usage.

Wallsten (2000), using a small sample of countries that have recently privatized their publicly owned telephone companies, shows that granting newly privatized companies "exclusivity" periods, during which time competitors are not allowed to enter the market, reduces investment in infrastructure when compared to competitive situations. While characterizing his results as preliminary, this evidence suggests that competition spurs investment in telecommunications equipment. Wallsten also shows that exclusivity periods increase the sale price of the public utility. He, therefore, reasons that an increase in short-term government revenue is a primary reason for granting exclusivity periods. An additional reason may be the protection of implicit subsidies put in place before privatization.

Bovenberg and Goulder (1996) show that taxes on inputs affect investment decisions. They examine the effect that carbon taxes have on overall economic efficiency. They find that taxes on carbon, rather than producing a "double dividend" as many claim, have a counteracting effect because of the distortionary impact that they have on input choices. Since telecommunications is an important input in many industries, universal-service taxes may lead to similar input-choice distortions. The overall effect of taxing telecommunications services to fund universal service may, therefore, result in significantly less efficient outcomes than would other funding mechanisms.

Universal-service programs attempt to ensure the provision of service to all consumers at "reasonable" rates. In the United States and other countries, this has resulted in a web of implicit cross-subsidies that serve to increase artificially the overall price of services to many consumers. This is done to reduce the price of connecting subscribers to the network. Such policies reduce the efficiency of the market, frustrate attempts to introduce widespread competition, and distort investment decisions in order to increase the number of people connected to the network.[2]

UNIVERSAL SERVICE IN THE UNITED STATES

In the United States, regulators have kept local connection rates "affordable" through implicit subsidies. In many countries, local rates are held at levels well below the long-run cost of providing connections to the network. Two primary mechanisms have been used to achieve this goal.

First, while the cost of connecting consumers to the network is inversely related to population density, regulators have adopted geographically averaged prices. These policies result in rates that are below the cost of service in rural areas and above costs in urban areas. A similar policy requires business customers to pay higher rates than residential customers, even when the cost of service is the same for both customers. A second mechanism has been to charge above-cost prices for long-distance calls. Such a scheme, however, ignores the value that consumers receive from making long-distance calls. Hausman, Tardiff, and Belinfante (1993) show that by keeping rates for long-distance services above costs, regulators may have actually decreased penetration rates. High long-distance rates decrease the surplus that consumers receive from connecting to the network. Moreover, because the demand for local services is relatively less elastic than the demand for long-distance,[3] the implicit tax on long-distance services is a departure from Ramsey pricing, which results in larger than necessary efficiency losses.

In the United States, universal-service policies have historically suffered from a number of problems. Most prominently, regulators have relied on hidden cross-subsidies to achieve their social goals. Such an approach results in a variety of problems that are difficult to solve after the program is put in place. In the United States, the implicit nature of a large portion of the subsidies does not allow competitors access to the subsidies. As a result, competition in high-cost areas is likely to be untenable because current prices do not allow competitors to cover the cost of serving these areas. Moreover, the use of implicit subsidies to fund universal-service programs puts the source of subsidies at risk when competitors are allowed to enter markets that generate the subsidy dollars.

The Telecommunications Act of 1996 requires that all implicit subsidies be removed from prices and that any universal-service programs be made explicit. Furthermore, the act requires that competitors have access to the subsidies available to incumbents or that the program be portable. To this end, the Federal Communications Commission reformed its high-cost universal service fund to meet these requirements.

In the United States, however, federal regulators have jurisdiction over about 25% of the costs and revenues associated with local telecommunications service.[4] Federal jurisdiction is limited, primarily, to interstate calling and recovery of a portion of local connection charges. State regulators, therefore, have a relatively larger role in regulating the industry. One of the states' primary roles is to set rates for local services, which allow consumers to connect to the network. Local services also typically allow consumers to make an unlimited number of calls within their local calling areas. In what follows, we examine how state regulators have addressed the act's directive to remove all implicit subsidies, including those embedded in local rates.

IMPLICIT SUBSIDIES AND LOCAL RATES

Regulators' responses to the introduction of competition are important for the ultimate development of competition. For example, some regulators may find that competition undermines their social-pricing policies. We might, therefore, expect to find that regulatory efforts to maintain and protect implicit cross-subsidies will have a large impact on the development of competition.

We begin by attempting to quantify the size of the implicit subsidies in the current setting. We extend the results of Rosston and Wimmer (2000) in three significant ways. In that paper we estimated the tax rates that state regulators would have to impose to subsidize high-cost areas and maintain various benchmark rate levels. We also showed that increasing the benchmark reduces tax rates substantially without seriously reducing subscribership. We add to these results by incorporating data on local telephone service rates. In addition, we examine data on collocation agreements in Bell Atlantic's wire centers. By using these additional data, we examine the question of the amount of rate rebalancing (i.e., aligning rates with costs) that is necessary to move toward an efficient and competitive local rate system. We can also make some predictions about where competition is likely to arise and, subsequently, test these assertions with data on competition by wire center. We begin with a discussion of the data.

Data

We use estimates of costs generated by the forward-looking hybrid cost proxy model (HCPM), developed by the FCC in connection with its universal-service proceedings.[5] For each of the 12,493 wire centers served by nonrural carriers, the model estimates the cost of the various components used to provide local telephone service: loop, switching, signaling and transport, and so on. Based on the differences in local conditions, population density, and other factors, the model estimates the cost of providing local service in each wire center.

We limit our attention to the lines served by the original Regional Bell Operating Companies (RBOCs). We have complemented the results of the cost model with two additional sets of data: demographic data on the number of households in each wire center that were headed by people of different races or ethnic groups; a breakdown by income, family type, and several other factors;[6] and data on local exchange-service prices for each wire center.

For each wire center, we obtained the rate for unlimited local residential[7] and business calling,[8] when available. The rates used are for the local calling area only.[9] Some states offer only measured service so we are forced to make usage assumptions based on FCC data. To estimate the number of calls that a customer with measured service in each wire center makes, we use information on total dial equipment minutes in a state and assumptions used in the HCPM.[10] In our analysis we use four-minute and five-minute business calls and five-minute residential calls. Overall, our results are not highly sensitive to the number of calls assumed.

We include data on the federal subscriber line charge (SLC) or end user common line (EUCL) as well as the primary interexchange carrier charge (PICC) to obtain the total revenues for local service, since these federal charges are independent of the number of local or long-distance calls.[11] We obtained these data for the most recently completed tariff period (July 1, 1999, to July 1, 2000) and the most recent (July 1, 2000) change in access charges due to the coalition for affordable local and long-distance services (CALLS) program.[12]

We also obtained data on collocation arrangements by wire center for Bell Atlantic, which includes the original Bell Atlantic and NYNEX territories, as of early August 2000. Bell Atlantic provides a list of collocation arrangements by wire center. We do not distinguish between the type of collocation, although these data are available, but simply use the fact that collocation has been requested. While not a perfect measure, the presence of a collocation agreement indicates that the local market served by a particular wire center has a degree of competition.

Relationship between Rates and Costs

There has been much discussion about the implicit subsidies in local telephone rates. We show in Wimmer and Rosston (2000) that density alone explains about 80% of the variation in local telephone costs in the HCPM model. Despite the strong, negative relationship between density and costs, a large number of states adopt so-called "value-based" pricing plans. Value-based pricing is a system where rates are positively related to the number of customers within a local calling area. For example, in South Carolina, (Table 8.1) there are seven different rate groups.

Table 8.1
Example of Rate Schedule: South Carolina Residential Rates

Rate Group	Number of lines	Basic Local Rate
1	7,000	$12.70
2	15,000	$13.15
3	28,500	$13.60
4	50,000	$14.05
5	78,000	$14.50
6	125,000	$14.95
7	Unlimited	$15.40

As Table 8.1 shows, rates go down as density decreases, which is exactly the opposite of cost-based pricing.

We have constructed a set of variables from the rate data to further examine the relationship between prices and costs. First, we have calculated average local revenue per line, which is equal to the sum of local rates, SLCs, and PICCs. To calculate the average revenue per line, we simply calculate the total revenues by type of line (i.e., multiple and single-line businesses, and primary and nonprimary residential lines multiplied by the appropriate rates[13]) and take the ratio of total revenue to total residential and business lines.

In addition to the average revenue per line, we estimate the average revenue per business and residential line. We find that the national average revenue per line, including federal PICCs and SLCs and our estimate of any variable revenues associated with measured service, is higher for business lines than for residential lines.[14] Table 8.2 summarizes these results.

Table 8.2
U.S. National Average Revenue per Line

	Total Lines	Average Revenue (4)	Average Revenue (5)
Business Lines	46,809,464	$39.14	$38.20
Residential Lines*	85,371,680	$18.29	$18.29
Overall	132,181,124	$25.67	$25.34

(4) Indicates that measured calls average four minutes per call.
(5) Indicates that measured calls average five minutes per call.
*Does not differ because number of residential calls is assumed to be constant.

Our results verify what is widely recognized—business rates are higher than local residential rates. Our data show that this difference is statistically significant. In an effort to avoid or minimize the debate about common-cost recovery, we take the entire amount of revenue from local service for both business and residential customers and assume that per-minute access is priced at cost.[15] Some parties may argue that residential lines should be treated as incremental in wire centers with primarily business lines. Under this assumption, the price of residential service need cover only its incremental cost. To avoid this problem, we examine total revenues to see if they cover the total cost of providing service within a wire center. For wire centers that do not cover costs, an infinite number of price changes and various combinations of prices could be used to allow full recovery of costs.[16]

After calculating the local revenue per line, we estimated the following equation:

$$\ln(\textit{Average Revenue}_i) = \alpha_{1n} + \alpha_2\ln(\textit{Average Cost}_i) + \alpha_3 \textit{ Measured Service}_i + \alpha_4 \textit{ Percent Business Lines}_i + \varepsilon_i$$

Average revenue is the average revenue earned per line and is calculated as discussed earlier. To account for state-specific fixed effects; we include a vector of constants, α_{1n}, that are allowed to vary across states. Average cost is the HCPM's estimate of the average cost per line. *Measured service* is a qualitative variable that is set equal to 1 if unlimited calling is not available to business or residential customers. Finally, *percent business lines* is simply the ratio of total business lines to total residential and business lines, multiplied by 100.[17] The α's are the respective coefficients, and ε_i is the random disturbance term.

Because we use average revenue per line as the dependent variable, the percentage of lines that are business lines is included in the analysis.[18] As shown earlier, average revenue per business line for local services only (not including any custom local area signaling services [CLASS] features or hunting) is substantially higher than the average revenue per residential line. A dummy variable capturing the presence of measured business service is also included. As discussed, the number of calls and their length are based on actual dial equipment minutes. When measured service is present, the number of calls and perhaps revenues are likely to be lower. Table 8.3 contains the results for regressions.[19]

The first two columns give the results of the regressions where state-specific fixed effects are not included. The final two contain those with fixed effects. We find that we can reject the null hypothesis that the fixed effects are jointly insignificant.[20] In all the specifications, we find an inverse relationship between average revenue and average cost. This relationship is statistically significant at standard levels in all specifications. In the case of average revenue, we find that a 10% increase in average costs is associated with approximately a 0.65% decline in average revenues when we account for state-specific fixed effects. The magnitude of the relationship is even greater when we do not account for fixed effects.

Table 8.3

Relationship between Average Revenue per Line and Average Cost

	ln(Ave Rev) (4 min)	ln(Ave Rev) (5 min)	ln(Ave Rev) (4 min) Fixed	ln(Ave Rev) (5 min) Fixed
ln (Cost)	-0.075	-0.076	-0.064	-0.066
	(13.73)	(14.01)	(15.75)	(15.63)
Measured	-0.052	-0.075	-0.123	-0.144
	(11.06)	(16.20)	(4.08)	(5.06)
Percentage Business	0.007	0.007	0.009	0.008
	(33.02)	(31.52)	(53.24)	(48.63)
Constant	3.232	3.24	3.177	3.19
	(138.36)	(138.8)	(151.33)	(149.6)
R^2	0.40	0.39	0.86	0.85
N Obs	8,026	8,026	8,026	8,026

The results also show that average revenue is affected significantly by the percentage of business lines. Again, concentrating on the fixed-effects model, we find that increasing the percentage of business lines by 10% increases average revenue per line by approximately 0.09%. Finally, measured rates in both the business and residential cases lead to a reduction in average revenue when either four- or five-minute calls are assumed. These results are consistent with the results generated when it is assumed that business callers make 200 five-minute calls per month.

Subsidies

For each RBOC wire center in the HCPM, we calculate the difference between the rate for flat-rate local residential service and the cost reported in the model. There is a wide dispersion in the differences between these numbers, both within and across states.

The weighted average cost per line for providing local service is $22.74.[21] The weighted average revenue for local residential telephone service (including SLCs and PICCs) is $18.28, not including any federal subsidy dollars. If we include federal subsidy dollars, average revenue increases to $18.51. The explicit universal-service funding applies to the high-cost wire centers according to a FCC formula. These dollars are added to the rates charged to consumers to determine overall revenue received in each wire center.[22]

The difference between the residential revenues and costs can be large and varies across states. For example, in Vermont, we estimate that the average revenue per line falls over $10 short of costs. We estimate that, in the aggregate, 17 states do not cover their costs for basic local service, as modeled by the HCPM, with revenues from local rates, federal SLCs, PICCs, and subsidies. The differences are even more pronounced when we examine revenue per residential line and compare this with estimated costs. Using this measure, only five states have a positive differential.[23] This is due to relatively little geographic disaggregation in rates, whereas costs vary widely. This is not simply a United States phenomenon—costs for phone service vary widely in India and any country where there are both urban and rural areas.

While it is interesting to see the results on a statewide basis, competitors are more likely to look at the results on a narrower basis. Competitors are likely to target rate centers where they can charge prices that cover costs. We, therefore, examine the results on a wire-center basis to understand the number of wire centers that have rates that cover the cost of local service.

Overall, only 31% of the 8,026 wire centers have an estimated revenue stream that exceeds its estimated costs. In 15 states, over 80% of the wire centers are estimated to have a shortfall, while only 3 states have over one-half of their wire centers covering estimated costs.[24] Such a simple comparison, however, may be misleading. As discussed earlier, costs are inversely related to density, while revenues are positively related to density. Thus, it is more reasonable to examine the number of lines receiving and contributing to our measure of implicit subsidy. Overall, 30% of lines are in wire centers that do not generate enough revenue to cover their costs. In Vermont, 73% of the lines are in wire centers where the contribution is negative. Nine states have more than half of their lines in wire centers where the contribution is negative. By contrast, in 38 of the 47 states examined, over half of the lines in the state have revenues that are sufficient to cover costs; and 22 have over 75% of their lines covering costs. According to these figures, the cross-subsidy problem, when the measure is based on total wire-center local revenue (i.e., including both business and residential lines), is concentrated in a relatively small number of states.

Simply counting the number of lines where revenues exceed or fall short of costs hides the magnitude of the problem because it may reflect only small differences. We, therefore, calculated these numbers using larger hurdles. First, to examine the source of cross-subsidies, we estimated the number of lines where revenues are greater than 125% of costs. This calculation shows that about 44% of the lines are in wire centers where revenues are greater than 125% of costs. On the other side, about 10% of the lines are in wire centers where revenues are less than 75% of costs. Again, the cross-subsidy problem is most severe in only a few states. Only five states have more than 25% of their lines in wire centers where revenues fall short of 75% of the costs. As in the early cases, the problem is most severe in Vermont, where 38% of the lines reside in wire centers where less than 75% of costs are recovered through local charges (including federal flat-rated charges).

These wide divergences mean two things. First, it is unlikely that competition will develop in wire centers where rates are below costs unless subsidies are made explicit and competitively neutral, rates change, or additional revenue sources are sufficient to make up the difference. However, because other rate centers implicitly subsidize these areas, we expect to see these contributing areas to be the targets of competitive entry.

COMPETITION

It is a basic tenet of economics that competitors enter markets when they expect to earn a profit. Competitors follow Willie Sutton's advice and target areas "where the money is." Typically, this leads to the result that the most efficient firms serve consumers. However, in the market for local telecommunications, the use of implicit cross-subsidies makes entry into many local markets untenable because prices are held below cost by regulatory fiat. To ensure that firms are fully compensated, regulators require firms to hold rates well above cost in other markets. It is not surprising, therefore, that anecdotal reports on the development of competition note that residential consumers are being passed over by new entrants in favor of dense, urban business districts. In this section we examine how these factors and others are influencing the development of competition. To accomplish this, we use data on the presence of collocation arrangements in the original Bell Atlantic and NYNEX service areas (hereafter, Bell Atlantic).

When entering a market, a competitor must interconnect with the incumbent's network. This may be accomplished in a number of ways, one of which is to place equipment in an incumbent's wire center. Such arrangements are known as collocation agreements. Collocation agreements are also required if the entrant is going to purchase unbundled loops or provide competitive high-speed digital services. Thus, one measure of competition is the presence of a collocation agreement. While this measure is somewhat broad—it does not measure the number of lines captured by a competitor or whether the entrant is serving business or residential customers—it does indicate whether or not a competitor has begun, or is planning, to offer service in an area. It also does not measure the amount of competition from wireless carriers, but that is currently less important in the United States than in other countries. As a result, the lessons are still applicable to countries where wireless competitors may have the ability to target high-profit opportunities.

Bell Atlantic has collocation agreements in place in approximately 57% of the 2,332 Bell Atlantic wire centers in our data set. These wire centers, however, account for over 90% of all the lines in the territory. Thus, while nearly a majority of the wire centers still do not have collocation, the vast majority of lines are served by wire centers that do have collocation.

Entrants using unbundled loops to provide service gain access to all the customers served by a particular wire center when they collocate. Using the FCC cost-model data, the number of lines in a wire center, including special access and public telephone lines, ranges from 11 to 407,207 lines. The average number of lines served in a wire center is 20,000, with a median of 6,735. In urban areas, several wire centers, many of which contain multiple switches, are used to serve a local area.[25] In more rural settings, a single switch is used to serve an entire town and its surrounding areas.

Using wire-center boundaries allows us to gather data on several characteristics of the local telephone market. The FCC's cost model gives us information on the average cost per line, number of lines, and the breakdown on the number of business and residential lines. The FCC also targets federal subsidy dollars to individual wire centers. We have augmented these data with demographic information from the 1990 census. In particular, we include data on the percentage of households in the census' top income category, those with an income in excess of $45,000 annually, in 1990 dollars. Finally, as discussed earlier, we have gathered price data on a wire-center basis. These data, combined with data on whether or not a particular wire center has a collocation agreement with an entrant, allow us to begin to examine the factors affecting the development of competition.

We begin our analysis by presenting basic summary statistics (Table 8.4). The data are presented according to the presence, or lack, of a collocation agreement.

Table 8.4
Summary Statistics for the Bell Atlantic Region

Variables	Collocation	No Collocation
Average Cost per Line	$19.41 (3.89)	$40.16 (21.75)
Average Revenue per Primary Residential Line	$19.17 (4.36)	$17.71 (5.82)
Average Revenue per Multiple Business Line	$41.60 (10.89)	$43.70 (8.98)
Percentage of Wire Centers Receiving Federal Support	4% (0.19)	23% (0.42)
Average Number Households in Wire Centers	15,483 (14,337)	2,204 (1,730)
Average Percentage of Business Lines in Wire Centers	31% (0.15)	11% (0.12)
Switching Access Charge (Interstate)	$0.0056 (0.002)	$0.0056 (0.002)
Average Percentage of Household in Top Income Group in Wire Center*	39% (0.16)	24% (0.13)
Percentage of Wire Centers with Measured Business Rates	44% (0.50)	37% (0.48)
Observations	1,341	991

* Because we use 1990 census data, two wire centers were listed as having no households in the census data. These wire centers are excluded from the analysis.

The average cost per line in the wire centers without collocation ($40) is more than double the cost ($19) of those with a collocation agreement. This is an indication that the former are less densely populated areas. This is confirmed by the difference in wire center size. In the data, the average number of households in wire centers with a collocation agreement is over seven times greater than those without. In addition, we find the average wire center with a collocation agreement has ten times as many lines as the average wire center without a collocation agreement (35,000 vs. 3,000). Also, the percentage of business lines in wire centers without collocation is significantly lower than in those with a collocation agreement (11% compared to 31%). We also find that in wire centers with a collocation agreement the percentage of households in the top income category (above $45,000) is much higher than in those wire centers without collocation.

Finally, we calculated the difference between our calculation of revenues (as described earlier) and the cost per line in these wire centers. Not surprisingly, we find that in wire centers with a collocation agreement the average differential is a positive $8.26, while those without a collocation agreement have an average differential of negative $17.66. This difference is driven by three factors. First, the average cost is higher in wire centers without a collocation agreement. Second, while multiple business lines earn a slightly higher amount, primary residential line revenues are lower in wire centers without collocation agreements. Finally, the percentage of business lines is much lower in wire centers without collocation agreements. In general, these data are consistent with the notion that competitors are taking advantage of the pricing structure in local telecommunications and are concentrating their entry in relatively dense, urban areas.

CONCLUSION

Because telecommunications development is important to economic growth, most countries are in the process of moving to more efficient systems of provision than state-owned monopolies. The move to more competitive, market-driven service provision is a first step for most countries. As countries move down this path, they will be forced to deal with the hidden distortions in the pricing system. Competitors will attack those areas where profit opportunities exist due to regulator-imposed supracompetitive pricing (provided the regulatory and competitive structure is in place to allow viable competition).

To obtain the largest benefits from this transition, regulators should reduce or eliminate artificial barriers to competition in rural areas and artificial inducements in urban areas. This requires allowing competitors equal access to the sources of subsidy available to incumbents. This is crucial to the efficient provision of service in rural areas. In urban areas, entrants should be required to make the same contributions to universal service funding that incumbents are required to make.

Because India can formulate universal service and competition policy on a centralized (federal) level, it can mandate consistent, explicit, nationwide subsidy programs. Of course, ensuring explicit and efficient subsidies through careful program design remains as an issue for regulators that need to also contend with the differential political power of different user groups—a difficult task, as evidenced in this chapter.

Even if the universal service funding for high-cost areas is explicit and competitively neutral, that does not mean that it is efficient or socially beneficial. The taxes needed to fund the program distort consumer choices. Telecommunications services will be underused when they are taxed to fund the program, while those receiving subsidies may be overused. In addition, because telecommunications is an input to other services, the funding mechanism may distort input choices, resulting in inefficiencies not associated with other potential funding programs.

When India thinks about its universal-service policies, especially to support the provision of service to remote villages, care should be taken to ensure that all competitive providers have the opportunity to provide service. In addition, regulators should, when feasible, allow prices to reflect the cost of providing service. Finally, the revenue used to fund any shortfalls should be raised in the least distortionary manner available.

NOTES

We would like to thank Rich Lerner, Tracy Waldon, and Jim Zolnierek of the Federal Communications Commission (FCC) for their help in gathering information on rates. We would also like to thank Rich Clarke and Ed Lowry, along with Robert McNary, for help provided on this project. All mistakes are, of course, ours alone.

1.   The causality of this relationship is, as shown by Cronin et al. (1991, 1993), likely to move in both directions. Increases in telephone penetration rates increase measures of income, and increases in income lead to higher levels of telephone penetration rates.

2.   We note that when penetration rates are low, increasing the number of subscribers may enhance the value of the network if network externalities exist. When this is the case, subsidizing connections to the network may improve economic efficiency, depending on how it is financed.

3.   See, e.g., Hausman, Tardiff, and Belinfante (1993).

4.   In the United States a complex dual jurisdictional regulatory scheme is in place where individual states set rates to recover approximately 75% of the local market. Federal regulators are responsible for the remainder. The respective shares are the result of legal decisions and, economically speaking, are arbitrary.

5.   The data are described more fully in Rosston and Wimmer (2001). In that we explain the effects of limiting the data analysis to the Regional Bell Operating Companies (RBOCs) and the matching process for the complementary data.

6.   For a fuller discussion of our use of the PNR data, see Wimmer and Rosston (2000).

7.   While nearly every state offers measured rate service for business and residential calling, we used the flat-rated option with unlimited calling when it was available. Each state has its own discount plans for measured service, making cross-state comparisons difficult. We also identified any differences between multiple-line and single-line business rates when the tariffs made a distinction. In the majority of states, the

rates are the same. In one case, Michigan, we used a plan that did not have unlimited calling but included a large number of local calls (400).

8. While many business customers may purchase "trunks" for use with PBXs and hunting service, we report only multiple-line and single-line rates. Additionally, many states explicitly note that, for two-way service, the business line rate is the same regardless of whether or not it is connected to a PBX. In short, we attempted to match rates to the cost of services modeled by the HCPM.

9. In approximately 3.8% of the wire centers, there are multiple rate centers, with different rates for residential and business customers, accounting for almost 7% of the total lines. This generally occurs in large wire centers serving both central cities and suburbs where the rates differ. In these cases, we take a simple average of the rates for the wire center. We take the simple average because, at this time, we do not have data on the number of lines within the wire center serving different rate centers.

10. We have rerun the regressions using a four-minute duration, and the results are very similar. We also assumed 100 calls per residential line and 200 calls per business line, which follows assumptions made by the FCC in its business-usage reports.

11. Even though the PICC charge is not charged directly to the end-user customer, we adopt the assumption that competition will force the consumer to ultimately pay this charge.

12. We report the results for rates before the CALLS program. Among other things, the CALLS program, at this time, reduces per-minute access charges and PICCs and increases SLCs. Thus, the overall change in flat-rated revenues, our concern in this study, is not large.

13. We have estimated the number of second lines in each wire center. This was completed by first multiplying the HCPM's estimate of households by the penetration rate reported by the FCC in its *Penetration Report* for 1999 to estimate the number of primary residential lines. We then used the difference between primary residential lines and total residential lines to estimate nonprimary lines. In five cases, this approach yielded more nonprimary lines than primary lines; the vast majority of the remaining wire centers are estimated to have less than 40% nonprimary residential lines. We estimate that approximately 16% of all lines are nonprimary lines. The appropriated SLCs and PICCs are assigned to lines based on these calculations.

14. In this calculation, we aggregate across primary and nonprimary residential lines, along with single and multiple business lines.

15. We realize that access is currently priced above cost, but the divergence has been narrowing significantly. Moreover, artificially high access charges are a source of implicit subsidy. Their inclusion would, therefore, interfere with our attempt to estimate the size of implicit-subsidy problems.

16. To avoid cross-subsidy, we could consider constraints that require that each line covers its incremental cost and that no price exceeds its stand-alone cost.

17. We omit special access lines and their cost.

18. Percentage of business lines is calculated by taking the ratio of total business lines to total lines (not including special access lines) and multiplying this ratio by 100.

19. We also ran, but do not report, regressions for residential and business revenues separately. These results are consistent with those reported.

20. In all cases, the F-statistic for this test exceeds 500.

21. This number differs slightly from the $23.84 reported in Rosston and Wimmer (2000) because the sample in this chapter is restricted to RBOC wire centers for which we were able to obtain rate data. The earlier paper included all nonrural, incumbent local exchange carriers (LECs) and all RBOC wire centers.

22. The FCC started targeting dollars to specific high-cost wire centers beginning in the third quarter of 2000.

23. Since our data focus exclusively on RBOCs, this does not mean that other states do not have significant rate-cost imbalances. States where the RBOC prices are close to costs may have service provided by other carriers that have significant imbalances.

24. We remind the reader that our data do not include revenues from CLASS features such as call waiting or any interstate or intrastate per-minute access charges.

25. For example, in the state of New York, in the *Local Exchange Routing Guide*, 12 wire centers list their locality as New York, and 16 list Brooklyn.

BIBLIOGRAPHY

Bovenberg, A., and L. Goulder. "Optimal Environmental Taxation in the Presence of Other Taxes: General Equilibrium Analyses." *American Economic Review* (September 1996): 985—1000.

Cronin, F. J., E. K. Colleran, P. L. Herbert, and S. Lewitzky. "Telecommunications and Growth." *Telecommunications Policy* (December 1993b): 677—690.

Cronin, F. J., E. K. Colleran, E. B. Parker, and M.A. Gould. "Telecommunications Infrastructure and Economic Growth." *Telecommunications Policy* (December 1991): 529—535.

Eisner, J., and Tracy Waldon. "The Demand for Bandwidth: Second Telephone Lines and On-Line Services." Unpublished manuscript, 1999.

Federal Communications Commission. "In the Matter of Federal–State Joint Board on Universal Service." CC Docket No. 96-45, Nineteenth Order on Reconsideration, adopted December 17, 1999, released December 17, 1999.

Greenstein, S., P. Spiller. "Modern Telecommunications Infrastructure and Economic Activity: An Empirical Investigation" *Industrial and Corporate Change* (December 1995) 4(4): 647—665.

Hausman, J., T. Tardiff, and A. Belinfante. "The Effects of the Breakup of AT&T on Telephone Penetration in the United States." *American Economic Review* (May 1993): 178—184.

Jipp, A. "Wealth of Nations and Telephone Density." *Telecommunications Journal* (July 1963): 199—201.

Madden, G., and S. Savage. "Measuring the Gains from Asia-Pacific Investment and Trade in Telecommunications." In S. Macdonald and G. Madden (eds.), *Telecommunications and Socio-Economic Development*, Chapter 4. Amsterdam: Elsevier Science, 1998.

Norton, Seth. "Transaction Costs, Telecommunications, and the Microeconomics of Macroeconomic Growth." *Economic Development and Cultural Change* 41 (October 1992): 175—196.

Rosston, Gregory L., and Bradley S. Wimmer. "The State of Universal Service." *Information Economics and Policy* 12 (2000): 261—283.

———. "From C to Shining C: Competition and Cross-Subsidy in Communications." In S. Greenstein, and B. Compaine, (eds.), "Communications Policy in Transition: The Internet and Beyond." Cambridge: MIT Press, 2001 available at: http://siepr.stanford.edu/papers/pdf/00-21.html.

Wallsten, Scott J. "Telecommunications Privatization in Developing Countries: The Real Effects of Exclusivity Periods." Stanford Institute for Economic Policy Research Working paper, SIEPR Policy paper No. 99-21, May 2000, available at: http://siepr.stanford.edu/papers/pdf/99-21.html

White, H. "A Heteroscedasticity-Consistent Covariance Matrix Estimator and a Direct Test for Heteroscedasticity." *Econometrica* 48 (1980): 817—838.

Wimmer, Bradley S. and Gregory L. Rosston. "Winners and Losers in the Universal Service Battle." In B. M. Compaine and I. Vogelsang (eds.), *The Internet Upheaval: Raising Questions, Seeking Answers in Communications Policy* (TPRC Proceedings), 387—412. Cambridge: MIT Press and TPRC, 2000.

Chapter 9

Regulation of the Mexican Telecommunications Markets

Cristina Casanueva

In the last two decades the Mexican telecommunications industry has experienced a substantial transformation. These changes have been triggered, to a large extent, by the privatization of Tel fonos de M xico (Telmex), the country 's original public telecommunications operator, and by the opening of the telecommunications markets to competition.

The profound changes in the Mexican telecommunications markets have been sometimes ushered in, and sometimes followed by, regulatory reform. However, some key aspects of the regulatory process have not resulted in the efficient use of the available infrastructure and its further expansion. Nor have they resulted in a higher penetration of telephone lines (mainly residential), which represents access by the end users to a more diversified array of telecommunications services, with better quality and lower prices.

The purpose of this chapter is to present an overview of this process, stressing the role played by the state regulators in the privatization and opening of Mexico's telecommunications sector. The chapter begins with a presentation of the background of the privatization of Telmex and emphasizes the main regulatory approach after privatization, embodied in Telmex's new license, which consisted of the policy of "regulating the monopoly" (1990).

The chapter later reviews and discusses the opening of the telecommunications markets and the regulatory changes associated with this change: the regulation for network interconnection (1994, 1996), the new Telecommunications Law, and the creation of an independent regulatory institution, the Federal Telecommunications Commission (Cofetel, 1995–1996). Finally the chapter analyzes the ongoing effort to implement "dominant carrier" regulation, aimed at leveling the playing field, after the recent declaration of Telmex as a market power operator (2000).

BACKGROUND AND OBJECTIVES OF THE PRIVATIZATION

As in many other developing countries, Mexico's state-owned telecommunications monopoly presented serious problems in service quality and reliability. Its operation was based on the use of obsolete technologies, compared to those already in use by other public telephone operators (PTO) in the world. By all usual performance standards, basic services were below the expected standards in other developing countries.

The administration of Telmex was, to a large extent, guided by political objectives and not by legitimate business interests or broad public goals. The government regarded Telmex as a source of revenue for projects in other policy areas and debt service. Telmex's operation was largely an instrument of fiscal and employment policy, with disregard for the efficient operation of the company in terms of the quality and reliability of service delivery (Casasús, 1994).

The breakdown of the state-run telecommunications system after the devastating earthquake of 1985, hindering relief activities, was the beginning of the end of the state monopoly (Casasús, 1994). The government's acknowledgment of the crisis led to the design of a telecommunications policy that began with a privatization project in 1989 and a plan for opening the sector to competition in the following years.

In September 1989, the government announced its intention to privatize Telmex, selling a majority position in the company's equity. The objectives of the privatization process were defined as:

- To achieve an efficient operation of the telecommunications system in Mexico

- To improve the quality of services and diversify the offerings

- To expand and upgrade network infrastructure

- To create a continuous flow of cutting-edge technology

- To establish the groundwork for the opening of markets

The reform and modernization of Telmex were part of an aggressive program of privatization in Mexico aimed, to a large extent, at generating a revenue flow for improving public finance. This objective created a policy dilemma of choosing between the possible policy measures that would introduce competition into the telecommunications markets. One approach would have been to structurally separate service delivery, through a company breakup, similar to the one experienced by the United States in 1984. This policy approach would have introduced vigorous competition in every telecommunications service market and introduced self-regulation on interconnection services provided by the local interconnection service providers, as a result of the breakup. The contrasting approach consisted of maintaining or creating market reserves to be exploited by the new owners, making the company more attractive to potential buyers.

The policy dilemma faced by decision makers was how to reconcile the macroeconomic objectives with the microeconomic efficiency objectives. The achievement of the macroeconomic objectives implied selling the company, with market reserves for specific services, allowing the establishment of a very high price for the company in order to fulfill revenue purposes. This approach, however, meant creating entry barriers for potential buyers and abandoning the structural separation that would have promoted vigorous competition.

Decision makers opted for the macro-oriented policy, selling the company at a very high price in order to fulfill the double purpose of generating a revenue flow and seeking telecommunications improvement. With the modification of Telmex's license, the purchasers were given a monopoly to operate long-distance service for six years.

The local and value-added service markets were open *de jure;* however, technical and regulatory barriers resulted in Telmex's facing little competition in most markets and almost no competition in local telephony.

The new Telmex license made this company operate, from the regulatory perspective, as a regulated monopoly. This translated into the establishment of the following operational goals:

- Setting an objective of 12% annual expansion of the network,

- Establishing quality and reliability indicators, in order to monitor the performance of the services delivered by the company, and

- Defining a program of social coverage by establishing universal service obligations within a time frame for their implementation.

The "new contract" embodied in Telmex's license established that Telmex must comply with antitrust provisions in some segments of the market, such as the commercialization of equipment, maintenance and installation services, radio-telephony, and value-added services. Telmex was asked to spin off separate firms for the provision of value-added network and mobile telephony services. The spirit of this regulation was to prevent cross-subsidies and other anticompetitive practices that would threaten fair competition with other companies in the markets in which Telmex engaged directly or indirectly through its affiliates or subsidiaries. These measures did not include the long-distance service, both national and international, which was provided exclusively by this company for the subsequent six years.

RATES REGULATION

Rates were to be set based on a price cap regulation, based on the average price of a basket of services. The basic principle was to allow rates to recover at least the long-run incremental cost. The basket of services included installation, rental charges, local services, and long-distance services, both domestic and international.

Between 1990 and 1996 Telmex agreed to rebalance its rates in order to stop subsidizing local service; however, given the definition of the elements of the basket used in calculating the average rate, it was unclear how the cross-subsidization was to be prevented. This was because the general price cap under which Telmex operated after privatization increased the probabilities of anticompetitive behavior. Since the cap covered prices in both competitive (long-distance services) and non-competitive markets (interurban access and local services), there was an incentive for Telmex to engage in anticompetitive cross-subsidization.

Although Telmex's license explicitly forbade pricing below incremental cost, there was room for an anticompetitive strategy consisting of recovering the burden of common costs in the local service, while reducing prices closer to incremental costs in the long-distance service (OECD, 1999a).

In effect, since the introduction of competition in the long-distance market, there has been constant allegation of anticompetitive practices and cross-subsidization, since the prices of the long-distance services have declined sharply, while local rates have increased (OECD, 1999a).

UNIVERSAL SERVICE

Telmex, due to its nature as a "regulated monopoly" and its ubiquitous presence as the only nationwide local service provider-operator, acquired social coverage obligations that can be summarized in the following obligations:

- To expand the number of basic telephone lines by a minimum of 12% per annum

- To reduce the waiting period for basic telephone service to a maximum of one month in the year 2000

- To provide telephone service to every town with more than 500 inhabitants and to increase the penetration of public telephone booths, from 0.5 per 1,000 to five per 1,000 by the end of 1998

Telmex complied with these requirements in the initial years after privatization (Table 9.1). However, local service, particularly residential service expansion, has lagged in subsequent years. Mexico currently has one of the lowest penetration rates of telephone lines in the Organization for Economic Corporation and Development (OECD).

Table 9.1

Mexico's Network Expansion (1990–1998)

	Mexico 1990	Mexico 1998
Lines/100 Inhab.	6.6	11.0
Digitalization	29%	98%
National long-distance Calls (millions)	951	2,511*
International long-distance Calls (millions)	169	627*

Sources: OECD (1999 a, b); Cofetel and Telmex Annual Reports.

*OECD estimations.

Mexico's telephone line penetration also appears low in comparison with its South American counterparts (taking into account the gross domestic product [GDP] per capita; see Table 9.2).

Table 9.2

Telecommunications Indicators in Latin America, 1998

Country	Mexico	Argentina	Chile	Venezuela	Brazil	Peru
Digitalization	98%	99%	100%	64%	69%	88%
Lines/100 inhab.	10	20	21	11.4	12	6.3
Residential/ 100 homes	29	60	73	46	29	28
Pay Phone/1000 inhab.	3.3	2.6	0.9	3.2	3	1.9
Mobile/100 inhab.	4	8	7	9	5	3

Source: Noll (2000); OECD (1999a, b).

For the last several years, Mexico has relied primarily on market forces to provide basic telephone service. As a result, although competition (or the expected opening of the markets) has resulted in an impressive expansion of its fiber-optic network (30,000 kilometers long) and level of digitalization, the overall penetration is low, and prices for basic services remain high.

INTERCONNECTION

Telmex's license required it to propose an interconnection plan to the new long-distance operators on January 1, 1994; however, Telmex's proposal did not contain the minimum requirements to guarantee conditions for competition and equal access for new long-distance operators. It was unacceptable to potential investors interested in participating in the long-distance services market.

The Ministry of Communications and Transportation, working in close collaboration with the Federal Competition Commission, issued an Interconnection Resolution in 1994 that included the following provisions:

- Guaranteed access to elements and functions of the Telmex network based on quality and nondiscrimination against new entrants

- Equal access to the rights-of-way

- Selection by the final user of its preferred network through dial-around

- Accounting separation and allocated costs

- Interconnection charges based on costs and in line with international references and standards

- A schedule established requiring Telmex to provide interconnection under conditions of "equal access," beginning with 60 cities in 1997 and covering the entire country by the year 2000

The new government Interconnection Resolution represented a key regulation to encourage license application, investment, and infrastructure construction by new entrants. The 1994 interconnection rules, in principle, established the technical, economic, and market conditions to create the expectation of a level playing field for competition.

In practice, however, the field for competition was not leveled. In 1996, after intense negotiations between the new long-distance companies and Telmex failed, the regulator stepped in and defined the interconnection rates, accepting Telmex's claim that it should be compensated for its local operation deficit. Telmex argued that it was entitled to receive a contribution in interconnection charges. In its 1996 Interconnection Resolution, the regulator imposed a relatively high interconnection charge equivalent to US5.3 cents per minute.[1] This charge included a basic rate of US2.5 cents and a surcharge on the termination of incoming international calls equal to 58% of the settlement rate.

Between 1996 and 1998 Telmex engaged in a rapid rebalancing of its local and long-distance prices, increasing local rates in real terms and reducing the deficit on the residential local service. Correspondingly, in December 1998, the regulator eliminated the 58% international surcharge, and by July 2000, interconnection charges represented the equivalent of US3.3 cents, per minute of use, at one end. However, this access charge did not include additional revenue from billing the customer directly for the local call component, an extra 5.7% for uncompleted calls, and the necessary network facilities for interconnection, such as circuits, ports, and (switches) collocation. These additional elements represented 20% more at each end.

Taking into account all additional elements in the access charge, they finally added up to the equivalent of US4.9 cents, per minute of use, at one end (Gil Hubert, 2000).[2] This access or interconnection charge remained very high compared to international standards, including in the United States, Mexico's main trade partner, and other developing countries in Latin America (Figure 9.1).

Table 9.3
Variable and Fixed Charges per Minute of Use to Local Operators in the United States and Mexico

Country	US (July 2000)	Mexico (July 2000)
Variable charges	US2.00 cents	US7.59 cents
Monthly fixed charges per minute of use	US0.00 cents residential subscribers US1.22 cents business, multiline	US0.00 cents
Fixed and variable charges	US2.00 cents residential subscribers US3.22 cents business, multiline Average US2.24 cents	US7.59 cents

Source: Gil Hubert (2000).

Figure 9.1
Interconnection Charges in Selected Latin American Countries, 2000

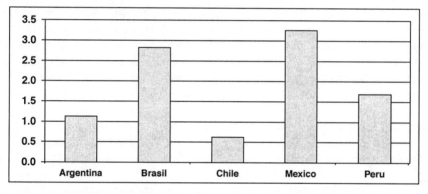

Source: Gil Hubert (2000).

The study by Gil Hubert (2000) showed that the definition of interconnection charges did not follow the interconnection regulation (1994 and 1998), allowing for anticompetitive practices such as a "price squeeze" and cross-subsidies by Telmex between its access or interconnection service and the other services in which Telmex faces competition. This may be due to the choice in Mexico of a different "balance" between the sources of revenue (monthly rental fees, local call usage fees, and interconnection charges) that are necessary to cover the costs of the local telephone service.

DISCUSSION OF CURRENT ISSUES

Telmex's Market Power

Telmex continues to benefit from its market power, and, although there has been entry into long-distance services, the entrants' infrastructure is still very modest, and they must rely on Telmex's capacity, both for their access to final consumers and to provide long-distance services on some routes. Telmex's vertical integration and its ability to set prices without other competitors being able to offset such power, as well as the existence of significant entry barriers, were taken into account in determining its dominant position.

Federal Telecommunications Law on Asymmetrical Regulation (1995)

The Federal Telecommunications Law adopted in 1995 incorporated central elements of effective regulation. The law codified the goal of promoting competition among providers, to benefit users through better services, diversity, and quality. The establishment of the Federal Telecommunications Commission (Cofetel) as a regulatory agency, separate from the secretary of communications and transportation, was an important step toward developing an independent and transparent regulatory framework in Mexico (OECD, 1999a).

In addition, the general competition or antitrust law applies to the telecommunications sectors, and thus the Federal Competition Commission (Mexico's antitrust agency) has the authority to provide competition policy advice. The regulator (Cofetel) was authorized to establish, for any public telecommunications network licensee, that in the opinion of the Federal Competition Commission had substantial power in the market, specific obligations related to rates, quality of service, and information.

The asymmetrical regulation on rates established that the rates for each service, capacity, or function, including those of interconnection, should allow the recuperation of at least the long-run incremental cost. Only by the application of this principle is it possible to prevent a "price squeeze" by the dominant operator in interconnection rates or interurban access.

The dominant carrier's control of the greater part of the access or interconnection services (bottleneck facility) makes discrimination in quality possible when this input is offered to competitors that terminate the service to the final user. Accordingly, the law aimed at regulating quality because of the incumbent's market power as the "essential facility," making it mandatory for the dominant carrier to provide information in order for its compliance to be overseen.

In 1998, Telmex was declared to have substantial power in five markets by the Federal Competition Commission. In effect, Telmex was considered dominant in the following markets, due to its high percentage of participation in these markets:

- Local service 99%

- National long-distance 78%

- International long-distance 65%

- Interconnection service 99%

- Wholesale (resale) domestic long-distance 98%.[3]

Cofetel Was Reluctant to Apply Dominant Carrier Regulation

For two years Cofetel did not accept the Federal Competition Commission's resolution, and the regulation of "Telmex dominance" was not applied. Telmex brought an "*amparo*" (constitutional claim) against this resolution, and by June of 1999 the definitive suspension of the application of the resolution was granted. Nevertheless, it was established that the competent authorities (Cofetel) could impose additional dominant carrier regulations. Cofetel was reluctant to apply dominant carrier regulation given the pressure brought by Telmex, arguing, among other things, the importance of their stock performance in the international financial markets.[4] In contrast to Cofetel, other policymakers who favor competition and economic efficiency argue that Telmex's stock performance should be based on productivity, rather than its market power based on regulatory barriers.

International Pressure for Asymmetrical Regulation Enforcement

The U.S. Trade Representative (USTR) and Federal Communications Commission (FCC) have pressured Mexican authorities since January 2000 to effectively open Mexico's markets to competition. The FCC has imposed fines on Telmex's company operating in the United States, and the USTR has brought a case within the World Trade Organization (WTO) against Telmex for lack of reciprocity. In the Forum Americas Telecom 2000, the International Telecommunications Union (ITU) declared itself in favor of dominant carrier regulation to prevent abuses of monopoly power, anticompetitive practices, and the creation of new obstacles to access, in particular in Latin America.

External pressure and opposition built up due to the lack of asymmetrical regulation, arguing:

- Lack of internal regulations,

- Proliferation of *amparos*, and

- Lack of definitions suggesting a regulatory vacuum.[5]

Finally, Cofetel Issues Dominant Carrier Declaration against Telmex

On September 12, 2000, Cofetel issued a Dominant Carrier Declaration, imposing 39 specific obligations on rates, quality of service, and information obligations. Telmex responded by threatening with new *amparos* (September–October 2000). The claims filed by this company are based on the unconstitutionality of the new Telecommunications Law and the Administrative Procedures Law, which allowed the creation of Cofetel.

The evolution and results of Telmex's filings against the government are not as yet clear. Much will depend on the presidency of Vicente Fox. However, what is clear is the paramount importance of the implementation of these additional regulations, in that they provide the regulator with an opportunity to improve the systems of price controls on Telmex by focusing the price controls on those services for which competition is limited.

Toward the Future

Mexico's president, Vicente Fox, has announced that his administration "Will introduce vigorous pro-competition activity" referring specifically to the strengthening of the regulatory institutions dealing with the telecommunications industry.[6]

The Federal Telecommunications Law (1995) incorporates central elements of effective regulation by:

- Promoting a market mechanism for the allocation of scarce spectrum rights,
- Establishing the framework for interconnection by rivals to the incumbent's public switched telephone network (PSTN),
- Establishing the basic principles of network expansion and universal service,
- Explicitly giving to Mexico's antitrust agency (Competition Commission) the right to provide competition policy advice, and
- Establishing a regulatory agency separate from the government.

However, much is left to be done by the administration of Vicente Fox.[7] Strong competition policy and efficiency-promoting regulatory measures are crucial to the performance and the future development of the industry. Giving real independence to Cofetel will give transparency and accountability to its decisions. There is a need for strengthening Cofetel's independence from regulated companies to further ensure transparent, fair, reasonable, and predictable decisions (OECD, 1999a; Noll, 2000).

NOTES

The author would like to acknowledge the invaluable assistance, positive criticism, and contributions to this chapter by Olga Briseño.

1. This charge was at each end of a long-distance call, not including additional revenue from billing the customer directly for the local call component.

2. Gil Hubert (2000) estimates the interconnection charge to be 9.99 cents, considering two ends and all the fixed and variable expenses charged by the local operator, per minute of use.

3. OECD (1999a).

4. Salomon Brothers, the investment bankers, insisted on Telmex's filing an "*amparo*" and thus delaying the imposition of the Dominance Regulations: "the only dark cloud that could shadow Telmex's performance expectations as a publicly traded company for the rest of 1999 and up to 2000" ("Telecomunicaciones Hoy," November 2, 1999).

5.   Wall Street Journal June 9, 2000. "A Final Test of Courage for Clinton and Zedillo."

6.   From "*El Financiero*" July 5, 2000, quoted by "*Hoy en Telecomunicaciones,*" July 7, 2000.

7.   Mexico's president, Vicente Fox, took office in December 2000.

BIBLIOGRAPHY

Casas s C. (1994). "Privatization of Telecommunications: The Case of Mexico." In B. Wellenieus and P. Stern, *Implementing Reforms in the Telecommunications Sector, Lessons from Experience,* Washington DC: World Bank.

Casanueva, C. (October 12, 2000). "*Regulaci n al Operador con Poder Substancial en el Mercado*", Inteligencia 2000, Desarrollo de Tecnolog a, Simposium Internacional de Electr nica y Telecomunicaciones. Instituto Tecnol gico de Estudios Superiores, Campus Ciudad de M xico (ITESM-CCM).

Cofetel. (July 1, 1994). *Resolución sobre el Plan de Interconexión con Redes Públicas de Larga Distancia.* http://www.cft.gob.mx/html/9_publica/pubindex.html.

Cofetel- SCT. (June 7, 1995). *Ley Federal de Telecomunicaciones.*

— — —. August 9, 1996). *Decreto por el que se crea la Comisión Federal de Telecomunicaciones.* http://www.cft.gob.mx/html/9_publica/pubindex.html

— — —. (April 26, 1996). *Resolución administrativa por la que la Secretaria de Comunicaciones y Transportes establece la regulación tarifaria aplicable a los servicios de interconexión de redes públicasde telecomunicaciones, autorizadas para prestar servicios de larga distancia.* http://www.cft.gob.mx/html/9_publica/pubindex.html

Gil, Hubert, J. (2000). La Interconexión en el Sector de las Telecomunicaciones en México a Partir de la Privatización de Telmex: un An lisis Te órico y Emp rico. Tesis para obtner el T tulo de Licenciatura en Econom a, México: Instituto Tecnológico Autónomo de México (ITAM).

Hoy en Telecomunicaciones. Miércoles November 7, 2000.

Hoy en Telecomunicaciones. Miércoles July 7, 2000.

Martin, I. (1994). "Interconnection and Equal Access: Principles and Practices." Paper presented at OECD Workshop on Network Interconnection and Equal Access in Central and Eastern Europe, Budapest, January 27-28.

Noll, R. (June 5, 2000). "Promoting Efficient Telecommunications in Mexico: Lessons from Recent Experience." Mimeo.

OECD   (1999a).   *Background   Report   on   Regulatory   Reform   in   the Telecommunications Industry,* in Regulatory Reform in Mexico. Paris: OECD.

OECD (1999b). *Communication Outlook.* Paris: OECD.

Wall Street Journal. "A Final Test of Courage for Clinton and Zedillo." (June 9, 2000).

Chapter 10

Pricing Interconnection and Universal Service

Yale M. Braunstein

PRICING INTERCONNECTION AND UNIVERSAL SERVICE IN A LIBERALIZED NETWORK: LESSONS FOR INDIA

As new entrants enter a telecommunications market, the problem of interconnection has two dimensions: technical and economic. This chapter focuses on the latter. Users wish to communicate with others regardless of which firm(s) provides them services and connects them to the network. The terms of interconnection between and among network operators directly influence both the costs to the users and the financial prospects of the operators, both incumbents and new entrants.

While operators seek to provide service to users who will generate sufficient revenues to cover the cost of service, there is often the view that it is in the national interest to encourage the widespread diffusion of the network and to promote access by users who might not be considered economically viable by operators for example, because of their income levels or location. There are various ways of encouraging this universal service, but it is likely that the specific mechanisms needed after liberalization will be different from those that have been used in a monopoly regime.

Interconnection and universal service are often linked by the practice of using interconnection fees that are higher than costs to generate additional revenues for the local carrier with the understanding, implicit or explicit, that these revenues will help finance the extension of service. This chapter describes several of the specific issues that arise in pricing interconnection and providing for universal service in a liberalized environment and draws on experiences in several countries. I start by describing the issues and the changes in industry structure that underlie them. I then use several sets of "stylized facts" from various countries to illustrate specific cases.

THE DIMENSIONS OF INTERCONNECTION

Historically, the standard model was to have a single provider of local telephone service, using central offices (switches) and wires to provide service to those regions in the service area that were profitable, at least on average, to serve. Local requirements and/or national policy may also have encouraged or required the provision of service to remote regions or to neighborhoods with lower purchasing power, thus extending the reach of telephone services. These local telephone operators then connected to trunk (long-distance) carriers and international carriers, which may or may not have had common ownership with the local carrier(s).

Domestic policies have, of course, varied from country to country, but it was common to see some or all of the following:

- Local tariffs were averaged across customers despite the fact that the cost of serving one region might be different from the costs of serving another. In addition, the non-traffic-sensitive portion of the tariff (the monthly subscriber fee or "line rental") was often kept artificially low.

- The tariffs for trunk calls were sufficiently higher than costs so as to enable the costs of local service to be kept low. This could be accomplished either by having an integrated entity with an implicit cross-subsidy or by having the trunk carriers pay call origination and/or termination fees to local carriers that were significantly above the costs of the local carriers.

- International rates were many times the cost of service. These high rates, when combined with a traffic imbalance on certain routes, led to a hard-currency inflow to monopoly carriers in several countries.

This pattern of tariffs had several effects. While it might have helped address national policy goals such as universal service (increasing the number of subscribers connected to the network), it also provided incentives for new entrants to provide services at below current price levels, thereby making the situation unstable.

(At this point it is useful to distinguish between efficient entry that is the result, for example, of a carrier with a new, lower-cost technology, and inefficient entry that is driven by an artificially high difference between costs and prices. Some consider a classic example of inefficient entry to be international "callback" operators who take advantage of the differences between inbound and outbound tariffs on certain routes.)

The picture that I have described has become increasingly more complex for two reasons: the liberalization in many countries of specific parts of the market, often starting with trunk and international services, and the growth of mobile services and new access technologies. In each case the payments between carriers (whether called access fees, settlements, termination charges, or interconnection fees) and the bases for those payments have become explicit and subject to scrutiny. At the same time, the entry of new carriers and new services, especially mobile telephony, has forced many regulatory and policy bodies to reopen the issue of how to finance universal service. This has also, in some cases, included the reexamination of what universal service means (or should mean) in the current circumstances.

TYPICAL INTERCONNECTION PRICING PHILOSOPHIES

Cost-based

If the old tariff and interconnection regime could be described as one in which a historically determined mix of policy and profit objectives either led to, or were used to justify, a set of prices, the current regimes in many countries might be characterized as seeking to have costs determine the various components of the pricing structure, with any remaining shortfalls being made up or redistributions being done explicitly. But prices, both the tariff schedules for subscribers and the terms of interconnection, remain complex. The integrated nature of the telecommunications network makes it difficult—and possibly impossible—to determine costs uniquely. Nevertheless, many regulatory authorities use some measure of costs as the benchmark for evaluating prices of all sorts. These cost-based approaches have the advantage of appearing to be fair and are viewed as consistent with the move toward increasing competition in all segments of the telecommunications service market.

Price-based

An alternative to a cost-based approach is one that is price-based. One version of this system starts with the terminating carrier's existing prices, which may have had regulatory approval and therefore are considered as meeting some policy objective. The originating carrier then pays the terminating carrier a fee based on this price. The standard can be the retail price, a wholesale price that includes volume discounts, or, at least in one case that will be described later, some prescribed fraction of the retail price.

Bill and Keep

Both the cost-based and price-based approaches assume that originating carriers, trunk carriers, and terminating carriers in some way compensate each other, possibly on a per-call or per-minute basis. It is common practice to do the accounting in this fashion and to base the payments (monthly or quarterly, in many cases) on the net flow. But this is not the only way that the business arrangements between, or among, carriers might be arranged. An alternative is to do away with the payments to the terminating carriers. Under a bill-and-keep system, each local carrier charges its subscribers for the calls that they originate, and no fees are paid to the carrier of the receiving party. This works as described if there is a direct interconnection between the two local carriers, typically with the two carriers sharing the costs of the link. If a third-party trunk carrier is used, it is paid a fee for its role.

Private Negotiation

A final alternative is to have negotiated private agreements between carriers without regulatory oversight. This is seen as consistent with the completely unregulated, free entry approach to telecommunications in countries such as New Zealand and Sweden. The interconnection agreements may be based, for example, on expected traffic, or actual call volumes, and may or may not have fixed monthly and/or traffic-sensitive components. They are left to the carriers to negotiate among themselves, but it is possible to have an appeals process to deal with allegations of anticompetitive behavior such as a refusal to interconnect.

IMPLEMENTATION CONCERNS

Each of the pricing systems has several problems, and many practical and philosophical issues need to be resolved regardless of which system is used. It is precisely these details that lead to voluminous regulatory proceedings. In this section I highlight a few of the concerns.

Equal Treatment and Symmetry Requirements

Whose costs should be used as the standard? Possibilities include the incumbent with the major market share, and the most efficient firm with the latest technology. To illustrate one aspect of this problem, consider two large carriers sending traffic to each other. If they have different cost structures, the termination fees could be based on the actual costs of the receiving carrier, even if they might differ, one from the other. Or the fees could be based on the average cost or average price. If an average is employed, one has to decide whether to use the relative volumes of the traffic as weights in calculating the average or to use a simple unweighted average.

Another issue arises when two or more trunk carriers interconnect to the originating and terminating carriers using different technologies with different cost structures. These cost differences can occur when one trunk carrier has collocated with a local carrier, but, whether due to call volumes or choice of technology, another trunk carrier chooses to use a tandem office and an inter-office trunk. In this situation the per-unit costs may vary (and depend differently on the traffic levels), but it is not obvious whether a requirement of nondiscriminatory interconnection fees means that the fees should vary with or be independent of, the actual costs. (This analysis also applies to questions involving legacy customers, who might have preexisting contracts or may have made investments based on former interconnection regimes and, as a result, have different cost structures.)

Preferences for Corporate Relatives

The common ownership of a local carrier and a trunk carrier, for example, introduces complications in the enforcement of equal treatment or symmetry requirements. These are in addition to those discussed earlier that may be the result of differing technologies or legacy interconnection arrangements. While it is possible to have a regulatory or statutory requirement for equal treatment, it may be difficult or impossible to detect if such a requirement is being met when one set of "transactions" is between two parts of the same corporate entity. Among the solutions that have been tried are efforts to force the creation of wholly owned subsidiaries and the use of line-of-business accounting methods. The underlying problem is compounded by the fact that there may, in fact, be economies from internalizing some transactions, thus avoiding complex metering and billing.

UNIVERSAL SERVICE

In the past the payments from trunk carriers and mobile operators to the local fixed carrier for origination and termination on the fixed network have often been at levels that were above the costs of that origination and termination. In addition, the lack of competition for local service has frequently allowed pricing plans that have artificially low fixed monthly fees and correspondingly higher usage-sensitive prices. Competitive entry has had the twin effects of making the various components of interconnection fees more visible and putting pressure on those fees to become increasingly cost-based. These changes raise the question of how to finance universal service obligations in the future.

There are no single definition of "universal" and no agreement on specifically which services should fall under a universal service obligation. Among the possible "definitions" are the following loosely stated concepts:

- Single-party, basic, switched, residential telephone service should be available to all geographic regions of a country for a common, reasonable monthly fee.

- Income and wealth levels should not be significant barriers to all (or a certain per cent of all) households' being able to afford residential telephone service.

- Every village of a certain size should have at least one public telephone.

- All local telephone providers should be able to interconnect to the national telephone network at reasonable rates.

My use of words such as "reasonable" and "certain" should highlight the judgmental nature of the decisions that are required to develop standards for universal service. Furthermore, as competition and new technologies are introduced into the telecommunications network, questions arise concerning which services should be included and who should be charged with providing these services.

A common approach is to charge the incumbent or dominant (these are frequently the same, of course) fixed operator with meeting either the geographic or income/wealth service requirements and to have all carriers contribute to the costs associated with this policy. Funds that are collected for these purposes are known as access deficit contributions (in the U.K.), universal service funds, or other similar names.

If such an approach is used, the next question becomes how to generate the sums required. From an economist's perspective, the problem is that no matter what basis for the calculation is chosen, some distortion will be introduced. For example, a fee per call ignores the fact that calls of different types (voice, fax, data) and to different regions may systematically vary in length, a per-minute fee ignores the non-usage-sensitive network costs, and so on. This list is endless.

Another problem is that the incentives for the chosen provider of universal service to act efficiently are reduced as others cover its share of the costs. It is in the interests of the carrier to argue that the costs are high and that it can't do as much as the government expects or that more of its coverage costs should be picked up by the universal service funds or both. One possible solution to encourage efficiency is to put well-specified components of the universal service obligation up for bid; a variation of such a system is used in Chile.

A FEW EXAMPLES

In each of the following cases, I use stylized facts: a mix of very general descriptions and only part of the current situation and data selected to illustrate one or more specific points.

Mobile-to-Fixed, Fixed-to-Mobile, and Mobile-to-Mobile in Israel

Israel has three mobile operators, all with national coverage. The sequential nature of their licensing has led to a changing mix of interconnection arrangements. Pelephone, the first cellular carrier, is 50% owned by Bezeq, the state-owned former integrated post, telephone and telegraph (PTT) system and the only fixed domestic operator. When the second cellular operator, Cellcom, was first licensed, it was originally required to pay Bezeq 90% of its retail rates to complete calls to the fixed network. Cellcom and Pelephone were allowed to negotiate a private interconnection agreement, but the original arrangement was that all mobile-to-mobile calls had to be carried over the Bezeq network.

In June 1996 the interconnection agreement between Cellcom and Bezeq was replaced by a new agreement that was not distance-dependent so long as more than 70% of the mobile-to-fixed calls were terminated as local calls on the Bezeq network. (This was to encourage interconnection at switches close to the terminating parties.) The interconnection fee for fixed-to-mobile calls was based on the average price for a retail, outgoing, airtime minute. The reason for this was the big difference between the prices of incoming and outgoing calls, with the first operator basing the fee for an incoming call to its network on its highest retail price for outgoing calls.

The interconnection fees included peak and off-peak rates. In the event that the 70% local termination requirement for mobile-to-fixed traffic was not met, that portion of the traffic that was not terminated locally would have interconnections fees that were 25% greater than normal.

The tender for the third carrier, won by Partner, included a provision that its mobile-to-mobile interconnection fees would be symmetrical. The interconnection fee was set at the average price for outgoing airtime minutes.

Retail tariffs have varied systematically across the cellular operators, with Pelephone, the first operator, having the highest subscriber fees, along with the best coverage, although the differences have become smaller over time. As a result, at least in part, average usage also varies across the operators. (See Table 10.1.) Recently, the Ministry of Communications announced a policy of uniform, declining, mobile-to-mobile interconnection fees, forcing Pelephone to reduce its interconnection fees for incoming calls to its network. Pelephone said that it will challenge this in the courts. (See Table 10.2.) (Israel has been a calling-party-pays country since 1994.)

Table 10.1
Average Number of Monthly Usage Minutes, Israeli Mobile Operators

Operator	1995	1996	1997	1998	1999
Pelephone	530	430	320	300	295
Partner					427 (Q4)

Source: Israel Ministry of Communications (September 2000).

Table 10.2
Current and Proposed Incoming Interconnection Rates, Israeli Mobile Operators

Operator	11/2000	Proposed 2000	Operator 2001	11/2000 2002	Proposed 2003
Pelephone	0.17	0.13	0.12	0.11	0.10
Cellcom	0.12		0.12	0.11	0.10
Partner	0.13	0.13	0.12	0.11	0.10

Note: All rates are per-minute, given in U.S. dollars at US$1 = Israel NIS 4.16.

Source: GLOBES Arena (September 2000).

Free Entry and Negotiated Interconnection in Sweden

Although Sweden's telecommunications law allows free entry and has basically no rate regulation, there is a second statute covering the use of the radio frequencies that requires licensing to encourage efficient use of the spectrum. In practice these laws had resulted in Telia, the state-owned former PTT, being able to enter any market segment, including mobile services, where the number of licenses is restricted. Telia is also able to freely set tariffs; its fixed-to-mobile tariffs have calls to subscribers on Telia's mobile networks priced below calls to mobile users who subscribe to other carriers. (See Table 10.3.) The interconnection fee agreements are not public, but comparisons are probably meaningless, as the Telia-fixed-to-Telia-mobile fees, if any, are intracompany transfers at arbitrary rates. (Sweden is a calling-party-pays country.)

Table 10.3
Fixed-to-Fixed and Fixed-to-Mobile Tariffs, Telia of Sweden

Destination	Base Plan		Bonus Plan	
	Peak	Off-peak	Peak	Off-peak
Domestic fixed	0.023	0.012	0.021	0.011
To Telia mobile	0.275	0.153	0.250	0.138
To Other mobile	0.301	0.229	0.301	0.229

Note: All tariffs are for residential service, on a per-minute basis, and include tax, given in U.S. dollars at US$1 = Sweden Krona (SEK9.81).

Source: Source: http://www.telia.se/bvo/info (October 2000).

Entry of Competition for International Calls in Israel

Bezeq had a monopoly on both domestic and international service until 1997. The traffic imbalance on one route (U.S.–Israel) was sufficiently high that it generated approximately $100 million annually to Bezeq. (Coincidentally, this was approximately the same magnitude as its profits.) These inflows, combined with a domestic tariff structure with relatively low monthly fees and high distance-sensitive per-minute prices for inland calls, encouraged widespread penetration of telephone service (approximately 50 lines per 100 population) but also led to extensive use of callback services. (There is no domestic long-distance as such, and Israel has just moved away from using a pulse system for pricing inland calls.)

The licensing of two new entrants as international carriers was accompanied by the institution of proportionate return and domestic termination fees of approximately $0.008 per minute (8/10ths of a cent). (The current fees are shown in Table 10.4.)

Table 10.4
Bezeq's Interconnection Rates

Time of day	Termination			Origination
	Local	Urban Toll	National	Toll
Peak	1.4	-	2.9	1.5
Intermediate	0.9	-	0.9	0.9
Off-peak	0.6	-	0.6	0.6
European Union Benchmarks	0.7-1	1-2	1.7-3	

Note: All rates are per-minute, given in U.S. cents at US$1 = Israel NIS 4.16

Source: Israel Ministry of Communications (September 2000).

In addition, the new entrants were required to pay an access deficit contribution to Bezeq to help maintain and expand its universal service obligation. The ministry and its advisers set the level of the contribution to be an amount based on the new entrants' expected share of the international market in the first year. They further decided that the contribution would decline to zero over a five-year period, and the annual levels were specified as part of the tender. An interesting footnote to this is that competition did lower international tariffs, outbound calling was stimulated, and the imbalance on the U.S. route disappeared after five months of competition. (Bezeq instituted some of the price drops before entry became a reality.) There has also been a rebalancing of Bezeq's domestic tariffs.

Calls to the Internet in the United States

The regulation of interconnection fees for calls between carriers within a LATA (local access and transport area—mostly single or adjacent metropolitan areas within a single state) is left to the state Public Utility Commissions. These fees vary across the states, with six of the states setting the fees at zero, essentially using a bill-and-keep approach. (This variation can be seen in Table 10.5.) With the growth of the Internet, some of the CLECs (competitive local exchange carriers, as opposed to incumbent local exchange carriers [ILECs]) have developed the business of serving ISPs (Internet service providers) in less-populated areas. This can be profitable because the telephone traffic to the ISPs is only in one direction, so there is an inherent imbalance between the ILEC who serves a wider, more populous area and the CLEC who serves the ISP. This imbalance results in significant payments from the ILECs to the CLECs and possibly helps keep prices to the ISPs low. The ILECs have asked many public utility commissions (PUCs) to review this issue and have supported a bill in Congress (H.R. 4442) to preempt the power of the states and eliminate termination fees on calls to the Internet.

Table 10.5
U.S. Intra- and Interstate Carrier Common Line Rates (CCLRs), 1990

State	1990
Highest (Texas)	0.0611
Median of those reporting CCLRs	0.0262
Lowest (South Dakota)	0.0121
Six states	0.0000
Interstate	0.0123

Source: Adapted from Vogelsang and Mitchell (1997).

Financing the Universal Service Organization (USO) and Rebalancing Domestic Tariffs in India

Currently, the margins on long-distance charges within India are used to cover the "access deficit" caused both by below-cost monthly fees for telephone service and by the costs of providing service to rural areas. The stated policy is to move to financing the universal service obligation by a levy based on a percentage of the revenues of all domestic operators (fixed, mobile, and cable). The policy is described in the New Telecom Policy of 1999:

> The government is committed to provide access to all people for basic telecom services at affordable and reasonable prices. The government seeks to achieve the following universal service objectives:
>
> • Provide voice and low speed data service to the balance of 2.9 lakh [290,000] uncovered villages in the country by the year 2002
>
> • Achieve Internet access to all district headquarters by the year 2000
>
> • Achieve telephone on demand in urban and rural areas by 2002
>
> The resources for meeting the USO would be raised through a universal access levy, which would be a percentage of the revenue earned by all the operators under various licenses. The percentage of revenue share toward universal access levy would be decided by the government in consultation with TRAI [Telecom Regulatory Authority of India]. The implementation of the USO obligation for rural/remote areas would be undertaken by all fixed service providers who shall be reimbursed from the funds from the universal access levy. Other service providers shall also be encouraged to participate in USO provision subject to technical feasibility and shall be reimbursed from the funds from the universal access levy.

TRAI, the regulator, has explicitly raised the issue of "whether interconnect charges [should] be also an instrument of subsidy to provide rural DELs [direct exchange lines] and low calling urban DELs as an alternative to the USF or complementary to it?" (*Consultation Paper*, p. 34.) The current fixed-service tariffs are rather complex; Table 10.6 presents a subset. Where multiple tariffs were available, I attempted to select those for the largest systems and for residential subscribers with the highest call volumes.

Table 10.6
Selected Residential Tariffs in India, 1999

	Urban	Rural
Registration	328.95	657.89
Installation	17.54	17.54
Monthly rentals	5.48	4.17
Per call charges		
<125 calls		0.00
126-225		0.01
226-250		0.02

Table 10.6 (continued)
Selected Residential Tariffs in India, 1999

	Urban	Rural
251-500		0.02
Above 500		0.03
<75	0.00	
76-200	0.02	
201-500	0.02	
Above 500	0.03	

Note: Given in U.S. dollars at US$1.00 = Rs. 45.6. Per-call charges are for the first three minutes.

Source: TRAI, as presented at http://www.DOTindia.com

Tariffs for trunk calls were reduced by 8% to 33% on October 1, 2000, and are calculated using a pulse measuring system. The tariffs include a classification system for call types, as shown in Table 10.7.

Table 10.7
Trunk Call Classes and Tariffs in India

Call Class	Tariff
Manual Standard	Rs. 5 plus tariff; one minute minimum
Urgent/Demand	Rs. 5 plus twice ordinary tariff
Lightning	Rs. 5 plus 8 times ordinary tariff

The interconnection fees on these calls are not available publicly. As the Israel case showed, it is common to see tariffs for trunk or international calls decline as competitive entry approaches.

CONCLUSION

The movement toward competition in telecommunications services has transformed the problem of setting interconnection fees and highlighted the linkage between those fees and the funding of universal service. Changes in one area affect the underlying economics of the other. One approach is to move interconnection fees toward becoming increasingly cost-based and to make the funding of universal service obligations more explicit. While it is important to get the prices "right," it is probably even more important to have the rules clear and fairly enforced.

BIBLIOGRAPHY

Frieden, Robert M. *International Telecommunications Handbook.* Artech House, 1996.

Hudson, Heather. "Universal Service in the Information Age" *Telecommunications Policy* 18 (1994): 658—667.

Johnson, Leland L. "Dealing with Monopoly in International Telephone Service: A U. S. Perspective." *Information Economics and Policy* 4 (1989/1991): 225—247.

Mitchell, Bridger M. and Ingo Vogelsang. *Telecommunications Pricing: Theory and Practice.* Cambridge University Press, 1991.

Mueller, Milton. "Universal Service in Telephone History: A Reconstruction." *Telecommunications Policy* 17, no. 5 (July 1993): 352—369.

――――. *Universal Service: Interconnection, Competition, and Monopoly in the Making of American Telecommunications.* AEI Series on Telecommunications Deregulation. MIT Press (1997).

――――. "Universal Service Policies as Wealth Redistribution," *Government Information Quarterly* 16, no. 4 (1999): 353—358.

Telecom Regulatory Authority of India. *Consultation Paper on Issues Relating to Universal Service Obligations.* Consultation Paper No. 2000/3, July 3, 2000.

U.S. Department of Commerce, National Telecommunications and Information Administration. *The NTIA Infrastructure Report: Telecommunications in the Age of Information.* NTIA Special Publication 91-26, 1991.

U.S. Federal Communications Commission, *Report and Order in the Matter of International Settlement Rates.* #97-280. Available at: http://www.fcc.gov/Bureaus/International/Orders/1997/fcc9728 0.html

――――. Common Carrier Bureau. "What Is Universal Service?" Available at: http://www.fcc.gov/ccb/universal_service/welcome.html

Valletti, Tommaso M. "Introduction: Symposium on Universal Service Obligation and Competition." *Information Economics and Policy* 12 (2000): 205s210. Available at: http://www.elsevier.nl/homepage/sae/econbase/iepol/menu.sht [The other papers in this special issue on universal service obligation and competition are all recommended.]

Vogelsang, Ingo and Bridger M. Mitchell. *Telecommunications Competition: The Last Ten Miles.* AEI Series on Telecommunications Deregulation. MIT Press, 1997.

Chapter 11

Universal Service in Densely Populated Developing Countries

Farid Gasmi, Jean-Jacques Laffont, and William W. Sharkey

The issue of the provision of universal service in a context of generalized liberalization of the telecommunications sector is the object of intense political and economic debates. Telecommunications has traditionally been supplied in a monopoly environment, and universal service has been funded by cross-subsidies running from urban to rural areas. While these subsidies have played a major historical role in the development of telecommunications networks, they are now threatened by the introduction of competition. Our study recognizes this threat but seeks to investigate conditions under which cross-subsidies may still prove to be a powerful tool for financing universal service under competition in developing countries, particularly those, such as India, that have densely populated rural areas.

A proper evaluation of any regulatory regime must take account of the asymmetry of information between telecommunications firms and/or competition (antitrust) authorities. Instances where the regulated firm (the agent) has information not available to the regulator (the principal) constitute the rule rather than the exception. This is most certainly the case in telecommunications, where the provision of increasingly sophisticated services, at an impressive pace, is made possible by a rapid technological progress. The availability of advanced technology allows incumbent firms to engage in vast programs of upgrading and modernization of their existing networks and also allows new entrants to invest in new facilities. In the investigation of precisely how the introduction of these new technologies affects costs, firms have a clear information advantage. Hence, under regulation, incumbent firms are able to extract informational rents on the basis of this advantage (by imitating firms of lesser efficiency). In the face of these dynamics, the regulator, being chiefly concerned with the best possible allocation of resources, should carefully account for these informational asymmetries while regulating the activities of incumbent firms and simultaneously consider policies that may encourage (efficient) entry and allow for eventual deregulation.

Regulatory authorities in developed countries are presently evaluating various policies that seek to maintain some form of universal service program, while simultaneously achieving the benefits of competitive entry into telecommunications markets. In both the United States and the United Kingdom, the regulatory agencies, the Federal Communications Commission (FCC) and the Office of Telecommunications (Oftel), respectively, have considered auctions as a means to allocate universal service funds to carriers.

While auctions represent a very attractive, market-based mechanism for determining the support needed to compensate telecommunications operators in high-cost service areas, serious technical difficulties in the design of these auctions have prevented a working scheme from being implemented.[1]

An alternative regulatory mechanism that has been pursued with more success is the use of engineering process models that allow computation of the (minimum forward-looking) cost of providing service. In the United States, these models rely on costing methods referred to as total element long-run incremental cost (TELRAIC), which is the practical counterpart of marginal cost (strictly speaking, average incremental cost) in a context of multiproduct firms producing with lumpy capital.

This chapter explicitly recognizes the existence of asymmetric information in the empirical analysis of the financing of universal service for telecommunications markets. We rely on a cost proxy model of the type described earlier to estimate a cost function, and we identify within the model elements that we use to model the incomplete information. This allows us to combine the model with the tools of modern regulatory economics in order to empirically analyze deregulation of the local telecommunications markets. We discuss the basic features of the theoretical framework that underlies our analysis and then present in a more formal way the specific theoretical alternatives that we use to analyze the issue of the financing of universal service, describe in some detail the empirical methodology, present the empirical results, and give some concluding remarks.

THEORY

Economic theory of regulation stresses the role of asymmetric information in the analysis of the regulator–regulated firm relationship.[2] In a framework where the regulator behaves as a (Stackelberg) leader, an important consequence of this asymmetry is that he must recognize the need to give up a rent to the firm (which has superior information) in order to provide it with (social welfare-enhancing) incentives to minimize costs. This is the fundamental rent-efficiency trade-off that regulators need to deal with when regulating public utilities. In this section, we present the basic ingredients of a conceptual framework of this regulator–regulated firm relationship and than proceed to describe how we use this framework to analyze the issue of the financing of universal service.

Supply is characterized by a cost function that gives the total cost of producing various levels of output. This technology is, however, better known by the firm than the regulating authority. The regulated firm may possess knowledge about a technological parameter, such as marginal cost, that is unavailable to the regulator. Further, the firm may invest in some cost-reducing activity, such as effort, to efficiently use production resources that the regulator cannot observe. In the former case the information problem concerns an exogenous variable (this leads to a so-called adverse selection situation), whereas in the latter case the information problem concerns an endogenous variable (this is a moral hazard situation). Hence, total cost of production is a function of these two variables as well.

The impact of production on consumers is modeled by specifying demand and associated gross consumer surplus. Assuming the firm's total costs are observable ex post, one can use (without loss of generality) the accounting convention that the regulator collects the firm's revenues, reimburses its production costs, and gives it a net transfer. The utility or the "rent" of the firm, which is assumed to value income and effort only, is then equal to the difference between this transfer and the "cost" to the firm of exerting effort (i.e., the disutility of effort). One of the main messages of the new regulatory economics is that, even though it is costly to society, because of asymmetric information and for efficiency reasons, this informational rent is strictly positive for all but the least efficient firm.

Let us now describe formally the way we apply this general framework to the specific situation that we analyze in this chapter.[3] We consider a territory composed of two distinct areas, an urban area (area 1) and a rural area (area 2), with N_1 and N_2 local telephone subscribers. For area $i = 1,2$, we denote by q_i, P_i (q_i) and S_i (q_i), respectively, output (usage), the inverse demand function, and the associated gross consumer surplus.[4]

Our first objective is to examine the relative technological efficiencies associated with two alternative entry scenarios. The first scenario is an urban-targeted entry scenario labeled *UT* in which entry, targeted toward the urban area only, leads to a split of the urban market in half between the entrant and the incumbent. The incumbent serves the entire rural area. The second scenario is a territory-constrained entry scenario labeled *TC* in which entry takes place in both the urban and rural areas, leading to an equal division of both markets between the two firms. We initially examine these two scenarios by imposing (socially efficient) marginal-cost pricing (*mc*) and financing, with public subsidies (*ps*), the implied deficit in each case.[5]

The cost function of an integrated monopolistic firm serving the whole territory is written:

$$C = C(\beta, e, q_1, q_2, ;N_1, N_2) \tag{1}$$

In Equation (1), β is a technological efficiency parameter assumed to belong to an interval [$\underline{\beta}$, $\bar{\beta}$], and *e* represents an endogenous efficiency parameter (the firm's effort), which may take any nonnegative value.[6] The value of β is private information to the firm, but the regulator knows the distribution function $F(\beta)$ and its density $f(\beta)$. An increase in the effort variable, *e*, decreases observable cost, *C*, but also imposes a cost on the firm's manager and workers, which we denote by the disutility of effort function $\psi(e)$. The level of effort carried out depends upon the regulatory mechanism implemented and the state of competition in the market.

Under *UT* duopoly, the cost function of the incumbent (firm 1) that serves half of the urban area and the entire rural area is:

$$C_1^{UT}(\beta, e_1, q_{11}, q_2) \equiv C(\beta, e_1, q_{11}, q_2; \frac{N_1}{2}, N_2) \tag{2}$$

where e_1 is the incumbent's effort and q_{11} is the incumbent's output in the urban area. The cost function of the entrant (firm 2) under this scenario is:

$$C_2^{UT}(\beta, e_2, q_{12}) \equiv C(\beta, e_2, q_{12}, 0; \frac{N_1}{2}, 0) \tag{3}$$

where e_2 is the entrant's effort and q_{12} is its output.[7]

Under *TC* duopoly the cost function of both the incumbent and the entrant ($j = 1,2$) is:

$$C_j^{TC}(\beta, e_j, q_{1j}, q_{2j}) \equiv C(\beta, e_j, q_{1j}, q_{2j}; \frac{N_1}{2}, \frac{N_2}{2}) \tag{4}$$

where q_{1j} and q_{2j} represent firm *j*'s output in the urban and rural area, respectively. Figure 11.1 illustrates the generic competitive market structures that are the focus of our analysis.[8]

Figure 11.1
Generic Market Structures

Monopoly

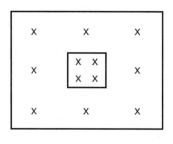

UT entry scenario
(destroys cross-subsidies)

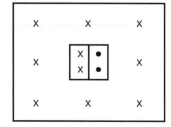

TC entry scenario
(allows some competition while preserving
cross-subsidies)

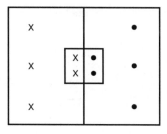

X - customers served by incumbent
• - customers served by entrant

We first consider a benchmark case in which the regulator has complete information, and there is marginal-cost pricing supplemented by public subsidies under the two types of duopoly markets discussed earlier. Scenario UT^{ps}_{mc} features (regulated) competition targeted toward the urban sector in which we assumed that an entrant captures half of the market, and the incumbent matches the entrant's price at marginal cost. Accordingly, the incumbent serves the other half as well as the whole rural area. Our benchmark hypothesis of complete information allows the regulator to impose optimal effort levels on both the incumbent (e_1*) and the entrant (e_2*).[9] Those firms solve, respectively, the first-order conditions, which require that marginal disutility of effort for each firm is equal to marginal benefit for cost-reducing activities and that prices are equal to marginal cost. These conditions are represented in Equations (5) to (8) where C_1^{UI} and C_2^{UI} are the cost functions of the incumbent and the entrant defined in (2) and (3), respectively.

$$\psi'(e_1) = -\frac{\partial C_1^{UT}}{\partial e_1}(\beta, e_1, q_{11}, q_2) \tag{5}$$

$$\psi'(e_2) = -\frac{\partial C_2^{UT}}{\partial e_2}(\beta, e_2, q_{12}) \tag{6}$$

$$p_1 = \frac{\partial C_2^{UT}}{\partial q_{12}}(\beta, e_2^*, q_{12}) \tag{7}$$

$$p_2 = \frac{\partial C_1^{UT}}{\partial q_2}(\beta, e_1^*, q_{11}, q_2) \tag{8}$$

Under our accounting convention, marginal-cost pricing creates an aggregate (financial) deficit, to be funded through public funds, given by:

$$D^{UT\,\frac{ps}{mc}} = C_1^{UT}(\beta, e_1^*, q_1, q_2) + C_2^{UT}(\beta, e_2^*, q_1) - N_1 p_1 q_1 - N_2 p_2 q_2 \tag{9}$$

where we make use of the fact that $q_{11} = q_{12} \equiv q_1$. Social welfare to be maximized with respect to q_1 ad q_2 is then given by:

$$SW^{UT\,\frac{ps}{mc}} = N_1 S_1(q_1) + N_2 S_2(q_2) - C_1^{UT}(\beta, e_1^*, q_1, q_2) - C_2^{UT}(\beta, e_2^*, q_1)$$
$$- \psi(e_1^*) - \psi(e_2^*) - \lambda[D^{UT\,\frac{ps}{mc}} + \psi(e_1^*) + \psi(e_2^*)] \tag{10}$$

The parameter λ, which represents the social cost of public funds, is generally assumed to range from a value of 0.3 in the most developed countries to 1 or higher in less developed countries (LDCs).[10]

In scenario TC^{ps}_{mc} , entry occurs in both the urban and the rural zones. Again, complete information allows the regulator to impose the (same) optimal level of effort on each firm, e_j**, which solves:

$$\psi'(e_j) = -\frac{\partial C^{TC}_j}{\partial e_j}(\beta, e_j, q_{1j}, q_{2j}) \tag{11}$$

where C^{TC}_j is the incumbent's (and the entrant's) cost function defined in (4). Marginal-cost pricing in both urban and rural areas amounts to:

$$p_1 = \frac{\partial C^{TC}_j}{\partial q_{1j}}(\beta, e_j^{**}, q_{1j}, q_{2j}) \tag{12}$$

$$p_2 = \frac{\partial C^{TC}_j}{\partial q_{2j}}(\beta, e_j^{**}, q_{1j}, q_{2j}) \tag{13}$$

and this leads to an aggregate deficit given by:

$$D^{TC\,^{ps}_{mc}} = 2C^{TC}(\beta, e**, q_{1,}q_2) - N_1 p_1 q_1 - N_2 p_2 q_2 \tag{14}$$

where, because of the symmetry of the problem, we make use of the fact that:

$e_1** = e_2** \equiv e**$, $q_{11} = q_{12} \equiv q_1$, $q_{21} = q_{22} \equiv q_2$ and $C_1^{TC} = C_2^{TC} \equiv C^{TC}$

Social welfare to be maximized with respect to q_1 and q_2 in this case is then given by:

$$SW^{TC\,^{ps}_{mc}} = N_1 S_1(q_1) + N_2 S_2(q_2) - 2C^{TC}(\beta, e**, q_{1,}q_2) \\ - 2\psi(e**) - \lambda[D^{TC\,^{ps}_{mc}} + 2\psi(e**)] \tag{15}$$

Let us now turn to competitive alternatives. Under competition, the regulator does not attempt to set either prices or effort levels. However, a profit-maximizing firm can be assumed to select a competitive price (we assume Bertrand competition) and for each price an optimal level of effort. The regulator's only role is to enforce a market segmentation according to the *UT* or *TC* scenarios. Firms must comply with the universal service obligation, that is, the obligation to provide service in (high-cost) rural areas at an affordable price, which we take here as meaning the same prices as in urban areas.[11] Second, we now impose a budget balance condition on the regulated firm and take account of the fact that public funds are a scarce resource.[12]

First, we examine once again the framework in which entry occurs in the urban sector only. Bertrand-like competition in the urban area is assumed to set the price of urban service at the average cost of the entrant who serves one-half of that market. If the incumbent matches this price in the urban area and serves the rural area at average (remaining) cost, then cross-subsidies going from the urban to the rural sector are, to a large extent, destroyed, and the incumbent cannot satisfy the universal service obligation.[13] One way to resolve this difficulty is to impose the urban price in the rural area and finance the subsequent incumbent's deficit through public subsidies. This is scenario UT^{ps}_{ac} which we derive next.[14]

Optimal output of the entrant in the urban sector (which is also that of the incumbent) q_1* maximizes:

$$\frac{N_1}{2} S_1(q_1) - C_2^{UT}(\beta, e_2*, q_1) \tag{16}$$

under the constraint:

$$\frac{N_1}{2} P_1(q_1) q_1 = C_2^{UT}(\beta, e_2^*, q_1) + \psi(e_2^*) \tag{17}$$

where e_2* is the entrant's optimal effort level that satisfies (6). This yields the optimal urban price p_1* which is matched by the incumbent. The (residual) rural cost function for the incumbent is:

$$C_1^{UT}(\beta, e_1*, q_1*, q_2) \, \psi(e_1*) - \frac{N_1}{2} p_1*q_1* \tag{18}$$

where e_1* is the incumbent's optimal level of effort that solves (5) and:

$$p_1* = S'_1(q_1*) \tag{19}$$

If the incumbent applies the same price in the urban and the rural areas, and its implied deficit is financed with public subsidies, then social welfare is given in this scenario by:

$$SW^{UT^{ps}_{ac}} = N_1 S_1(q_1^*) + N_2 S_2(q_2^*) - C_1^{UT}(\beta, e_1^*, q_1^*, q_2^*) - \psi(e_1^*)$$

$$- C_2^{UT}(\beta, e_2^*, q_i^*) - \psi(e_2^*) \tag{20}$$

$$- \lambda[C_1^{UT}(\beta, e_1^*, q_i^*, q_2^*) + \psi(e_1^*) - \frac{N_1}{2} p_1^* q_1^* - N_2 p_1^* q_2^*]$$

where q_2^* is determined by:

$$p_1^* = S'_2(q_2^*) \tag{21}$$

An alternative view of competitive entry with balanced-budget (as already seen in scenario TC^{ps}_{mc} earlier) would be to assume that the whole territory is divided in half. In this scenario, labeled TC_{ac}, social welfare is given by:

$$SW^{TC_{ac}} = \max_{q_1, q_2} \left\{ N_1 S_1(q_1) + N_2 S_2(q_2) - 2[C^{TC}(\beta, e^{**}, q_1, q_2) + \psi(e^{**})] \right\} \tag{22}$$

s.t.

$$P_1(q_1)N_1 q_1 = P_2(q_2) N_2 q_2 = 2[C^{TC}(\beta, e^{**}, q_1, q_2) + \psi(e^{**})] \tag{23}$$

and

$$P_1(q_1) = P_2(q_2) \tag{24}$$

where the cost function C^{TC} is the one that is defined in (4) and e^{**} satisfies (11).

Both of the preceding (competitive) scenarios satisfy the universal service obligation (i.e., uniform pricing across the urban and rural areas). However, while TC_{ac} uses urban-to-rural cross-subsidies, UT^{ps}_{mc} relies on public subsidies to finance universal service. Clearly then, the relative attractiveness of these scenarios depends upon the cost of public funds λ applicable to UT^{ps}_{mc}, in relation with the distortions created by the cross-subsidies in TC_{ac}. This issue is addressed in our empirical analysis.

Still another way to finance universal service is by using explicit taxes or surcharges.[15] In fact, since it imposes average-cost pricing, TC_{ac} may be interpreted as a scenario that imposes a particular (implicit) tax on the low-cost urban subscribers through price-averaging. Moreover, one can also rely on explicit taxes applied to the urban sector in a *UT*-type entry scenario to finance universal service, that is, to cover the incumbent's deficit from using uniform pricing over the whole territory. Let us succinctly describe the main features of such a scenario, which we label UT_{ac}^{τ} .

Let τ designate the tax rate applied in the urban sector. Note that since the incumbent has to match the entrant's price in the urban area and apply that same price in the rural area, we have $q_{11} = q_{12} \equiv q_1$ and $P_1(q_1) = P_2(q_2)$. Furthermore, assuming that P_1 represents the after-tax price (which is then applied across the whole territory), the firms per unit revenue in the urban and rural markets is given by $P_1/(1+\tau)$. This yields the following budget balance constraint for the entrant:

$$\frac{\frac{N_1}{2} P_1(q_1)q_1}{1+\Gamma} = C_2^{UT} (\beta, e_2^*, q_1) + \psi(e_2^*) \tag{25}$$

where e_2^* is the entrant's optimal effort which satisfies (6). Now, assume that only a fraction δ of the tax revenues collected from the urban subscribers is kept within the system, or, equivalently, that a fraction $(1-\delta)$ is driven out of the system for private motives (through corruption or waste). Then, the incumbent's budget balance condition (which requires that the incumbent's revenues from telephone service provision in half of the urban area and the whole rural area augmented by the tax revenues collected from the urban population be equal to the incumbent's total cost) is given by:

$$\delta \left(\frac{\Gamma}{1+\Gamma}\right) P_1(q_1)q_1 N_1 + \frac{\frac{N_1}{2} P_1(q_1)q_1}{1+\Gamma} + \frac{N_2 P_2(q_2)q_2}{1+\Gamma} = C_1^{UT} (\beta, e_1^*, q_{1,} q_2) + \psi(e_1^*) \tag{26}$$

where e_1^* is the incumbent's optimal effort level, which satisfies (5), and q_2 is its output in the rural area. Comparing the levels of social welfare achieved under this scenario $SW^{UT_{ac}^{\tau}}$ with SW^{TCac} gives us some indication on the relative importance of the distortions associated with implicit (TC_{ac}) and explicit (UT_{ac}^{τ}) taxation, accounting for the fact that in the latter case tax money is vulnerable to corruption.

The final step of the analysis consists in taking account of the p with respect to the firms' technologies. There are various ways to introduce competition in the context of asymmetric information. In order to make the most favorable case for competitive entry into the urban sector only, we assume that the entrant has the most efficient technology, corresponding to β, and that the incumbent is regulated as in scenario UT_{ac}^{ps} , that is, still with complete information. This scenario will be designated by $\underline{UT}_{ac}^{ps}$ and social welfare achieved by $SW^{UT_{ac}^{ps}}$. We then compare this scenario with the optimal price cap (*PC*) with asymmetric information obtained when the whole territory is divided in half (scenario *TCPC* yielding social welfare SW^{TCPC}).[16] This allows us again to assess the value of cross-subsidies as a means of financing universal services when asymmetric information is taken into account.

EMPIRICAL METHODOLOGY

As the formal analysis of the previous section makes clear, a detailed specification of the cost function of a representative local exchange telecommunications firm is required for our empirical analysis. In order to calibrate the cost function for local exchange markets, we use a detailed engineering process model known as LECOM (local exchange cost optimization model), developed by Gabel and Kennet (1991). Our use of a cost proxy model, instead of a more traditional approach to empirical analysis, using econometric techniques with historical data, is part of a larger research project that is more fully reported in Gasmi, et al. (2001).[17]

By specifying appropriate input parameters, LECOM allows us to model the cost of a representative local telephone company, which serves a central business district, a medium-density district, and a residential district (see Figure 11.1). Our analysis of entry, however, also requires a method of accounting for the costs of traffic that originates on one network and terminates on a different network. We rely on our cost proxy model to estimate these interconnection costs.

Consider the case of a duopoly equilibrium where each firm supplies service to the subscribers of one-half of the whole territory, as in the case of a *TC*-type entry scenario. Figure 11.2a, illustrates a stylized representation of a LECOM simulation for a representative duopolist. The relevant costs include the cost of access lines that connect each subscriber to a local switch, as well as the cost of the switching and interoffice transport capacity necessary to provide the assumed level of usage demand among all subscribers in the duopolist's network. Figure 11.2b, illustrates the network that the duopolists would construct assuming that each operator carried only the traffic that both originates and terminates on its own network. In order to approximate the increase in switching and interoffice transport capacity that would be required to carry internetwork traffic, we treat the combined network as if it were a monopoly and run a constrained LECOM simulation of the resulting costs. More specifically, we take the exact set of switched locations and levels of network investment that LECOM produces for the duopoly firms in isolation and perform a new simulation to compute total network cost, assuming that the monopoly network is constrained to use the duopoly investments. The resulting network is illustrated in Figure 11.2c.

Figure 11.2
Interconnection Costs

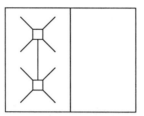

(a) Optimal network for one firm assuming
targeted entry.

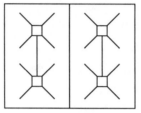

(b) Optimal network for both firms ignoring
interconnection costs.

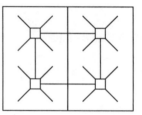

(c) A monopoly network (based on douopolists' switch locations)
that includes all appropriate switching and transport costs.

As a final step in the analysis, we take the ratio of both switch and interoffice transport traffic costs in the constrained monopoly scenario to the unconstrained duopoly case. This exercise allows us to compute a multiplier for both switching and transport that can be used to proxy the true cost of interconnection. We find that switching costs are higher by a negligible amount (approximately 1%) and that transport costs are higher by 12% under the constrained monopoly scenario than under duopoly. Assuming that these cost gaps can, for the most part, be attributed to internetwork connection, we adjusted the data from LECOM for the isolated duopoly by multiplying switching costs by 1.01 and transport costs by 1.12 for each simulation. Then we used these data to obtain a translog representation of a duopolistic cost function that accounts for interconnection costs. A similar exercise was performed to adjust for interconnection costs under a *UT*-type entry scenario. We found a multiplier of 1.01 for switching costs and 1.13 for transport cost.

We use LECOM to simulate each of the cost functions, which are implied by one of our scenarios. As a measure of output, we use traffic volume, expressed in units of hundreds of call seconds, common channel signalling system (CCS7).[18] LECOM allows for the dependent specification of demands for access, switch local and toll usage, and local and toll private line services. In order to keep the analysis and the number of simulations within tractable limits, however, we hold the number of subscribers fixed, and we constrain the other outputs to vary proportionally with our measure of traffic volume, which is measured on a per-line basis.

As a measure of technological efficiency, β, we use a multiplicative shift term for the price of capital, which is one of the user-supplied inputs for LECOM. The effect of this multiplier is to scale the cost of those inputs that are sensitive to the cost of capital in a linear manner. In a similar manner, we use a multiplier for the price of labor as a measure of the effect of managerial effort on total cost. In this interpretation, an increase in "effort" leads to a reduction in the price of labor, which we interpret as an increase in the efficiency units of labor associated with a given size of workforce. The underlying assumption is that effort is primarily directed toward efficiently utilizing labor inputs.

Our (generic) LECOM cost function is therefore defined in terms of three independent variables: outputs, technology, and effort. Holding all other LECOM inputs fixed, we are able to simulate the cost functions by repeatedly running LECOM for a range of plausible values of the arguments of interest. By appropriately specifying internal LECOM parameters to reflect each of our assumed market structures, we are able to generate different cost data sets that we use to estimate a cost function appropriate to each entry scenario.

In order to evaluate social welfare, we must specify both the inverse demand functions and the cost of public funds λ. We use the exponential form that has been widely used in empirical studies of local telecommunications markets (see Taylor, 1994) for the demand functions. We calibrate this functional form for both urban and rural customers, taking account of the substantially lower income per household that we assume prevails in the rural sector. As to the cost of public funds, we consider values that range from below 0.3, which is taken to reflect the relative efficiency of taxation systems in the most advanced economies, to high values above 1.0, which correspond to the much less efficient taxation systems in developing countries.

Clearly, much less is known about the disutility of effort function ψ than about consumer demand, since this function is, by definition, unobservable. Nevertheless, it is possible to assume a functional form that is consistent with theory, that is, increasing and convex. We calibrate a disutility of effort function of a specific quadratic functional form. The pair of parameters associated with this quadratic disutility is found by relying on two assumptions. First, under cost-plus regulations, the marginal disutility of effort is equal to zero. Second, under deregulation, the marginal disutility of effort is equal to marginal cost-saving.[19]

EMPIRICAL RESULTS

Before presenting the results for the financing of universal service in the case of countries with densely populated rural areas, which is the case of interest in this chapter, we summarize the results of our previous study in which we assumed a rural area with low density (Gasmi, Laffont, and Sharkey, 2001). Throughout our study we have assumed that universal service technically amounts to imposing uniform pricing across the urban and rural areas despite the difference in the cost of serving a typical customer in those two areas. This rules out, therefore, any price discrimination based on cost of service. This uniform pricing constraint creates, one way or another, economic distortions the extent of which depends upon the unit cost of making the transfers necessary to offset those distortions. Comparing social welfare achieved under the various scenarios allows us to obtain some estimates of the magnitude of these distortions.

An analysis of the performance of the UT and TC scenarios in an economic, distortion-free environment provides us with useful information on the relative attractiveness of these two industry organizations on the basis of technological efficiency only. This was the purpose of the preliminary exercise performed in which we compared the marginal cost pricing scenarios UT^{ps}_{mc} and TC^{ps}_{mc}. From the full standpoint of technological efficiency, we found that these two scenarios were quite close, with the urban-targeted scenario slightly dominating for larger values of the cost of public funds λ. Then, we imposed performance of scenario UT^{ps}_{ac} (funding of universal service organization [USO] through urban to rural cross-subsidies or equivalently through implicit taxation of the urban sector) which turned out to show that the distortions associated with the TC solution are rather small, corresponding to a shadow cost of public funds in the 0.1 to 0.2 range. In other words, since the TC scenario does not rely on public subsidies and is, therefore, not sensitive to the cost of public funds, we found that this scenario dominates the UT scenario whenever λ is greater than (approximately) 0.15. This implicit cost of public funds reflects the deadweight loss created by explicit taxation of the urban sector in an urban-targeted framework (UT^{T}_{ac}), which uses all of the tax revenues to finance the USO.

A comparison of scenario $\underline{UT}^{ps}_{ac}$ (an improved version of UT^{ps}_{ac} in which the entrant is the most efficient firm in our grid) with scenario $TCPC$ (which allows for cross-subsidies, or implicit taxation of the urban sector, under price cap regulation) yields a shadow cost of the distortions created by the TC solutions in the 0.3 to 0.4 range. While, under complete information, the distortions associated with the cross-subsidies in the TC solution turned out to be small, socially costly informational rents increase them quite a bit (from the 0.1 to 0.2 range to the 0.3 to 0.4 range) and hence made this solution noticeably less attractive than explicit taxation of the urban sector. However, we found that, when a fraction of the tax revenues close to 20% is taken out of the USO financing system, the TC solution becomes desirable. More specifically, under a regime with this level of waste (or corruption), the TC scenario was again superior to the UT scenario in spite of the informational rents associated with price-cap regulation and the assumed technological superiority of the entrant.

While the results of our previous study have strong policy implications for developing countries, in that they show that cross-subsidies are useful for financing universal service, two important aspects of our design of the serving territory might not reflect the situation of many of these countries, namely, the structure of demand and the density in rural areas. Indeed, in many of these countries rural areas are regions that are very densely populated by low-income households.[20] In the remainder of this section, we present the results of an empirical experiment that attempts to account for this important feature of developing countries such as India.

In order to incorporate this key aspect of same developing countries, we used a higher rural density than in our previous exercise and calibrated demand for the urban and rural sectors with average elasticity equal to -0.2 and -0.6, respectively.[21] The higher rural elasticity corresponds to a lower level of disposable income, which is reflected in a willingness to pay approximately one-third that of the urban area at any level of consumption.[22]

Many of the qualitative results found in our previous analysis, in particular, the relative attractiveness of cross-subsidies for developing countries, remain valid in this new setting. In fact, the new results, clearly driven by the fact that the rural area is highly populated, strengthen even further the case for the use of cross-subsidies in developing countries. Our preliminary comparison of the two alternative scenarios from a purely efficiency point of view (i.e., when marginal-cost pricing is imposed over the whole territory, and public subsidies are used to cover the implied deficits), shows that the territory constrained scenario (*TC*) achieves a slightly higher level of social welfare than the urban-targeted scenario (*UT*) for any value of the cost of public funds (Figure 11.3).

Figure 11.3
***UT* versus *TC* under Marginal-Cost Pricing**

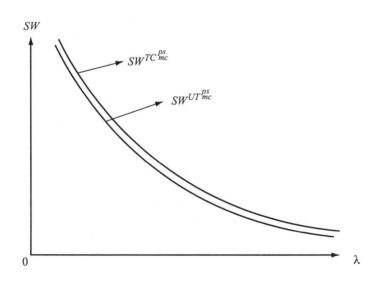

We next examine these two industry configurations when both the universal service obligation and the balanced-budget constraints are binding. To this purpose, we compare scenario UT^{ps}_{ac}, in which the incumbent has to match the entrant's average-cost price in the urban area and relies on public subsidies to cover its deficit from applying the same price in the rural area, to scenario TC_{ac} in which universal service is financed internally through cross-subsidies imposed on both the incumbent and the entrant by budget balance. We find that only for values of λ smaller than 0.05 is the UT-type scenario preferred to the TC-type scenario from a social welfare point of view (Figure 11.4). This very small value of the cost of public funds shows the superiority of the latter mode of organization of entry for developing countries with demographic characteristics such as India. In contrast to our previous results, cross-subsidization appears to be an efficient mechanism for funding universal service, even when the system of tax collection is extremely efficient.

Figure 11.4
***UT* versus *TC* under Average-Cost Pricing**

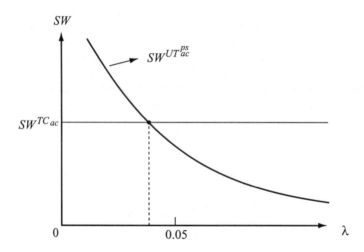

When introducing the social cost of asymmetric information within the TC framework by assuming that the incumbent is under price-cap regulation and allowing the entrant under UT framework to possess the most efficient technology, we make the best case for the latter organization of competition. Despite this, we find that the UT scenario is preferred only for values of λ less than 0.1 (Figure 11.5).

Finally, the introduction of taxation of the urban sector as a means of financing universal service leads to results that are even more favorable to cross-subsidies than in our previous study. Indeed, the task of subsidizing the highly populated rural sector by the urban sector is now so large that even if only a small fraction of the tax revenues (smaller than 10%) is taken out of the system, there is no viable solution that could use explicit taxation of the urban customers to fund universal service.

Figure 11.5
UT under Average-Cost Pricing versus TC under Price-Cap Regulation with Asymmetric Information

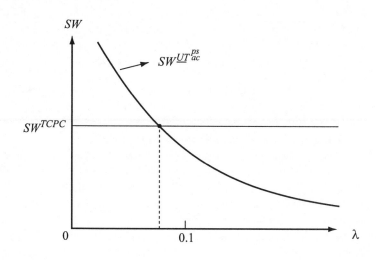

CONCLUSION

The main empirical finding of this chapter is that, even in the context of a generalized liberalization of the telecommunications sector, cross-subsidies may still be regarded as a valuable instrument for funding a universal service policy in developing countries, particular those with densely populated rural sectors. In the territory-constrained scenario that implements the cross-subsidies in our analysis, prices in both urban and rural markets are significantly higher than the corresponding prices in the urban-targeted scenario. The high price in the urban sector is used to generate internal funds within the firm, which allow for the subsidization of the high-cost rural sector. These prices are in excess of marginal cost, and they therefore introduce distortions away from the first-best marginal pricing outcome. Our analysis has revealed, however, that at least for the particular demand functions that we have assumed, these price distortions are less significant than the distortions associated with financing the assumed universal service obligation entirely with costly public funds, even when the shadow cost of raising public funds is extremely low. This result is driven, in large, part by the relative inelasticity of demand for telephone usage in the urban sector. Our previous analysis has confirmed that as the urban elasticity increases, the distortions associated with the territory-constrained scenario correspondingly increase, and so the urban-target scenario becomes more attractive for any given value of λ.[23] For developing countries with inefficient or corrupt taxation systems, however, cross-subsidies appear to remain a potentially valuable instrument for universal service policy for most plausible values of the elasticity.

Our methodology builds on a combination of an engineering process model of the local exchange network and the tools of modern industrial organization. Data scarcity and rapid industry dynamics in telecommunications lead us to use a flexible, state-of-the-art technology engineering process model, LECOM, in order to generate cost pseudo data that we use to fit flexible form cost functions. Furthermore, by appropriately specifying some internal parameters of this engineering process model, we customize the cost data sets to various market structures and proxy (asymmetric) information on the technology that regulators might not possess.

We have modeled deregulation through various entry scenarios and explicitly investigated the issue of providing service in the rural part of a territory composed of an urban and a rural area. We considered two prototype configurations of the industry: a scenario in which entry is targeted toward the profitable urban center, the urban-targeted (UT) entry model, and one in which an entrant is constrained to provide service in both the urban and the rural areas of the territory, the territory-constrained (TC) model. In both of these entry scenarios, the issue of the funding of universal service, taken as the provision of service over the whole territory, is raised.

Operating such a transfer is costly to society, and while in the UT framework the regulator relies on either funding from the national budget (at an explicit cost of public funds) or taxation of the urban telecommunications sector (at an implicit cost of public funds associated with the deadweight loss due to distortionary taxes), in the TC-type scenario this funding is allowed by urban-to-rural cross-subsidies (with yet a different form of implicit cost created by distorting away prices from cost).

The main empirical contribution of the analysis conducted in this chapter is to provide thresholds for the cost of public funds beyond which cross-subsidies constitute a powerful tool for financing universal service. The main policy implication of the results is that developing countries, in particular, those with densely populated rural areas, often satisfy those thresholds.

NOTES

We thank R. Dossani for useful comments on an earlier draft.

1.   On the difficulties in designing auctions for natural monopoly services generally, see Williamson (1976). Milgrom (1996) discussed many of the particular issues in universal service auctions.

2.   See Laffont and Tirole (1993).

3.   For additional details, see Gasmi et al. (2001), Chapter 8.

4.   Demand functions (where quantity is telephone use per subscriber) are defined on a per subscriber basis. Aggregate revenue and social welfare are determined by multiplying the per subscriber revenue and consumer surplus by the number of subscribers

in each market. In the case of duopoly, which will be the main focus of our analysis, q_{ij} will designate output of firm j in area i.

5.   Although the focus of this chapter is to compare the performance of alternative competitive scenarios, for clarity of exposition it is useful to start from a monopoly framework. At this point, the reader might find it useful to take a glance at Figure 11.1, which visualizes the generic market structure that we consider in the empirical analysis.

6.   Since, in our analysis, the urban and rural subscribers' populations N_1 and N_2 are held constant, they will be kept as arguments of the various cost functions considered only when necessary. We noted that this approach does not allow consideration of the issue of subscriber participation, since fixed fees for access to the network do not vary with our entry scenarios. This analysis, therefore, ignores the possible effect that usage-based prices have on the decision to subscribe to the network.

7.   Unless indicated otherwise, we assume that the entrant has the same technological efficiency parameter β as the incumbent.

8.   For reference, the top of Figure 11.1 shows a monopolistic situation.

9.   Optimal effort equates marginal disutility and marginal cost saving.

10.   In order to make transfers to the firm, the regulator needs to collect money from consumers through taxes. These taxes create distortions, the importance of which depends on the efficiency of the taxation system. For developed economies, empirical work (see Ballard, Shoven, and Whalley, 1985) has shown that each dollar collected through taxation cost society 30¢. Note that the cost of public funds is not to be compared with the nominal or real interest rate.

11.   This interpretation of universal service may be oversimplifying, to some extent, the policy initiatives in both developed and developing countries. For example, in the United States, universal service is currently interpreted as the right to purchase a set of services (voice grade plus access to advanced services) at a bench price that does not necessarily equal the price of the low-cost urban area. However, in many countries universal service entails uniform pricing.

12.   In this chapter, we designate by "balanced-budget" regulating a regulation that saturates the firm's participation constraint without transfers from the regulator. Such a participation constraint means that revenues must recover production cost as well as the disutility of effort.

13.   In fact, our empirical analysis shows that in this case the (residual) rural average cost function is consistently above the inverse demand function.

14.   The subscript "ac" indicates that average-cost pricing is used.

15.   Excise taxes on telecommunications services have been imposed in the United States at the federal level and by various state and local authorities. In the implementation of the 1996 Telecommunications Act, a universal service fund was funded through surcharges on revenues of all telecommunications carriers as defined in the act.

16. A simple description of price cap is as follows. Under this regulatory mechanism, the price (output) decision is decentralized. Hence, the main objective of the regulator under this type of regulation is production efficiency, which should be a consequence of the fact that the firm is the residual claimant of any cost reductions (hence, the firm chooses the optimal level of effort). In order to prevent the firm from exercising its monopoly power, the regulator sets a price ceiling $\bar{p}$. The firm may, however, choose

its monopoly price p^M if the ceiling turns out to be not binding. The regulatory mechanism seeks to determine the level of this cap that maximizes aggregate expected social welfare. For more technical details on this regulatory mechanism see Gasmi, Laffont, and Sharkey (1999).

17. See, in particular, Chapters 1 and 2 for a discussion of the advantages of the cost proxy model approach and a full description of LECOM.

18. The first C is the Roman numeral for 100. This measure gives, in hundreds of seconds, the time during which an average line is used per hour. Its relation to the standard engineering measure of traffic, the Erlang, is given by $Erlang = 36CCS$.

19. This calibration of the disutility of effort function has been used in our previous work (see Gasmi, Laffont, and Sharkey, 1997, 1998, 1999).

20. Note that this may be the case for some, but not necessarily all, developing countries. For instance, in some developing countries high-income households live in rural areas (e.g., in rich farms) or own secondary houses in those areas.

21. Our demand functions were calibrated so that these elasticities hold for the price-output combinations that generate revenue equal to the cost per subscriber as determined by the cost proxy model.

22. An examination of the urban and the rural inverse demand functions shows that the latter is consistently below the former for any output level in our simulations.

23. See, in particular, Gasmi et al. (2001, Table 8.3).

BIBLIOGRAPHY

Ballard, C., J. Shoven, and J. Whalley. 1985. "General Equilibrium Computations of the Marginal Welfare Costs of Taxes in the United States." *American Economic Review* 75: 128—138.

Gabel, D., and M. Kennet. 1991. "Estimating the Cost Structure of the Local Telephone Exchange Network." National Regulatory Research Institute Report N$7810, Institute for Policy Analysis, University of Toronto.

Gasmi, F., J.J. Laffont, and W. W. Sharkey. 1997. "Incentive Regulation and the Cost Structure of the Local Telephone Exchange Network." *Journal of Regulatory Economics* 12: 5—25.

———. 1998. "The Natural Monopoly Test Reconsidered: An Engineering Process-Based Approach to Empirical Analysis of Telecommunications," *International Journal of Industrial Organization*.

———. 1999. "Empirical Evaluation of Regulatory Regimes in Local Telecommunications Markets." *Journal of Economics and Management Strategy* 8(1): 61—93.

———. 2001. *Cost Proxy Models and Telecommunications Policy—A New Approach to Empirical Regulation.*

Laffont, J. J., and J. Tirole. 1993. *A Theory of Incentives in Procurement and Regulation.* Cambridge MA, MIT Press.

Milgrom, P. 1996. "Procuring Universal Services: Putting Auction Theory to Work." Lecture at the Royal Swedish Academy of Sciences, December 9.

Taylor, L. D. 1994. *Telecommunications Demand in Theory and Practice.* the Netherlands, Kluwer Academic.

Williamson, O. 1976. "Franchise Bidding for Natural Monopolies-in General and with Respect to CATV." *Bell Journal of Economics* 7: 73—104.

Chapter 12

Parvathagiri, Andhra Pradesh: A Rural Case Study

*Uday Kumar, Joseph Pernyeszi, E. Madanmohan Rao,
and P. Yadagiri*

As of 1999, there were four telecom connections per 1,000 people in rural areas of India (http://www.DOTindia.com, New Telecom Policy 1999 document). This compares with the government's target of 4% by 2010 (New Telecom Policy, 1999). With 75% of India's population living in approximately 600,000 villages (1991 census figures), improving rural telephone density is, therefore, an important policy goal. By September 1999, the Department of Telecommunications reported that 340,000 villages—or about 60% of the total—had telecom services, almost invariably as a single public telephone in each connected village (www.DOTindia.com).

This chapter presents the results of an undertaking between July and October 2000 in Parvathagiri mandal of Andhra Pradesh, done by the Rural Telecom Foundation.[1] The objective of this chapter is to use the Parvathagiri data to clarify issues in Indian policy on rural telecommunications. The chapter first presents data on the growth of cable television (TV) in Parvathagiri. These are used as benchmarks for the growth of telecommunications services in Parvathagiri. The chapter concludes with a discussion of needed policy changes; the argument is made that several simple changes in policy can rapidly increase rural teledensity in India. This is a contrast with the policymakers' view that rural telecommunications is the biggest challenge to policymakers in the sector driven by lack of affordability.[2]

CABLE TV IN PARVATHAGIRI MANDAL, ANDHRA PRADESH STATE

Pavathagiri Mandal[3] is in the Warangal District of Andhra Pradesh. Warangal District, an agricultural area close to the state capital, Hyderabad, is considered a backward area by the definitions of the Indian government. The district has over 1,000 villages grouped into 50 mandals.

Per the 1991 census, Warangal District had a population of 2.8 million, with around 80% of its population living in rural areas. The typical wage of agricultural labor was around Rs.40 per day, or around Rs.1,200 per month (US$1 = Rs.46.7, as of March 31, 2001). The literacy rate was 39% (http://www.andhrapradesh.com/).

Cable TV's wider spread relative to telephones in Parvathagiri may be seen from Table 12.1.

Table 12.1
Telephone and Cable TV Lines in Parvathagiri Mandal

Village Name	Telephone Lines	Cable TV Lines	Households	Population*
Vadlakonda	1	100	433	1,940
Ravoor	0	37	243	1,287
Burugamadla	2	52	376	1,827
Rollakal	3	10	353	1,764
Somaram	24	80	476	2,268
Kalleda	43	100	503	2,566
Parvathagiri**	242	649	1,433	6,775
Gopanapalle	0	80	424	1,925
Choutpalle	15	50	610	2,706
Konkapaka***	19	151	654	2,783
Enagal	1	175	1,125	5,295
Chinta-nekkonda	3	165	871	4,001
Annaram-sharif	0	126	509	2,494
Total	353	1,775	8,010	37,631

* 1991 census data.
** Parvathagiri village includes Daulatanagar hamlet.
*** Parvathagiri and Konkapaka villages have telephone exchanges with 318 and 35 access lines, respectively.

Source: Rural Telecom Foundation.

There are 34 cable operators and as many dish antennae, with 1,775 household connections in 13 villages and 5 hamlets. The twin villages of Parvathagiri and Kalleda account for 42% of the cable television connections. The investment required to start business varies from Rs.5,000 to Rs.35,000, and the cable providers' subscribers vary between 6 and 300. The providers are franchisees of large firms that supply channels over satellite.

The channels offered vary from a minimum of one to a maximum of four. The technology used is nonstandard and of low quality because the markets are small, and consumer awareness for quality is low. Most of the cable TV providers operate from their own residences.

Connections to tribal villages and their households account for 17% of the total cable TV connections, although scheduled castes and tribes make up 40% of the population of the mandal. In comparison, there is only one tribal telephone subscriber in the entire mandal.

Cable service providers charge Rs.50 per month per subscriber (there is no up-front fee) and supply 4 cable channels (in nearby Hyderabad city, a user would typically pay the same charge of Rs.50 per month and receive 40 channels). Providers surveyed generally consider the cable business to be growing.

The operators earn an income of Rs.1,200 per month on average. The total billed amount per month works out to Rs.88,750 from 1,775 connections at the rate of Rs.50 per subscriber. Collection is labor-intensive, and about 10% of the billed amount is uncollectable and is written off as bad debt. The collection of cable subscriber charges is not regular and follows the agricultural season.[4]

None of the 34 operators carry commercial advertisements or use scrolling on the screen to convey local information to villagers. However, they use an "audio-mode" channel to make public announcements such as due dates for the payment of electricity bills and meetings of Mythri Sangam, a police-to-community interface group.

RURAL TELECOM IN PARVATHAGIRI

Telephone services in the mandal are provided by Bharat Sanchar Nigam Ltd. (BSNL), a central government-owned company. Typically, BSNL lays a line to the village from the nearest town (Figure 12.1) and franchises an individual to operate a public call office (PCO). Some of the larger villages have private lines, but most have just (one or more) public call offices (refer to Table 12.1 and Figure 12.1).

As Table 12.1 shows, there is greater variation in teledensity in Parvathagiri than in cable TV. Part of the reason may lie in the high fixed costs of telecommunications access (consisting of an up-front registration fee) relative to the cost of cable access (the latter is zero). The high elasticity of telecommunications demand to fixed costs can be seen from responses to changes in fixed charges. In October 1999, the registration fee was reduced from Rs.1,000 to Rs.500 for the festival season. After the end of the festival season in November, the charge was raised back to its old rate. It was again reduced to Rs.500 in May 2000. As Table 12.2 shows, there was a strong response to the cut in fees (the implementation time of about two months between registration and connection explains the lag).

Figure 12.1
Rural Line Layout Strategy of the State-Owned Provider

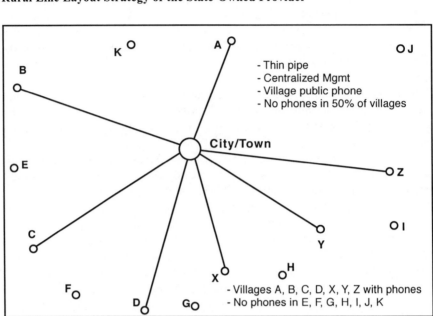

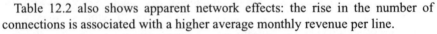

Table 12.2 also shows apparent network effects: the rise in the number of connections is associated with a higher average monthly revenue per line.

The survey done by the Rural Telecom Foundation is covered next.

Users Farther Away from the Central Switch Tend to Less Readily Receive Connections

The higher costs incurred by the DOT for more distant connections are probably the reason for this outcome. This may explain the almost total neglect of tribal residents in the mandal since they typically reside in small hamlets away from the village center.

Table 12.2
Monthly Revenue for Parvathagiri Exchange

Month	Individual Rev.(Rs)	Public Phone Rev. (Rs)*	Total Rev. (Rs)	Access Lines	Avg. Monthly Rev. per Line
Sep-99	28,070	0	28,070	146	192
Oct-99	28,070	0	28,070	146	192
Nov-99	24,450	0	24,450	146	167
Dec-99	24,450	0	24,450	146	167
Jan-00	25,500	0	25,500	180	142
Feb-00	25,500	0	25,500	180	142
Mar-00	25,400	0	25,400	180	141
Apr-00	25,400	3,730	29,130	180	162
May-00	47,130	15,777	62,907	222	283
Jun-00	47,130	22,101	69,231	222	312
Jul-00	56,230	16,406	72,636	293	248
Aug-00	56,230	15,537	71,767	293	245

* Revenue for public telephones after deducting commissions.

Source: Department of Telecommunications (DOT)

Spatial Analysis and Perceived Network Value

Villagers surveyed ranked their preferences for telecom service in descending order as: intervillage (within their cluster), village-to-district headquarters, intervillage (outside their cluster), and intravillage.

Figure 12.2 describes the perceived value of the telephone network as a function of distance for a resident of Parvathagiri village. The highest value, as noted, is placed on intervillage person-to-person communication. This intervillage traffic was observed to be equally for personal and business reasons. The value of the telephone call is best measured by its opportunity cost: the cost of either a walk or public transportation to the next village. The second highest value is observed to be for village-to-district headquarters traffic. In this case the telephone call could save commute costs and money lost in wages. The lowest value is observed to be intravillage traffic. In this case, the telephone call saves a small amount of time but is more of a convenience, and a replacement to walking to a person's house.

Figure 12.2a shows an approximate spatial map of Parvathagiri village (identified by the letter P), and Warangal town (identified by the letter W), which is the district headquarters. Small circles identify the villages and hamlets surrounding Parvathagiri village.

Figure 12.2
Spatial Telephone Network Value for Parvathagiri Mandal

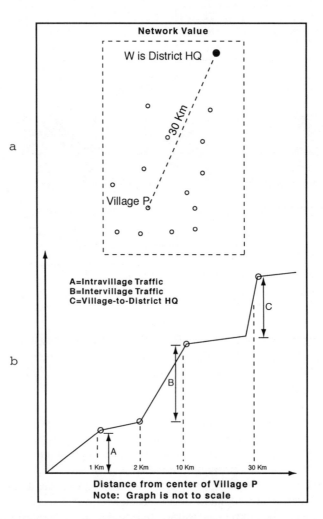

Figure 12.2b shows a hypothetical situation of changes in network value, if one locates a telephone switch at the center of Parvathagiri village and gradually begins to increase telephone coverage radially from the village center. The X-axis shows the radial distance from the center of Parvathagiri village, and on the Y-axis is the perceived telephone network value to the residents of Parvathagiri. There is a rise in network value from the zero to 1 kilometer radial distance because of the intravillage traffic. Between 1 kilometer and 2 kilometers there is a flattening out of network value reflecting the typical case that the nearest village is around 2 kilometers from the village center. Beyond 2 kilometers, intervillage traffic begins, and network value rapidly increases up to the cluster

(typically 10 kilometers). Beyond 10 kilometers, business and personal connections begin to fade, and the network value of intervillage traffic begins to flatten until it reaches the 30 kilometer point, the typical distance to the district headquarters. At the 30 kilometer point, the village-to-district headquarters traffic starts, and network value rises. Beyond the district headquarters, the value of the telephone network to a villager is very marginal.

Implementation of Universal Service Policy Is Inefficient

Universal access is defined for rural areas by the government as providing a public telephone in every village (National Telecom Policy, 1994). Its implementation is as shown in Figure 12.1. The policy envisions creating thin pipes of one to two lines from the nearest town going to a village. One of these lines is earmarked for a public telephone, and the other line usually goes to the most affluent or influential person in the village. The problem with this policy is that most residents have limited use for the public telephones because they cannot terminate intervillage person-to-person calls. For example, village H will get connected to the main city/town only when enough funds are allocated for this. Instead of this, a more efficient policy would be to create a higher-bandwidth connection from, say, X to the city, while connecting up G, X, and H in a cluster. This is shown in Figure 12.3.

Figure 12.3
An Efficient Network Layout

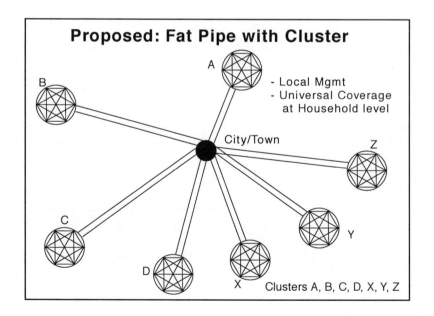

IMPLICATIONS FOR RURAL TELECOMMUNICATIONS POLICY

The preceding analysis suggests the following policy prescriptions. (1) Regulators should ask state-owned providers to concentrate on village-to-village connections, followed by village-to-headquarters (HQ) connections; this should replace the current policy of only village-to-HQ connections. Such a policy would increase revenues for the entire network. (2) There is substantial heterogeneity within villages and rural districts. This should be exploited by allowing wealthier users to access higher-quality services such as private lines, whereas poorer villages should access public lines. This is contrary to current policy, which does not distinguish among rural users and which has led to the current policy of providing only public call access in a village. (3) Private and stakeholder provision of services at different geographic levels should be seriously considered. As United States experience with cooperative and small firms shows, it is possible for small telecommunications companies serving limited geographic areas to be profitable where large ones may not be. See Table 12.3.

Table 12.3
Financial Information on Rural Telecommunications in Colorado State 1999

Average Number of Access Lines for the Telephone Companies/ Cooperatives*	1852
Average Gross Plant in Service per Access Line	$4,943
Average Annual Net Operating Revenue per Access Line	$1,450
Average Monthly Net Operating Revenue per Access Line	$121
Average Annual Total Operating Expenses per Access Line	$1,058
Average Monthly Total Operating Expenses per Access Line	$88
Average Annual Net Operating Income per Access Line	$82

* All Colorado wired-telephone companies excluding U.S. West/Qwest and Century Telephone of Eagle.

India has mostly had a bad experience with cooperatives due to political interference. Recent changes in Indian cooperative law in some states, such as the Andhra Pradesh Mutually Aided Societies Act, 1995, will help boost the long-term viability of cooperatives by giving them greater levels of autonomy. (4) Since a portion of a landowner's need for services is filled by cheap labor provided by tribals and other underprivileged segments, it may make sense to charge wealthier users an interconnection charge when they call poorer villages. The interconnection charge can then be used to subsidize poorer users within rural areas (see also Chapter 10 in this volume). (5) Calls to the nearest district headquarters should be at a reduced charge relative to a village of the same distance, given its greater value. (Current policy is based on a slab system, where rates depend on distance—see Chapter 4 in this volume.) (6) Private/stakeholder providers, if allowed, should be given flexibility to set prices. In this respect, stakeholder provision can save regulatory costs by allowing providers to set rates subject only to member approval. This will allow a provider to charge rates based on quality of service and costs. For example, daytime rates could be set higher than nighttime rates in order to encourage the use of bandwidth during the times when it is most available.

CONCLUSION

Indian telecommunications policy for universal access has been through three distinct phases, treating it first as a luxury good subject to heavy taxation (until 1984), then as an essential service offered through public call offices (until 1999), and, most recently, as a citizen's right, though unaffordable and, therefore, best delivered by subsidized, state-owned providers. This chapter has shown that, in the reformed environment, there can be rapid improvements in teledensity even in backward rural areas if simple policy changes are implemented. Chief among these are the allowance of stakeholder provision through cooperatives at the village level, pricing flexibility to allow quality and price to vary together, and the setting of interconnection charges to reflect differential ratios of incoming to outgoing calls. This will allow latent demand to be expressed through the development of cluster-based networks rather than the existing system of radial networks.

NOTES

1. Rural Telecom Foundation, a nonprofit organization that supports public policy for improving rural telecom access in India, funded the Telecom and Cable TV Survey in Parvathagiri Mandal. The foundation is also interested in creating new business and technology models and decentralized structures that are rapidly scalable and manageable at the village level.

2. Comment by DOT secretary Shyamal Ghosh at Stanford University India Telecom Conference, November 9–10, 2000.

3. A mandal is an administrative area comprising a cluster of about 20 villages. In Andhra Pradesh state of India, there are 23 districts (larger administrative areas), and within each district there are around 50 mandals (decentralized administrative areas).

4. The mandatory government license fee is invariably evaded; in return, all government officials and those who matter in the village are kept "in good humor" by giving them free connections.

BIBLIOGRAPHY

Bhatnagar, Subhash. Enhancing Telecom Access in Rural India: Some Options. Indian Institute of Management, Ahmedabad, August 2000.

Colorado Public Utilities Commission, Annual Reports of Telephone Companies.

Department of Telecommunications, National Telecom Policy, 1994. (http://www.DOTindia.com)

Department of Telecommunications, New Telecom Policy, 1999. (http://www.DOTindia.com)

Dossani, Rafiq. Rural Telephony: Rationale for a Focus on Local Service. Asia/Pacific Research Center, Stanford University. August 2000.

Garcia, D. Linda, and Neal R. Gorenflo. *The First Mile of Connectivity, Rural Networking Cooperatives: Lessons for International Development and Aid Strategies.* Washington, DC: Foundation for Rural Service

Henderson, Byron. Ensuring Rural and Remote Telecommunications Access: Technology, Community and History. Acrossworld Communications, August 2000.

Putnam, Robert D. "The Prosperous Community: Social Capital and Public Life," *The American Prospect,* no. 13 (Spring 1993).

Rural America, Connections to the Future: A Historical Perspective of Public Policy, Independent Telephone Companies and Universal Service by John N. Rose, President, Organization for the Promotion and Advancement of Small Telecommunications Companies (http://www.OPASTCO.org)

Appendix A: National Telecom Policy—1994

INTRODUCTION

(1) The new economic policy adopted by the government aims at improving India's competitiveness in the global market and rapid growth of exports. Another element of the new economic policy is attracting foreign direct investment and stimulating domestic investment. Telecommunications services of world class quality are necessary for the success of this policy. It is, therefore, necessary to give the highest priority to the development of telecom services in the country.

OBJECTIVES

(2) The objectives of the New Telecom Policy will be as follows:

    (a) The focus of the Telecom Policy shall be telecommunication for all and telecommunication within the reach of all. This means ensuring the availability of telephone on demand as early as possible.

    (b) Another objective will be to achieve universal service covering all villages as early as possible. What is meant by the expression universal service is the provision of access to all people for certain basic telecom services at affordable and reasonable prices.

    (c) The quality of telecom services should be of world standard. Removal of consumer complaints, dispute resolution and public interface will receive special attention. The objective will also be to provide widest permissible range of services to meet the customer's demand at reasonable prices.

    (d) Taking into account India's size and development, it is necessary to ensure that India emerges as a major manufacturing base and major exporter of telecom equipment.

    (e) The defence and security interests of the country will be protected.

PRESENT STATUS

(3) The present telephone density in India is about 0.8 per hundred persons as against the world average of 10 per hundred persons. It is also lower than that of many developing countries of Asia like China (1.7), Pakistan (2), Malaysia (13) etc. There are about 8 million lines with a waiting list of about 2.5 million. Nearly 1.4 lakh (1 lakh/lac = 100,000) villages, out of a total of 5,76,490 villages in the country, are covered by telephone services. There are more than 1 lakh public call offices in the urban areas.

REVISED TARGETS

(4) In view of the recent growth of the economy and the reassessed demand, it is necessary to revise the VIII Plan (1992—1997) targets as follows:

  (a) Telephone should be available on demand by 1997.

  (b) All villages should be covered by 1997.

  (c) In the urban areas a PCO [public call office] should be provided for every 500 persons by 1997.

  (d) All value-added services available internationally should be introduced in India to raise the telecom services in India to international standard well within the VIII Plan period, preferably by 1996.

RESOURCES FOR THE REVISED TARGETS

(5) The rapid acceleration of telecom services visualized above would require supplementing the resources allocated to this sector in the VIII plan. The total demand (working connections + waiting list) showed a rise of nearly 50% from 7.03 million on 1.4.1992 to 10.5 million on 1.4.1994 over a three year period. If the demand grows at the same rate for the next three years, it would touch about 15.8 million by 1.4.1997. The actual rate of growth is likely to be higher as the economy is expected to grow at a faster pace. Achieving the target of giving telephone on demand by 1997 would thus imply releasing about 10 million connections during the VIII Plan as against the existing target of 7.5 million. Release of 2.5 million additional lines alone would require extra resources to the tune of Rs. 11,750 crores (1 crore = 10 million) at a unit cost of Rs.47,000 per line at 1993–1994 prices. To this must be added the requirement on account of additional rural connections of Rs.4,000 crores.

(6) Even with the comparatively modest targets of the VIII Plan, as originally fixed, there is a resource gap of Rs.7,500 crores. The additional resources required to achieve the revised targets would be well over Rs.23,000 crores. Clearly this is beyond the capacity of government funding and internal generation of resources. Private investment and association of the private sector would be needed in a big way to bridge the resource gap. Private initiative would be used to complement the Departmental efforts to raise additional resources both through increased international generation and adopting innovative means like leasing, deferred payments, BOT, BLT, BTO (build, operate, transfer; build, lease, transfer; build, transfer, operate), etc.

HARDWARE

(7) With the objective of meeting the telecom needs of the country the sector of manufacture of telecom equipment has been progressively relicensed. Substantial capacity has already been created for the manufacture of the necessary hardware within the country. The capacity for manufacture of switching equipment, for example, exceeded 1.7 million lines/year in 1993 and is projected to exceed 3 million line/year by 1997. The capacity for manufacture of telephone instruments at 8.4 million units per year is far in excess of the existing or the projected demand. Manufacturing capacities for wireless terminal equipment, multi-access radio relay (MARR) for rural communication, optical fiber cables, underground cables etc. have also been established to take care of the requirements of the VIII Plan. With the revision of the targets demand would firm up and there would be an incentive to expand the capacities to meet the extra requirement.

VALUE-ADDED SERVICES

(8) In order to achieve standards comparable to the international facilities, the sub-sector of value-added services was opened up to private investment in July 1992 for the following services:

(a) Electronic Mail

(b) Voice Mail

(c) Data Services

(d) Audio Text Services

(e) Video Text Services

(f) Video Conferencing

(g) Radio Paging

(h) Cellular Mobile Telephone

(9) In respect of the first six of these services companies registered in India are permitted to operate under license on non-exclusive basis. This policy would be continued. In view of the constraints on the number of companies that can be allowed to operate in the area of Radio Paging and Cellular Mobile Telephone Service, however, a policy of selection is being followed in grant of licenses through a system of tendering. This policy will also be continued and the following criteria will be applied for selection:

(a) Track record of the company;

(b) Compatibility of the technology;

(c) Usefulness of the technology being offered for future development;

(d) Protection of national security interests;

(e) Ability to give the best quality of service to the consumer at the most competitive cost; and

(f) Attractiveness of the commercial terms to the Department of Telecommunications.

BASIC SERVICES

(10) With a view to supplement the effort of the Department of Telecommunications in providing telecommunication services to the people, companies registered in India will be allowed to participate in the expansion of the telecommunication network in the area of basic telephone services also. These companies will be required to maintain a balance in their coverage between urban and rural areas. Their conditions of operation will include agreed tariff and revenue sharing arrangements. Other terms applicable to such companies will be similar to those indicated above for value-added services.

PILOT PROJECTS

(11) Pilot projects will be encouraged directly by the government in order to access new technologies, new systems in both basic as well as value-added services.

TECHNOLOGY AND STRATEGIC ASPECTS

(12) Telecommunication is a vital infrastructure. It is also technology intensive. It is, therefore, necessary that the administration of the policy in the telecom sector is such that the inflow of technology is made easy and India does not lag behind in getting the full advantage of the emerging new technologies. An equally important aspect is the strategic aspect of telecom, which affects the national and public interests. It is, therefore, necessary to encourage indigenous technology, set up a suitable funding mechanism for indigenous R&D [research and development] so that the Indian Technology can meet the national demand and also compete globally.

IMPLEMENTATION

(13) In order to implement the above policy, suitable arrangements will have to be made to (a) protect and promote the interests of the consumers and (b) ensure fair competition.

Appendix B: New Telecomm Policy—1999

1.0 PREAMBLE

1.1 Importance of Telecommunications

The Government of India (Government) recognizes that provision of world class telecommunications infrastructure and information is the key to rapid economic and social development of the country. It is critical not only for the development of the Information Technology industry, but also has widespread ramifications on the entire economy of the country. It is also anticipated that going forward, a major part of the GDP [gross domestic product] of the country would be contributed by this sector. Accordingly, it is of vital importance to the country that there be a comprehensive and forward looking telecommunications policy which creates an enabling framework for development of this industry.

1.2 NTP 1994 Objectives and Achievements

In 1994, the Government announced the National Telecom Policy (NTP), which defined certain important objectives, including availability of telephone on demand, provision of world class services at reasonable prices, ensuring India's emergence as major manufacturing/export base of telecom equipment and universal availability of basic telecom services to all villages. It also announced a series of specific targets to be achieved by 1997. As against the NTP 1994 target of provision of 1 PCO [public call office] per 500 urban population and coverage of all 6 lac villages, DOT [Department of Telecommunications] has achieved an urban PCO penetration of 1 PCO per 522 and has been able to provide telephone coverage to only 3.1 lac villages. As regards provision of total telephone lines in the country, DOT has provided 8.73 million telephone lines against the eighth plan target of 7.5 million lines.

NTP 1994 also recognized that the required resources for achieving these targets would not be available only out of Government sources and concluded that private investment and involvement of the private sector was required to bridge the resource gap. The Government invited private sector participation in a phased manner from the early nineties, initially for value-added services such as Paging Services and Cellular Mobile Telephone Services (CMTS) and thereafter for Fixed Telephone Services (FTS). After a competitive bidding process, licenses were awarded to 8 CMTS operators in the four metros, 14 CMTS operators in 18 state circles, 6 basic telephone service (BTS) operators in 6 state circles and to paging operators in 27 cities and 18 state circles. VSAT [very small aperture terminal] services were liberalized for providing data services to closed user groups. Licenses were issued to 14 operators in the private sector out of which only nine licensees are operational. The Government has recently announced the policy for Internet Service Provision (ISP) by private operators and has commenced licensing of the same. The Government has also announced opening up of global mobile personal communications by satellite (GMPCS) and has issued one provisional license. Issue of licenses to other prospective GMPCS operators is under consideration.

The Government recognizes that the result of the privatization has so far not been entirely satisfactory. While there has been a rapid rollout of cellular mobile networks in the metros and states with currently over 1 million subscribers, most of the projects today are facing problems. The main reason, according to the cellular and basic operators, has been the fact that the actual revenues realized by these projects have been far short of the projections and the operators are unable to arrange financing for their projects and therefore complete their projects. Basic telecom services by private operators have only just commenced in a limited way in two of the six circles where licenses were awarded. As a result, some of the targets as envisaged in the objectives of the NTP 1994 have remained unfulfilled. The private sector entry has been slower than what was envisaged in the NTP 1994.

The government views the above developments with concern as it would adversely affect the further development of the sector and recognizes the need to take a fresh look at the policy framework for this sector.

1.3   Need For a New Telecom Policy

In addition to some of the objectives of NTP 1994 not being fulfilled, there have also been far reaching developments in the recent past in the telecom, IT [information technology], consumer electronics and media industries world-wide. Convergence of both markets and technologies is a reality that is forcing realignment of the industry. At one level, telephone and broadcasting industries are entering each other's markets, while at another level, technology is blurring the difference between different conduit systems such as wireline and wireless. As in the case of most countries, separate licenses have been issued in our country for basic, cellular, ISP, satellite and cable TV operators each with separate industry structure, terms of entry and varying requirement to create infrastructure. However this convergence now allows operators to use their facilities to deliver some services reserved for other operators, necessitating a relook into the existing policy framework. The new telecom policy framework is also required to facilitate India's vision of becoming an IT superpower and develop a world-class telecom infrastructure in the country.

2.0   OBJECTIVES AND TARGETS OF THE NEW TELECOM POLICY 1999

2.1   The Objectives of the NTP 1999 Are as Under

* Access to telecommunications is of utmost importance for achievement of the country's social and economic goals. Availability of affordable and effective communications for the citizens is at the core of the vision and goal of the telecom policy.

* Strive to provide a balance between the provision of universal service to all uncovered areas, including the rural areas, and the provision of high-level services capable of meeting the needs of the country's economy.

* Encourage development of telecommunication facilities in remote, hilly and tribal areas of the country.

* Create a modern and efficient telecommunications infrastructure taking into account the convergence of IT, media, telecom and consumer electronics and thereby propel India into becoming an IT superpower.

* Convert PCO's, wherever justified, into Public Teleinfo centers having multimedia capability like ISDN [integrated services digital network] services, remote database access, government and community information systems etc.

* Transform in a time bound manner, the telecommunications sector to a greater competitive environment in both urban and rural areas providing equal opportunities and level playing field for all players.

- Strengthen research and development efforts in the country and provide an impetus to build world-class manufacturing capabilities.

- Achieve efficiency and transparency in spectrum management.

- Protect the defense & security interests of the country.

- Enable Indian Telecom Companies to become truly global players.

2.2   In Line with the Above Objectives, the Specific Targets that the NTP 1999 Seeks to Achieve Would Be [to]

- Make available telephone on demand by the year 2002 and sustain it thereafter so as to achieve a teledensity of 7 by the year 2005 and 15 by the year 2010;

- Encourage development of telecom in rural areas making it more affordable by suitable tariff structure and making rural communication mandatory for all fixed service providers;

  - Increase rural teledensity from the current level of 0.4 to 4 by the year 2010 and provide reliable transmission media in all rural areas;

  - Achieve telecom coverage of all villages in the country and provide reliable media to all exchanges by the year 2002;

  - Provide Internet access to all district headquarters by the year 2000;

  - Provide high-speed data and multimedia capability using technologies including ISDN to all towns with a population greater than 2 lac by the year 2002.

3.0   NEW POLICY FRAMEWORK

New Policy Framework must focus on creating an environment, which enables continued attraction of investment in the sector and allows creation of communication infrastructure by leveraging on technological development. Toward this end, the New Policy Framework would look at the telecom service sector as follows:

- Cellular Mobile Service Providers, Fixed Service Providers and Cable Service Providers, collectively referred to as 'Access Providers';

- Radio Paging Service Providers;

- Public Mobile Radio Trunking Service Providers;

- National long-distance Operators;

- International long-distance Operators;

- Other Service Providers;

- Global Mobile Personal Communication by Satellite (GMPCS) Service Providers;

- V-SAT based Service Providers.

3.1   Access Providers

3.1.1   Cellular Mobile Service Providers

The Cellular Mobile Service Providers (CMSP) shall be permitted to provide mobile telephony services including permission to carry its own long-distance traffic within their service area without seeking an additional license. Direct interconnectivity between licensed CMSP's and any other type of service provider (including another CMSP) in their area of operation including sharing of infrastructure with any other type of service provider shall be permitted. Interconnectivity between service providers in different service areas shall be reviewed in consultation with TRAI [Telecom regulatory Authority of India] and the same would be announced by August 15, 1999 as a part of the structure for opening up national long-distance. The CMSP shall be allowed to directly interconnect with the VSNL [Videsh Sanchar Nigam Ltd.] after opening of national long-distance from January 1, 2000. The CMSP shall be free to provide, in its service area of operation, all types of mobile services including voice and non-voice messages, data services and PCOs utilizing any type of network equipment, including circuit and/or packet switches, that meet the relevant International Telecommunication Union (ITU) / Telecommunication Engineering Center (TEC) standards.

CMSP would be granted separate license, for each service area. Licenses would be awarded for an initial period of twenty years and would be extendible by additional periods of ten years thereafter. For this purpose, service areas would be categorized into the four metro circles and Telecom circles as per the existing policy. CMSP would be eligible to obtain licenses for any number of service areas.

Availability of adequate frequency spectrum is essential not only for providing optimal bandwidth to every operator but also for entry of additional operators. Based on the immediately available frequency spectrum band, apart from the two private operators already licensed, DOT/MTNL [Mahanagar Telephone Nigam Ltd.] would be licensed to be the third operator in each service area in case they want to enter, in a time bound manner. In order to ensure level playing field between different service providers in similar situations, license fee would be payable by DOT also. However, as DOT is the national service provider having immense rural and social obligations, the Government will reimburse full license fee to the DOT.

It is proposed to review the spectrum utilization from time to time keeping in view the emerging scenario of spectrum availability, optimal use of spectrum, requirements of market, competition and other interest of public. The entry of more operators in a service area shall be based on the recommendation of the TRAI who will review this as required and no later than every two years.

CMSP operators would be required to pay a one-time entry fee. The basis for determining the entry fee and the basis for selection of additional operators would be recommended by the TRAI. Apart from the one time entry fee, CMSP operators would also be required to pay license fee based on a revenue share. It is proposed that the appropriate level of entry fee and percentage of revenue share arrangement for different service areas would be recommended by TRAI in a time-bound manner, keeping in view the objectives of the New Telecom Policy.

3.1.2 Fixed Service Providers

The Fixed Service Providers (FSP) shall be freely permitted to establish "last mile" linkages to provide fixed services and carry long-distance traffic within their service area without seeking an additional license. Direct interconnectivity between FSP's and any other type of service provider (including another FSP) in their area of operation and sharing of infrastructure with any other type of service provider shall be permitted. Interconnectivity between service providers in different service areas shall be reviewed in consultation with TRAI and the same would be announced by August 15, 1999 as a part of the structure for opening up of national long-distance. The fixed service provider (FSP) shall be allowed to directly interconnect with the VSNL after the opening up of national long-distance from January 1, 2000. The FSP may also utilize last mile linkages or transmission links within its service area made available by other service providers. The FSP shall be free to provide, in its service area of operation, all types of fixed services including voice and non-voice messages and data services, utilizing any type of network equipment, including circuit and/or packet switches, that meet the relevant International Telecommunication Union (ITU)/ Telecommunication Engineering Center (TEC) standards.

The FSP shall be granted separate license, on a non-exclusive basis, for each service area of operation. Licenses would be awarded for an initial period of twenty years, which shall be extended, by additional periods of ten years thereafter. The FSPs shall be eligible to obtain licenses for any number of service areas.

While market forces will ultimately determine the number of fixed service providers, during transition, number of entrants have to be carefully decided to eliminate non-serious players and allow new entrants to establish themselves. Therefore, the option of entry of multiple operators for a period of five years for the service areas where no licenses have been issued is adopted. The number of players and their mode of selection will be recommended by TRAI in a time-bound manner.

The FSP licensees would be required to pay a one-time entry fee. All FSP licensees shall pay license fee in the form of a revenue share. It is proposed that the appropriate level of entry fee and percentage of revenue share and basis for selection of new operators for different service areas of operation would be recommended by TRAI in a time-bound manner, keeping in view the objectives of the New Telecom Policy.

As in the case for cellular, for WLL [wireless-in-local-loop] also, availability of appropriate frequency spectrum as required is essential not only for providing optimal bandwidth to every operator but also for entry of additional operators. It is proposed to review the spectrum utilization from time to time keeping in view the emerging scenario of spectrum availability, optimal use of spectrum, requirements of market, competition and other interest of public.

The WLL frequency shall be awarded to the FSPs requiring the same, based on the payment of an additional one-time fee over and above the FSP entry fee. The basis for determining the entry fee and the basis for assigning WLL frequency shall be recommended by the TRAI. All FSP operators utilizing WLL shall pay a license fee in the form of a revenue share for spectrum utilization. This percentage of revenue share shall be over and above the percentage payable for the FSP license. It is proposed that the appropriate level of entry fee and percentage of revenue share for WLL for different service areas of operation will be recommended by TRAI in a time-bound manner, keeping in view the objectives of the New Telecom Policy.

3.1.3 Cable Service Providers

Under the provisions of the Cable Regulation Act, 1995, Cable Service Providers (CSP) shall continue to be freely permitted to provide "last mile" linkages and switched services within their service areas of operation and operate media services, which are essentially one-way, entertainment related services. Direct interconnectivity between CSPs and any other type of service provider in their area of operation and sharing of infrastructure with any other type of service provider shall be permitted. Interconnectivity between service providers in different service areas shall be reviewed in consultation with TRAI and the same would be announced by August 15, 1999 as a part of the structure for opening up national long-distance. In view of convergence, it is highly likely that two-way communication (including voice, data and information services) through cable network would [be] emerge in a significant way in future. Offering of these services through the cable network would tantamount to providing fixed services. Accordingly, in case the above two-way communication services are to be provided by CSPs utilizing their network, they would also be required to obtain an FSP license and be bound by the license conditions of the FSPs, with a view to ensure level playing field.

3.2   Internet Telephony

Internet telephony shall not be permitted at this stage. However, Government will continue to monitor the technological innovations and their impact on national development and review this issue at an appropriate time.

3.3 Radio Paging Service Providers

The radio paging service providers (RPSP) shall be permitted to provide paging services within their service area of operation. Direct interconnectivity between licensed RPSPs and any other type of service provider in their area of operation including sharing of infrastructure shall be permitted. Interconnectivity between service providers in different service areas shall be reviewed in consultation with TRAI and the same would be announced by August 15, 1999 as a part of the structure for opening up of national long-distance.

The RPSP shall be granted separate license, on a non-exclusive basis, for each service area of operation. Licenses would be awarded for an initial period of twenty years and will be extended by additional periods of ten years thereafter. For this purpose, the service areas would be categorized as per the existing structure. The RPSP shall be eligible to obtain licenses for any number of service areas.

Availability of adequate radio frequency spectrum is essential not only for providing optimal bandwidth to every operator but also for entry of additional operators. It is proposed to review the spectrum utilization from time to time keeping in view the emerging scenario of spectrum availability, optimal use of spectrum, requirements of market, competition and other interest of public. The entry of more operators in a service area shall be based on the recommendation of the TRAI who would review this as required and no later than every two years.

The radio-paging licensees shall pay a one-time entry fee. The basis for determining the entry fee and the basis for selection of additional operators will be recommended by the TRAI. All radio-paging licensees shall pay license fee as a revenue share. It is proposed that the appropriate level of entry fee and percentage of revenue share for different service areas of operation will be recommended by TRAI in a time-bound manner, keeping in view the objectives of the New Telecom Policy. Further, TRAI may also examine and recommend the revenue sharing arrangements between RPSP and other access providers, subject to technical feasibility.

3.4 Public Mobile Radio Trunking Service Providers

The Public Mobile Radio Trunking Service Providers (PMRTSP) shall be permitted to provide mobile radio trunking services within their service area of operation. Direct interconnectivity between licensed PMRTSP's and any other type of service provider in their area of operation shall be permitted after examining the legal implications in view of the CMSP licenses.

The PMRTSP shall be granted separate license, on a non-exclusive basis, for each service area of operation. Licenses would be awarded for an initial period of twenty years and will be extended by additional periods of ten years thereafter. For this purpose, the service areas would be categorized as per the existing structure. The PMRTSP shall be eligible to obtain licenses for any number of service areas.

PMRTSP licensees would be required to pay a one-time entry fee. The basis for determining the entry fee and the basis for selection of additional operators will be recommended by the TRAI. Apart from the one time entry fee, PMRTSP licensees would also be required to pay license fee based on a revenue share. It is proposed that the appropriate level of entry fee and percentage of revenue share arrangement for different service areas would be recommended by TRAI in a time-bound manner, keeping in view the objectives of the New Telecom Policy.

3.5   National Long-Distance Operator

National long-distance service beyond service area to the private operators will be opened for competition with effect from January 1, 2000. To promote setting up long-distance bandwidth capacity in the country, provide a choice to consumers and promote competition, all NLDOs [national long distance operators] should be able to access subscribers. With a view to achieve the above, all access providers shall be mandatorily required to provide interconnection to the NLDOs resulting in choice for subscribers to make long-distance calls through any operator. For this purpose, the terms and conditions and other modalities would be worked out in consultation with TRAI and the same will be announced by August 15, 1999. The terms and conditions would also specify the number of operators, license conditions on revenue sharing basis and other related issues.

Usage of the existing backbone network of public and private power transmission companies / Railways / Gas Authority of India, Ltd. (GAIL), Oil and Natural Gas Commission (ONGC), etc. shall be allowed immediately for national long-distance data communication and from January 1, 2000 for national long-distance voice communications.

Resale would be permitted for domestic telephony, announcement for the modalities thereof to be announced along with the opening up of national long-distance by August 15, 1999. Resale on international long-distance will not be permitted till the year 2004.

3.6   International Long-Distance Services

The subject of opening up of international telephony service to competition will be reviewed by the year 2004.

3.7   Other Service Providers

For applications like tele-banking, tele-medicine, tele-education, tele-trading, e-commerce, other service providers will be allowed to operate by using infrastructure provided by various access providers. No license fee will be charged but registration for specific services being offered will be required. These service providers will not infringe on the jurisdiction of other access providers and they will not provide switched telephony.

3.8   Global Mobile Personal Communication Services

The Government has opened up the GMPCS market in India and has issued a provisional license. The terms of the final license would need to be finalized in consultation with TRAI by June 30, 1999. All the calls originating or terminating in India shall pass through VSNL gateway or in case of bypass; it should be possible to monitor these calls in the Indian gateways. VSNL is also to be compensated in case gateway is bypassed.

The GMPCS operators shall be free to provide voice and non-voice messages, data service and information services utilizing any type of network equipment, including circuit and/or packet switches that meet the relevant International Telecommunication Union (ITU)/Telecommunication Engineering Center (TEC) standards. However, the licenses [will] be awarded after the proposals are scrutinized from the security angle by the Government.

The appropriate entry fee/revenue sharing structure would be recommended by TRAI, keeping in view the objectives of the New Telecom Policy.

3.9   SATCOM Policy

The SATCOM [satellite communication] Policy shall provide for users to avail of transponder capacity from both domestic/foreign satellites. However, the same has to be in consultation with the Department of Space.

Under the existing ISP policy, international long-distance communication for data has been opened up. The gateways for this purpose shall be allowed to use SATCOM.

It has also been decided that Ku frequency band shall be allowed to be used for communication purposes.

3.9.1 VSAT Service Providers

The VSAT Service Providers shall be granted separate license, on a non-exclusive basis for an initial period of twenty years and will be extended by additional periods of ten years thereafter. Interconnectivity between service providers in different service areas shall be reviewed in consultation with TRAI and the same would be announced as a part of the structure for opening up national long-distance by August 15, 1999.

The VSAT service providers shall be granted separate license, on a non-exclusive basis. Licenses would be awarded for an initial period of twenty years and will be extended by additional periods of ten years thereafter.

VSAT licensees would be required to pay a one time entry fee. The basis for determining the entry fee and the basis for selection of additional operators will be recommended by the TRAI. Apart from the one time entry fee, VSAT licensees would also be required to pay license fee based on a revenue share. It is proposed that the appropriate level of entry fee and percentage of revenue share arrangement would be recommended by TRAI in a time-bound manner, keeping in view the objectives of the New Telecom Policy.

3.10 Electronic Commerce

On line Electronic Commerce will be encouraged so that information can be passed seamlessly. The requirement to develop adequate bandwidth of the order of 10 Gb on national routes and even terrabits on certain congested important national routes will be immediately addressed so that growth of IT as well as electronic commerce will not be hampered.

3.11 Resolution of Problems of Existing Operators

The New Policy Framework, which seeks to significantly redefine the competitive nature of industry, would be applicable to new licensees.

There are, however, multiple licenses that have been issued by the Government for cellular mobile services, basic services, radio paging services, Internet services etc. It is the Government's intention to satisfactorily resolve the problems being faced by existing operators in a manner, which is consistent with their contractual obligations and is legally tenable.

4.0 RESTRUCTURING OF DOT

World-wide, the incumbent, usually the Government owned operator plays a major role in the development of the telecom sector. In India, DOT is responsible for the impressive growth in number of lines from 58.1 lakh on April 1, 1992 to 191 lakh in December 1998, showing a CAGR of 20%. DOT is expected to continue to play an important, and indeed, dominant role in the development of the sector.

Currently, the licensing, policy making and the service provision functions are under a single authority. The Government has decided to separate the policy and licensing functions of DOT from the service provision functions as a precursor to corporatisation. The corporatisation of DOT shall be done keeping in mind the interests of all stakeholders by the year 2001.

All the future relationship (competition, resource raising etc.) of MTNL / VSNL with the corporatised DOT would be based on best commercial principles.

The synergy of MTNL, VSNL and the coporatised DOT would be utilized to open up new vistas for operations in other countries.

5.0 SPECTRUM MANAGEMENT

With the proliferation of new technologies and the growing demand for telecommunication services, the demand on spectrum has increased manifold. It is, therefore, essential that spectrum be utilized efficiently, economically, rationally and optimally. There is a need for a transparent process of allocation of frequency spectrum for use by a service and making it available to various users under specific conditions.

The National Frequency Allocation Plan (NFAP) was last established in 1981, and has been modified from time to time since. With the proliferation of new technologies it is essential to revise the NFAP in its entirety so that it could become the basis for development, manufacturing and spectrum utilization activities in the country amongst all users. The NFAP is presently under review and the revised NFAP-2000 would be made public by the end of 1999, detailing information regarding allocation of frequency bands for various services, without including security information. NFAP shall be reviewed no later than every two years and shall be in line with radio regulations of International Telecommunication Union.

Relocation of existing Spectrum and Compensation:

- Considering the growing need of spectrum for communication services, there is a need to make adequate spectrum available.

- Appropriate frequency bands have historically been assigned to defense & others and efforts would be made toward relocating them so as to have optimal utilization of spectrum. Compensation for relocation may be provided out of spectrum fee and revenue share levied by Government.

    - There is a need to review the spectrum allocations in a planned manner so that required frequency bands are available to the service providers.

There is a need to have a transparent process of allocation of frequency spectrum, which is effective and efficient. This would be examined further in the light of ITU guidelines. For the present, the following course of action shall be adopted.

- Spectrum usage fee shall be charged.

- Setting up an empowered Inter-Ministerial Group to be called as Wireless Planning Coordination Committee (WPCC) as part of the Ministry of Communications for periodical review of spectrum availability and broad allocation policy.

- Massive computerization in the WPC Wing will be started during the next three months' time so as to achieve the objective of making all operations completely computerized by the end of year 2000.

6.0   UNIVERSAL SERVICE OBLIGATION

The Government is committed to provide access to all people for basic telecom services at affordable and reasonable prices. The Government seeks to achieve the following universal service objectives [USOs]:

- Provide voice and low speed data service to the balance 2.9 lac uncovered villages in the country by the year 2002.

- Achieve Internet access to all district head quarters by the year 2000.

- Achieve telephone on demand in urban and rural areas by 2002.

The resources for meeting the USO would be raised through a "universal access levy", which would be a percentage of the revenue earned by all the operators under various licenses. The percentage of revenue share toward universal access levy would be decided by the Government in consultation with TRAI. The implementation of the USO obligation for rural/remote areas would be undertaken by all fixed service providers who shall be reimbursed from the funds from the universal access levy. Other service providers shall also be encouraged to participate in USO provision subject to technical feasibility and shall be reimbursed from the funds from the universal access levy.

7.0   ROLE OF REGULATOR

The Telecom Regulatory Authority of India (TRAI) was formed in January 1997 with a view to provide an effective regulatory framework and adequate safeguards to ensure fair competition and protection of consumer interests. The Government is committed to a strong and independent regulator with comprehensive powers and clear authority to effectively perform its functions.

Toward this objective the following approach will be adopted:

- Section 13 of the TRAI Act gives adequate powers to TRAI to issue directions to service providers. Further, under Section 14 of the Act, the TRAI has full adjudicatory powers to resolve disputes between service providers. To ensure level playing fields, it will be clarified that the TRAI has the powers to issue directions under Section 13 to Government (in its role as service provider) and further to adjudicate under Section 14 of the Act, all disputes arising between Government (in its role as service provider) and any other service provider.

- TRAI will be assigned the arbitration function for resolution of disputes between Government (in its role as licensor) and any licensee.

- The Government will invariably seek TRAI's recommendations on the number and timing of new licenses before taking decision on issue of new licenses in future.

- The functions of licensor and policy maker would continue to be discharged by Government in its sovereign capacity. In respect of functions where TRAI has been assigned a recommendatory role, it would not be statutorily mandatory for Government to seek TRAI's recommendations.

8.0   OTHER ISSUES

8.1   Standardization

To enable the establishment of an integrated telecommunication network, common standards with regard to equipment and services would be specified by the Telecommunications Engineering Center (TEC). TEC would also continue to grant interconnect and interface approvals for various service providers.

8.2   Telecom Equipment Manufacture

With a view to promoting indigenous telecom equipment manufacture for both domestic use and export, the Government would provide the necessary support and encouragement to the sector, including suitable incentives to the service providers utilizing indigenous equipment.

8.3   Human Resource Development and Training

Human resources are considered more vital than physical resources. Emphasis would be placed on the development of human resources for all fields related to telecommunications and the dispersal of this expertise to the related fields. Such expertise shall also be made available to other countries.

8.4   Telecom Research and Development

Recognizing that telecommunications is a prime pre-requisite for the development of other technologies, telecommunications research and development (R&D) activities would be encouraged. Government would take steps to ensure that the industry invests adequately in R&D for service provision as well as manufacturing. Indigenous R&D would be actively encouraged with a view to accelerate local industrial growth and hasten transfer of technology. Premier technical institutions would be encouraged to undertake R&D activities on a contribution basis by the telecom service providers and manufacturers so as to develop multi-dimensional R&D activities in telecommunications and information technology.

8.5   Disaster Management

International co-operation in the use of terrestrial and satellite telecommunications technologies in the prediction, monitoring and early warning of disasters, especially in the early dissemination of information would be encouraged. Financial commitment to disaster management telephony and the development of appropriate regulatory framework for unhindered use of trans-boundary telecommunications would be put in place.

8.6   Remote Area Telephony

Rural Telephony, areas of North East, Jammu & Kashmir and other hilly areas, tribal blocks, etc. may be identified as special thrust areas for accelerated development of telecommunications. The Ministry of Defense shall be assigned a more active role in the development of telecommunications in such remote areas as are identified for accelerated development of telecommunications.

8.7   Export of Telecom Equipment and Services

Export of telecom equipment and services would be actively incentivised. Synergies among the various telecom players (manufacturers and service providers) would be exploited and used to provide integrated solutions for exports.

8.8 Right Of Way

Government recognizes that expeditious approvals for right-of-way clearances to all service providers are critical for timely implementation of telecom networks. The Central/State Government/Local bodies/Ministry of Surface Transport, etc. shall take necessary steps to facilitate the same.

9.0 CHANGES IN LEGISLATION

The Indian telecommunications system continues to be governed by the provisions of the Indian Telegraph Act, 1885 (ITA 1885) and the Indian Wireless Act, 1933. Substantial changes have taken place in the telecommunications sector since 1992. ITA 1885 needs to be replaced with a more forward-looking Act.

Index

About the Editor and Contributors

RAFIQ DOSSANI is a Senior Research Scholar at Stanford University's Asia/ Pacific Research Center, responsible for developing and directing the South Asia Initiative. His research interests include financial, technology, and energy-sector reform in India. He has undertaken projects on the upgradation of information technology in Indian start-ups, the institutional phasing-in of power-sector reform in Andhra Pradesh and telecommunications reform in India. He serves as an advisor to (1) India's Securities and Exchange Board in the area of venture-capital reform, (2) the Council of Strategic and International Studies and (3) the Knowledge Trade Initiative of the US India Business Council. Dr. Dossani earlier worked for the Robert Fleming Investment Banking group, first as CEO of its India operations and later as head of its San Francisco operations. He has also been the deputy editor of the Business India Weekly, and a Professor of Finance at Pennsylvania State University. His recent publications include *Reforming Venture Capital in India: Creating the Enabling Environment for Information Technology* (International Journal of Technology Management, 2000) and (co-authored with Lawrence Saez) *Venture Capital in India* (International Journal of Finance, 2000). He has a Ph.D. in Finance from Northwestern University.

CONTRIBUTORS

YALE M. BRAUNSTEIN is a Professor at the School of Information Management and Systems at the University of California at Berkeley. He has been a consultant to the FCC, Israel's Ministry of Communications and Sweden's National Telecommunications Agency. He was a contributing author to "Issues in Information Policy," National Telecommunications and Information Administration, 1981, which was the first U.S. government statement on information policy. Dr. Braunstein was previously a professor of economics at Brandeis University and at New York University. He is the author or co-author of over forty scholarly papers in economics and information science. Dr.Braunstein is also a director of Kalba International, Inc. He has a Ph.D. in Economics from Stanford University.

CRISTINA CASANUEVA is a Professor in the Division of Management and Social Sciences at the Monterrey Institute of Technology in Mexico City where she does research and policy analysis on telecommunications management. Dr. Casanueva has been involved in telecommunications policy since 1991, when she worked at Mexico's Trade Office, during the North America Free Trade Agreement negotiation, and prepared the negotiation agenda for this industry. She has also worked at the Federal Competition Commission, Mexico's anti-trust agency, representing this office in the design of the Rules of Interconnection, that led to the opening of the telecommunication markets after the privatization of the National Telephone Company (Telmex). In 1995, Dr. Casanueva worked for the Secretary of Communications, where she participated in the preparation of the proposal of the new Federal Telecommunications Law, presented by the Executive and approved the same year.   She has also worked in the telecommunications industry, in the regulatory and legal affairs department of Avantel, MCI partner in Mexico. Dr. Casanueva obtained her Ph.D. at Stanford University's School of Education and an M.A. in policy analysis from Harvard University.

FARID GASMI is a member of the research staff of the Institut D'Economie Industrielle (IDEI) in Toulouse, France and a Professor of Economics at The Universit des Sciences Sociale de Toulouse. Previously, he was a Member of Technical Staff at Bell Communications Research (Bellcore). His research fields are mainly theoretical and empirical industrial organization and regulation. Professor Gasmi holds M.S. and Ph.D. degress from The California Institute of Technology.

SHYAMAL GHOSH is Secretary, Department of Telecommunications, and Chairman, Telecom Commission of the Government of India. He belongs to the Indian Administrative Services and has held various administrative positions at the District and State levels in his initial years of service. He has held various senior positions, including Director General of Foreign Trade in the Ministry of Commerce; Secretary, Department of Electronics and Secretary, Ministry of Textiles, Government of India. He has also been Managing Director, Gujarat State Petrochemicals Corporation, Chief Secretary/Principal Secretary, Finance, Industry & Agriculture, and Additional Chief Secretary in the Government of Gujarat. Mr. Ghosh has an M.S. in Economics from Calcutta University and is a Parvin Fellow in Public Administration from Princeton University, USA.

HEATHER E. HUDSON is the Director of the Telecommunications Management and Policy Program in the School of Business Administration at the University of San Francisco.   Dr. Hudson is a Governor of the International Council for Computer Communications (ICCC) and Member of the Board of the

Pacific Telecommunications Council and the Telecommunications Policy Research Conference. She has been a member of Advisory Committees of the Federal Communications Commission, the Department of Commerce and the Office of Technology Assessment, and was a special advisor to the International Commission on Worldwide Telecommunications Development (the Maitland Commission). Dr. Hudson has worked on communication projects in more than 50 countries in Africa, America, Asia and the Pacific and the Middle East and consulted for the World Bank and the ITU. She is the author of numerous books, including *Global Connections: International Telecommunications Infrastructure and Policy* (1997); *Electronic Byways: State Policies for Rural Development through Telecommunications* (1992) (with Edwin Parker) and *Communication Satellites: Their Development and Impact* (1990). Hudson has a Ph.D. in Communication Research from Stanford University, and a J.D. from the University of Texas at Austin.

ASHOK JHUNJHUNWALA is a Professor and the Head of the Department of Electrical Engineering, Indian Institute of Technology, Madras, India. Dr. Jhunjhunwala leads the Telecommunications and Computer Networks Group (TeNeT) at IIT, Madras. This group works with industry and IIT alumni in the development of Telecommunications and Computer Network Systems. Their products include corDECT Wireless in Local Loop system, Fiber Access Network, Direct Internet Access System, Remote Access Switches, Ethernet Switches, IP Switches, V5.2 Stack and Network Management Stack. He was an Assistant Professor of Electrical Engineering with Washington State University until 1981. Since 1981, he has been teaching at IIT, Madras. Dr. Jhunjhunwala was awarded the Shanti Swarup Bhatnagar Award for outstanding contributions in the field of Engineering Sciences in 1998, the Hari Om Ashram Prerit Dr.Vikram Sarabhai Research Award for the year 1997 and the Millennium Medal at the Indian Science Congress in the year 2000. He is a Fellow of the Indian National Academy of Engineering, Indian National Science Academy and National Academy of Science and a Governor of the International Council for Computer Communications (ICCC). Jhunjhunwala has a B.Tech from IIT, Kanpur, India, and an M.S. and Ph.D. in Electrical Engineering and Computer Science from the University of Maine.

VINOD KHOSLA was a co-founder of Daisy Systems and founding Chief Executive Officer of Sun Microsystems, where he pioneered open systems and commercial RISC processors. He serves on the boards of Asera, Centrata, Juniper Networks, Redback, QWEST Communications and Zaplets, plus several other private companies. Mr. Khosla is also a General Partner at Kleiner Perkins Caufield & Byers. He is widely considered the premier venture capitalist on telecommunications in Silicon Valley. He has a B. Tech in Electrical Engineering from the Indian Institute of Technology, Delhi, an M.S. in Biomedical Engineering from Carnegie Mellon University and an MBA from the Stanford Graduate School of Business.

UDAY KUMAR is co-founder of Rural Telecom Foundation, a nonprofit organization that is dedicated to improving telecom access in rural India. He is also a Principal Consultant at BEA Systems, an E-business infrastructure software company. Prior to working at BEA Systems, he held positions at Hewlett-Packard and Advanced Micro Devices. He has a B. Tech in Electrical Engineering from the Indian Institute of Technology, Kanpur, an M.S. in Electrical Engineering from Louisiana State University, and an MBA from the University of California, Berkeley.

JEAN-JACQUES LAFFONT obtained his Ph.D. from Harvard University in 1975. Since 1979 he has been Professor of Economics at the University of Toulouse. He has held visiting positions at the California Institute of Technology, the University of Pennsylvania, Harvard University and the Australian National University. He was President of the Econometric Society (1992) and of the European Economic Association (1998). In 1990, he created the Institut d'Economie Industrielle, of which he is still the Director, which has become one of Europe's leading centers for economic research. He has published 12 books and over 300 scientific articles. He has made contributions to most areas of microeconomics, including the economics of incentives, public economics, the theory of regulation, the economics of development. His book "A Theory of Incentives in Procurement and Regulation," co-authored with Jean Tirole, is an authoritative statement of the "New Economics of Regulation." More recently he published "Competition in Telecommunications" with Jean Tirole and "Incentives and Political Economy."

S. MANIKUTTY is a professor at the Indian Institute of Management, Ahmedabad, India. He has 10 years of experience in teaching Business Policy and Strategy at IIMA and is a member of the Centre for Telecom Policy Studies at the Indian Institute of Management, Ahmedabad. His current areas of research include different aspects of telecommunications policy and competitive responses of organizations, especially family organizations and firm level strategies. Professor Manikutty was a visiting scholar at Cornell University between April-May 2000. He has published widely in international and national journals. His recent papers include "Who Needs Subsidy? A Study of Telephone Users in Gujarat" (1999), and "WTO: Opportunity or Constraint? Some Lessons from the Experiences of Mexico and China" (2000). Manikutty holds a doctorate in Business Policy from IIM, Ahmedabad.

JOSEPH PERNYESZI is an independent consultant specializing in semiconductors, high voltage integrated circuits and telecommunications systems. He holds several patents in telecommunications and high-voltage circuits. He holds an M.S. Electrical Engineering from Technical University of Budapest, Hungary and a B.S. in Chemistry from PL Chemical College in Budapest, Hungary.

E. MADANMOHAN RAO is co-founder of Rural Telecom Foundation, a non-profit organization that is dedicated to improving telecom access in rural India. He is also a senior journalist at United News India and a specialist in rural public policy. He holds a B.A. in Economics from the University of Chennai, and an M.A. in Economics from Osmania University, Hyderabad, India.

GREGORY L. ROSSTON is the Deputy Director of the Stanford Institute for Economic Policy Research at Stanford University. He is also a Lecturer in Economics at Stanford University. Dr. Rosston served as Deputy Chief Economist at the Federal Communications Commission working on the implementation of the Telecommunications Act of 1996 and he helped to design and implement the first ever spectrum auctions in the United States. He has also served as a consultant to various organizations including the World Bank and as an advisor to high technology and startup companies in the area of auctions, business strategy, antitrust and regulation. Dr. Rosston has written extensively on the application of economics to telecommunications issues and is the co-editor of two books relating to telecommunications. Rosston has a Ph.D. in Economics from Stanford University.

WILLIAM W. SHARKEY is currently Senior Economist with the Common Carrier Bureau of the Federal Communications Commission in Washington, D.C. Earlier, he was a visiting professor at the Institut d'Economie Industrielle in Toulouse and the Ecole Polytechnique in Paris, and was a member of the economics research group at Bellcore and at Bell Laboratories. While at the FCC he has directed the development of a staff model of the cost of local exchange telecommunications. As a consultant to the World Bank he is also assisting in the development of cost models in developing countries. His research interests include the economics of regulation, the economics of telecommunications, cooperative game theory, cost allocation, and the economics of networks. Dr. Sharkey has also been a visiting professor at the Universities of Arizona, Pennsylvania and Roosevelt University, Chicago. He has published a number of papers, written a number of books and is one of the acknowledged leaders of his field. He has also been a referee for a number of reputed journals. Sharkey has a Ph. D. in economics from the University of Chicago.

J.P. SINGH is an Assistant Professor at the Communication, Culture & Technology Program of Georgetown University, having earlier taught at the American University and the University of Mississippi. Dr. Singh's publications include the books *Leapfrogging Development: The Political Economy of Telecommunication Restructuring (1999)* and (with James N. Rosenau) *Information Technologies and Global Politics: The Changing Scope of Power and Governance (2001)*. His position at the University of Mississippi, 1993-98, funded by The BellSouth Foundation, entailed research and teaching related to international telecommunications policy. He has a Ph.D. in Political Economy and Public Policy from the University of Southern California.

M.S. VERMA is the Chairman of the Telecom Regulatory Authority of India (TRAI). TRAI is a statutory body established by an Act of Parliament to regulate telecommunication services in India. In his long and distinguished career, Verma has held several important posts, including the chairmanship of the State Bank of India, India's largest commercial bank, from which he retired in 1998. He has also been Advisor to the Reserve Bank of India, and is presently the Non-Executive Chairman of the Board of Directors of the IDBI Bank, Chairman of the Primary Markets Advisory Committee of the Securities and Exchange Boards of India, Member of the Governing Council of the National Council of Applied Economic Research, Member of the Academic Council of Indira Gandhi National Open University and Member of the Steering Committee of the World Bank-sponsored South Asian Forum of Infrastructure Regulators. Verma has an M.A. in Philosophy from Patna University.

BRADLEY S. WIMMER is an Assistant Professor of Economics at the University of Nevada, Las Vegas.   His research interests include telecommunications deregulation and the effects that universal service programs have on the development of competition. He has also published articles relating to the effect that asymmetrical information has on market outcomes, minimum-wage legislation and issues related to franchising. Before joining the faculty at UNLV, Bradley served as the Acting Chief Economist of the Common Carrier Bureau, which regulates interstate telecommunication services, and as the Chief Economist in the Division that oversees Universal Service Programs at the Federal Communications Commission. While at the Commission, Bradley worked primarily on issues related to implementation of the Telecommunications Act of 1996. Recent publications include *The State' of Universal Service* (Information Economics and Policy, 2000) and *The ABC's of Universal Service: Arbitrage, Big Bucks, and Competition* (Hastings Law Journal, 1999), both co-authored with Gregory L. Rosston. He has a Ph.D. in Economics from the University of Kentucky.

P. YADAGIRI is co-founder of Rural Telecom Foundation, a non-profit organization that is dedicated to improving telecommunications access in rural India. He is also a cable television media analyst and an independent journalist. He holds a B.A. in Economics and an M.A. in Political Science from Osmania University in Hyderabad, India.